The GEORGE RAFT Films

By
James L. Neibaur

The George Raft Films
By James L. Neibaur
Copyright © 2022 James L. Neibaur
No part of this book may be reproduced in any form or by any means, electronic, mechanical, digital, photocopying, or recording, except for inclusion of a review, without permission in writing from the publisher or Author.
No copyright is claimed for the photos within this book. They are used for the purposes of publicity only.

Published in the USA by:
BearManor Media
1317 Edgewater Dr #110
Orlando, FL 32804
www.bearmanormedia.com

Perfect ISBN: 978-1-62933-995-5
Case ISBN: 978-1-62933-996-2
BearManor Media, Orlando, Florida
Printed in the United States of America
Book design by Robbie Adkins, www.adkinsconsult.com

Table of Contents

GEORGE RAFT: THE EARLY YEARS 1
SCARFACE AND THE EARLY FILMS 3
NIGHT AFTER NIGHT 9
IF I HAD A MILLION 17
UNDER-COVER MAN 22
PICK-UP 27
MIDNIGHT CLUB 34
THE BOWERY 38
ALL OF ME 49
BOLERO 53
THE TRUMPET BLOWS 60
LIMEHOUSE BLUES 65
RUMBA 70
STOLEN HARMONY 75
THE GLASS KEY 80
EVERY NIGHT AT EIGHT 87
SHE COULDN'T TAKE IT 94
IT HAD TO HAPPEN 102
YOURS FOR THE ASKING 109
SOULS AT SEA 114
YOU AND ME 124
SPAWN OF THE NORTH 131
THE LADY'S FROM KENTUCKY 137
EACH DAWN I DIE 142
I STOLE A MILLION 149
INVISIBLE STRIPES 155
THE HOUSE ACROSS THE BAY 164
THEY DRIVE BY NIGHT 171
MANPOWER 180

BROADWAY 191
BACKGROUND TO DANGER 199
FOLLOW THE BOYS 208
NOB HILL 219
JOHNNY ANGEL 228
WHISTLE STOP 234
MR ACE 240
NOCTURNE 246
INTRIGUE 253
CHRISTMAS EVE 261
RACE STREET 266
OUTPOST IN MOROCCO 273
JOHNNY ALLEGRO 278
RED LIGHT 284
A DANGEROUS PROFESSION 291
LUCKY NICK CAIN 296
LOAN SHARK 300
I'LL GET YOU 306
THE MAN FROM CAIRO 310
ROGUE COP 315
BLACK WIDOW 321
A BULLET FOR JOEY 327
SOME LIKE IT HOT and the LATER FILMS 333
BIBLIOGRAPHY 338
INDEX 342

ACKNOWLEDGEMENTS

First and foremost, as always, I must give my deepest appreciation to film historian and essayist Katie Carter, who takes time out of her own busy writing and reviewing schedule to work on my books. She lives every book with me, watching each film and carefully going over each chapter to fix my (many) typos and offer her own valuable insights.

And there is also the support and encouragement I received from:

Gary Schneeberger, Terri Lynch, Peter Jackel, Kelly Parmelee, Ted Okuda, Richard Finegan, Amanda Grinstead, Farran Nehme, Kim Morgan, Jill Blake, Sheree Homer, Phil Hall, Kat Lively, Lee Gambin, and to the memory of my dear son Max Neibaur who inspires everything I do.

DEDICATION

I discovered George Raft back in high school when my best friend Brian Weiher and I saw *Souls at Sea* on the late show. We thereafter tried to catch every George Raft movie that showed up on TV. Brian died in 2019. He was an important person from a significant time in my life. This book is fondly dedicated to his memory.

INTRODUCTION

George Raft entered films at the same time as other noted movie tough guys Edward G. Robinson and James Cagney. While he arguably did not have the same level of acting ability, he had a very strong presence, an understanding of subtle nuance, and the ability to be imposing and compelling, even in small roles. After his striking portrayal of a henchman in Howard Hawks' *Scarface* (1932), Raft rather quickly reached leading man status. At Paramount Pictures he scored in everything from gangster dramas (*The Glass Key*), to sea adventures (*Souls at Sea, Spawn of the North*), to musicals (*Bolero, Rumba*) where he could show off his dancing prowess.

Later at Warner Brothers, George appeared in films with Humphrey Bogart, Edward G. Robinson, and James Cagney, but the studio's attempts to star him in his own movies met with difficulty. Raft turned down the roles he was offered in several films, including, notably, *High Sierra* and *The Maltese Falcon*, both of which were subsequently instrumental in making Humphrey Bogart a star.

Raft then decided to freelance, making films for various independent producers, even forming his own production company. Choosing films that best suited his own vision of his screen persona, Raft was able to maintain stardom pretty consistently if not at a top tier level, then at least to the point where, with few exceptions, his films made money.

However, by the end of the 1940s, George Raft's films were no longer generating the same level of box office, and he ended up on poverty row, appearing in potboilers for Lippert pictures during the 1950s. After teaming with Edward G. Robinson in *A Bullet for Joey* in 1955, a film that flopped despite its cast, Raft was thereafter reduced to supporting parts and bit roles. This meant good cameos in films like Billy Wilder's *Some Like it Hot* and *Ladies Man* with Jerry Lewis, but walk-ons in movies like *For Those Who Think Young*,

The Patsy, and *Skiddoo* were a big comedown for a former top billed movie star.

This book will discuss George Raft's early roles, including *Scarface*, and then examine each of his starring films, one-by-one, from the early 1930s into the mid 1950s. A concluding chapter on his later supporting roles and cameos will explore what he did at the end of his career (Raft remained semi-active until his death in 1980). This book will cover George Raft's choices, both good and bad, his actual underworld connections, his response to changes in filmmaking, the situations that made him happy, or unhappy, and what he did in television, from producing his own series to appearing as himself in commercials.

However, we will also look at George Raft the actor. Raft's economy of movement and low key verbal delivery have been unfairly defined as wooden and limited, when, in fact, when given the right script and director, his style was nuanced and effective. As previously indicated, post-war crime dramas, dark mysteries that have since been identified by the sub-genre term film noir, were good for Raft's style of acting, and his best films in this field, especially those directed by Edwin L. Marin, hold up quite well.

George Raft's film career is a fascinating study, including top level stardom, and demeaning walk-ons, from being in demand, to being forgotten, from success as a movie tough guy with real life connections to the underworld, to actually sobbing as an old man on TV about his personal economic troubles. Triumphs and tragedies are abounding in the life and career of this colorful, fascinating, decidedly underrated actor.

GEORGE RAFT: THE EARLY YEARS

There have been some conflicts over the years as to when George Raft was born. When he died in November of 1980, most obituaries listed him as being 85 years old. That is because most biographies claim he was born September 26, 1895. As recently as seven months before his death, Raft told Mike Douglas on the latter's syndicated afternoon talk show on television that the 1895 birth year was correct. However, further investigation has revealed that Raft was born George Ranft to German-Jewish immigrants Eva and Conrad Ranft on September 26, 1901, in Manhattan.

Growing up in the roughest area of what was known as Hell's Kitchen, Raft joined the teenage gang The Gophers and became friends with British born Owney Madden, who later became a noted racketeer during the Prohibition era. When Owney was sent to prison for manslaughter, the Gophers were rudderless and disbanded.

When Raft was young he worked at his uncle's barber shop, shining shoes and sweeping hair from the floor. Raft recalled that his uncle was hard taskmaster who beat him when he felt the boy didn't perform his duties well enough. Raft hated it there, the only fun he got was becoming familiar with his uncle's clients, which included several Broadway actors, and he ran away. He slept in pool halls and abandoned buildings, tried his hand at boxing, and at semi-pro baseball, was not at all good at either, and gravitated toward dancing. During this same time, he also acted as the personal driver to Owney Madden, who, after his release from prison, began bootlegging and eventually opened The Cotton Club

Changing his name to Raft (though not legally until 1935), George frequented the dance halls and soon realized he had a natural talent, despite no training. His only experience was having danced with his parents in local carnivals, his mother having taught him some basic steps as a child. Raft quickly mastered the popular Charleston, and teamed up with female dancers and later Lily Field for a few limited tours in the New England area. He then became part of the vaudeville team Pilcer, Douglas, and Raft, touring in the Paramount Publix circuit and honing his skills.

During the 1920s, George Raft met Max Greenburg, who, as Mack Gray, would remain connected with the actor for the remainder of his life. He also became friendly with Jimmy Durante, who was then the piano player at a place called the College Inn. It was in 1925 when George Raft made his Broadway debut in *The City Chap*, while also appearing in nightclubs as a specialty dancer. He became known as "the world's fastest Charleston dancer," continuing on Broadway in shows like *Gay Paree, Madhattan, Palm Beach Nights* and *Padlocks of 1927*.

Working in a club run by Texas Guinan, Raft was hired to be her bodyguard when she traveled to Hollywood to star in the early talkie *Queen of the Nightclubs* (1929), a movie loosely based on her life. Raft ended up with a small part in the movie. *Queen of the Nightclubs* is a lost film, so we can't really judge George Raft's work in his movie debut, or even if he appears in the final film. Some studies claim his part was cut from the movie, while others believe he appears in a few isolated scenes. A clip from this film would later be used as stock footage in the James Cagney vehicle *Winner Take All* (1932), thus preserving at least some of its footage. Texas Guinan and George Raft are both seen in this clip.

Not long after this, Raft secured a very small part as a gangster in the early RKO talkie *Side Street* (1929), which is notable as the only movie in which all three Moore brothers – Tom, Owen, and Matt – appear together in the same film. When he returned to New York, the stock market crashed, and the night life had quieted down considerably.

Owney Madden believed George Raft had a future in Hollywood and provided the finances needed for him to move there permanently. Having difficulty finding acting work, Raft supported himself with sporadic nightclub appearances until a chance meeting with writer-director Rowland Brown resulted in his being cast in the 1931 film *Quick Millions*. George Raft's motion picture career had just begun.

SCARFACE AND THE EARLY FILMS

George Raft made many appearances in small, supporting roles before securing the part in Howard Hawks' *Scarface* (1932), that truly launched his career as a leading man. In fact, George Raft's movie career was almost cut short early when his mob connections raised the suspicions of Hollywood police and he was nearly forced to leave town.

Rowland Brown was just beginning to establish himself as a screenwriter, having penned the gangster drama *Doorway to Hell* (1930) which featured James Cagney in an early supporting role and netted Brown an Oscar nomination. Brown would later be nominated for writing a far more notable Cagney movie, *Angels With Dirty Faces* (1938). Brown wrote and also directed *Quick Millions*, the first of only three films the screenwriter directed in his career.[1]

When Brown hired George Raft for *Quick Millions*, it was based on having seen him dance on stage, and running into him, by chance at the Brown Derby restaurant. Brown wanted a gangster who was tough but could exude sensuality for the supporting role. Raft later told Lewis Yablonsky: "I was very erotic. I used to caress myself as I danced. I never felt I was a great dancer. I was more of a stylist, unique. I was never a Fred Astaire or a Gene Kelly, but I was sensuous."[2]

Quick Millions was a tough gangster drama released at a time when such films were quite popular. Fox released it in April of 1931, and its popularity followed the Warner Brothers releases of *Little Caesar* in January of that year, and *The Public Enemy*, which came out the same month as *Quick Millions*. Each of these films

---

[1] The others being *Hell's Highway* (1932) and *Blood Money* (1933). Brown was also replaced as a director on some projects he started, notably *The Devil is a Sissy* (1936), on which he was replaced by W.S. Van Dyke.

[2] Yablonsky, Lewis. *George Raft*. NY: McGraw-Hill, 1974

George Raft and Spencer Tracy in Quick Millions

made stars out of their leading men; Edward G. Robinson in *Little Caesar*, James Cagney in *The Public Enemy*, and Spencer Tracy in *Quick Millions*.

Despite being seventh-billed, George Raft had a solid supporting role in *Quick Millions* and reviewers took notice. The review in the *Los Angeles Evening Express* stated: "George Raft former vaudeville headliner turns in the slickest gangster character seen in a long time lies cool deceptive in manner and just what one expects of a deadly killer.[3]" While Raft would have small parts in several more films, it was *Quick Millions* that was most instrumental in his eventually securing the part in *Scarface*.

---

3 Quick Millions review. *Los Angeles Evening Express.* March 28, 1931

George Raft and Miriam Hopkins are Dancers in the Dark

George Raft was barely noticeable in a brief bit as a pickpocket in his next film, *Goldie* (1931), which also starred Spencer Tracy and featured Jean Harlow. Then Raft was cast in *Hush Money* in a small supporting role. The star of *Hush Money* (1931) was Joan Bennett. She and Raft met on this film and became friendly. They'd go on to co-star in three more films later on.

It was when he was about to start filming *Hush Money* when George Raft was brought in by police who thought he might be an advance man for the mob. They accused him of robbing the home

George Raft and Paul Muni in Scarface

of actress Molly O'Day, whom Raft had once dated. Threatening to make him leave town, the police backed off when Fox's head of production, Winfield Sheehan, contacted the District Attorney and intervened on George Raft's behalf, indicating that he had a contract to act in a movie at the studio, and was intent on a motion picture career.

Raft played another henchman in the Eddie Cantor comedy *Palmy Days* (1931), and then had a brief but memorable bit in *Taxi* (1932) which starred James Cagney and Loretta Young. As a dancer who competes with his partner against Cagney and Young in a contest, Raft's character makes a cutting remark and gets punched. Cagney and Raft had known each other from the New York days, and were friendly. They would later co-star in one of the best films for either actor.

George Raft certainly was comfortable settling into his role in *Dancers in the Dark* (1932). The world of dancers and gangsters was quite familiar to Raft and he turned in one of his better performances from this early in his screen career. This film was shot after *Scarface* but released earlier, and Raft's role features him as particularly ruthless.

Scarface was completed in 1931 but withheld from release until April of 1932. Although it was just another role as a tough henchman, not unlike the parts Raft had been playing, director Howard Hawks worked with him, expanding his limitations as an actor with nuanced bits, most notably the coin-flipping which became an act that would define quietly simmering gangster henchmen.

Grittier and more violent than even the Warner Brothers gangster films released the year before that had inspired it, *Scarface* was something of a dichotomy for the trade magazines. While many of the reviews decried its brutality, these same magazines named it one of the best films of 1932. However, shortly after the film was in release, the censor board wanted to ban the movie all together. Moviegoers wrote to the trades in protest, the July 1932 issue of *Photoplay* containing the following Letters to the Editor:

Why does the censor board wish to ban a great picture that every American should see? I am referring to the greatest gangster picture ever made, *Scarface*.

Scarface is not only a picture it is modern history. Almost every incident is something I have read about, discussed with others, and pondered over. Not until I saw *Scarface* did I really come to realize what's going on in gangland.

I sincerely think the government owes Howard Hughes a vote of thanks instead of criticism for *Scarface*. It gives the public such a realistic portrayal of organized crime.[4]

At least one letter singled out George Raft himself for special praise, in spite of an inaccurate prediction:

I discovered George Raft for myself about a year ago when he was an extra on the screen. The first time I saw him, I knew he would make good. He is more like Valentino in looks than any

---

4 Letters. Photoplay July, 1932

other actor. In a very short time, he ought to make Clark Gable look silly.[5]

George Raft made so much of an impact, he was listed on theater marquees alongside the film's star, Paul Muni, despite his small role. By contrast, Vince Barnett, who also plays a henchman, has about as large a role as Raft, and plays his part for comedy, remains firmly in his capacity as support. Raft's charisma was enough to elevate him to marquee billing alongside the star. Articles on Raft appeared in the trades, many of them with inaccurate details (many erroneously stated he was half-Italian).

Raft's Rinaldo is pretty calm and cool throughout the film, and yet he and his relationship with Ann Dvorak's character is the catalyst for so much of the film's angst, especially between Ann's Cesca and Tony, who is her brother. So, even though Raft isn't in the movie that much and technically doesn't do much in it, a lot of important things that happen in the film revolve around him.

After his stint in *Scarface*, George Raft appeared in a couple more supporting roles. He has a small part in *Night World* (1932) with Lew Ayers and Boris Karloff; and a few scenes in *Madame Racketeer* (1932) with Alison Skipworth. However, once the success of *Scarface* began to register at the box office, it resulted in Raft being offered contracts by several studios. He accepted a contract from Paramount, and preparations began for his first film as a leading man, *Night After Night*.

---

5 Letters. Photoplay July, 1932

NIGHT AFTER NIGHT

Directed by Archie Mayo
Assistant Director: Henry Hathaway
Screenplay by Vincent Lawrence, from the story Single Night by
    Louis Bromfield, with additional dialog by Mae West.
Produced by William LeBaron
Cinematography by Ernest Haller

Cast:

George Raft	Joe Anton
Constance Cummings	Miss Jerry Healy
Wynne Gibson	Iris Dawn
Mae West	Maudie Triplett
Alison Skipworth	Miss Mabel Jellyman
Roscoe Karns	Leo
Louis Calhern	Dick Bolton
Bradley Page	Frankie Guard
Al Hill	Blainey
Harry Wallace	Jerky
George "Dink" Templeton	Patsy
Marty Martyn	Malloy
Tom Kennedy	Tom the bartender
Dick Rush	Bolton - Private Detective
Phillips Smalley	Mr. Wilson
Dick Gordon	Nightclub Patron
Carl M. Leviness	Nightclub Patron
Edmund Mortimer	Nightclub Patron
Patricia Farley	Hatcheck Girl
Theresa Harris	Ladies' Room Attendant
Bill Elliott	Escort
Dennis O'Keefe	Drunk Sleeping on a Table
Anderson Lawler	Lonely Drunk
Leo White	Kitchen Staff

Released October 30, 1932
Paramount Pictures
Running time: 73 minutes
Black and White

After the gritty, brutal gangster dramas like *Little Caesar, The Public Enemy,* and, of course, *Scarface,* filmmakers got the idea that a gangster having more layers to his character might be of some interest. One of the various approaches to that concept was to feature a racketeer who had made enough money and wanted to explore some level of refinement. Such is the case for *Night After Night,* in which George Raft marks his first starring role by playing the familiar gangster with a more expanded personality than would be found in *Quick Millions, Dancers in the Dark,* or *Scarface.*

George Raft plays Joe Anton, an ex-boxer turned racketeer, who has achieved success and now rests easily as the owner of a successful speakeasy that operates inside of Joe's palatial mansion. Rival gangsters who had previously run the territory want to buy his place for $50,000. Unafraid, he refuses to sell for less than $250,000. Joe is pursuing an education through a private tutor who teaches at an exclusive school. Once per week, Ms. Mabel Jellyman (Alison Skipworth) comes to give Joe lessons in current events, culture, and diction. Tiring of the earthy type of women he's used to dealing with, Joe falls for a refined-looking lady who frequently comes to his speakeasy alone "night after night." Joe discovers that the woman's name is Miss Healy (Constance Cummings) and the place was once her childhood home. Her father lost it in the 1929 stock market crash. While he is showing her around, the two are confronted by his jealous former girlfriend Iris (Wynne Gibson) who pulls a gun and threatens to shoot Joe. He takes the gun away, but it fires, hitting a mirror near Miss Healy. She is excited by the action and kisses Joe before leaving. Joe never hears from her again, and when he seeks her out, he discovers she is living with a wealthy associate of his, Joe Bolton (Louis Calhern), whom she admits she does not love, but still plans to marry. Joe realizes she is a mere gold digger like all the other women he's known and tells her off. Meanwhile, the rival gang compromises with Joe on the sale of his place at

Movie ad for Night After Night

$200,000. But when he makes his discovery about Miss Healy, Joe tries to back out of the deal. Miss Healy comes to the speakeasy and confronts Joe about the things he said to her, and they end up kissing passionately as she realizes her love for him. When the rival racketeers come to bust up the place, Joe tells them he now does plan to sell and all is well.

George Raft and Mae West in Night After Night

Within the context of this story is the appearance of Mae West, making her film debut, as Maudie, an old friend of Joe's who stops by to see him during his first dinner party with Miss Healy. Joe has also invited Ms. Jellyman to the same dinner so that she may engage him in sophisticated conversation. Maudie sits down and despite her aggressive, boorish manner, not only does she not disrupt the setting negatively, but both women find her delightful. She and the cultured Ms. Jellyman especially hit it off. It is interesting how Joe feels like he needs to change and behave more sophisticatedly to win over Miss Healy when in reality his main appeal for her was his ruggedness, and that includes the company he kept with people like Maudie.

At first, George Raft felt playing the lead role would be daunting and suggested that he continue to work in supporting parts. The studio kept getting letters from fans who wanted to see Raft in his own movie, so they talked him into taking the lead. A quick study, Raft reportedly didn't look at his scenes until he was on his way to the studio. He and Mack Gray would go over the day's shooting script in the limousine and Raft would be ready with his lines upon arrival.

Even though he was a comparative newcomer, George Raft also had an understanding of how his character should be played. He always wanted to maintain a consistent low-key expression and reaction. He stated in later years

> I was always calm, always spoke slowly, and I never yelled on the screen. I told the coaches and directors, "Don't ask me to shout or talk too fast. Let me be myself." The minute they asked me to do anything I wasn't totally comfortable with, I refused.[6]

And while many faulted Raft for his limited expressions, in close-ups as well as medium shots he was able to exhibit a great deal of acting nuance. Howard Hawks stated, "When George thought something on the screen, the audience knew what he was thinking."

The part of Maudie was originally written for Texas Guinan, and Raft was pleased for his old friend, believing the role could launch a career doing character parts in movies. However, when producer William LeBaron decided Guinan would be too old for the part at 48,[7] Raft then suggested Mae West, not yet 40, and, he felt, perfect for the part. Mae West had no experience with movies, but was quite notorious for her edgy stage presentations like *Sex* and *Diamond Lil*. The studio on one hand was reticent about hiring a controversial entertainer like West, but also realized she was right for the part. West was hired and allowed to write her own dialog.

---

6 Yablonsky, Lewis. *George Raft*. NY: McGraw-Hill, 1974

7 Guinan died the following year of amoebic dysentery after drinking tainted water at a Chicago hotel.

George Raft and Roscoe Karns in Night After Night

In her first scene, West enters the speakeasy with a flourish and when the hat check girl exclaims, "Goodness, what lovely diamonds," West famously replies "Goodness had nothing to do with it dearie." It was quite an impactful debut, and Mae West is delightful. George Raft would later recall, "She stole everything but the cameras." Whereupon Mae West stated, "George dominated all the scenes. In any scene where George appears, you're not aware of anyone else."

The cast is rounded out by such welcome veterans as Al Hill, playing one of Joe Anton's bodyguards who menaced his way through several small gangster roles in the 1930s and 1940s; and fast-talking Roscoe Karns, as Joe's right-hand man. Karns' rat-a-tat line delivery helps maintain the pace of the film, and he is one of the more appealing characters among the supporting cast. Wynne Gibson also registers strongly as Iris, the former girlfriend who would rather Joe be dead than with another woman.

Critic Kaspar Monahan in his review for *The Pittsburgh Press* noticed both Raft and West:

> As in *Scarface*, Mr. Raft is given to swell apparel. His hair is brilliant with a patent-leather sheen. About him is that air of deadly menace. And his voice has the hard, metallic ring of a fellow who would slay you if you dared block his path. The difference comes from within. Mr. Raft this time has a soul that yearns for beauty and for romance of the ethereal brand. The best scene in the film is provided by Mae West and Alison Skipworth when both imbibe too deeply. Mae West is Diamond Lil again in every undulation of her generous anatomy and in every inflection of her coarse strident voice.[8]

While the reviewer in *The New York Daily News* also called out Mae West's performance while praising Raft and Constance Cummings:

> Besides the smooth performances given by George Raft and Constance Cummings, the picture sponsors the film debut of Mae West, who, like Jimmy Durante, has the sort of personality that clicks on her first appearance in a scene. Her part in *Night After Night* isn't a big one, but she dominates every scene she's in, even when she is playing against such a veteran scene-stealer as Alison Skipworth, who does more than her bit to make the picture a howling success.[9]

As a result of her impact in this film, Mae West was given a contract to do more films for Paramount, and, especially during the pre-code era, her self-penned scripts resulted in a series of hit movies like *She Done Him Wrong* (1933) and *I'm No Angel* (1933). In fact, George Raft was supposed to be her co-star in the 1934 film *Belle of the Nineties*, but this was one of many parts the actor notoriously turned down.

Night After Night proved that George Raft was indeed leading man material, and the studio banked on his rugged toughness as well as his sensual quality (there is a scene in this film where he's

---

8 Night After Night review. *The Pittsburgh Press*. October 15, 1932.
9 Night After Night review. *The New York Daily News*. October 29, 1932

taking a bath, and Raft insisted on playing the scene naked). Raft was not classically handsome, but he had an earthy charisma that attracted female moviegoers, while his tough no-nonsense style appealed to men.

For his next film appearance, George Raft appeared in one of many vignettes for the all-star Paramount ensemble piece *If I Had a Million*, which explored how various types would react if given a million dollars with no strings attached. As a forger whose reputation would not allow him to cash the perfectly legitimate check, Raft turns in an emotionally stirring performance as his character gradually descends in to madness.

IF I HAD A MILLION

Directors: James Cruze, H. Bruce Humberstone, Ernst Lubitsch, Norman Z. McLeod, Stephen Roberts, William A. Seiter, Norman Taurog
Screenplay: Robert Sparks, Grover Jones, William Slavens McNutt, Lawton Mackall, Joseph L. Mankiewicz, Oliver H.P. Garrett, Harvey Gates, Claude Binyon, Malcolm Stuart Boylan, Whitney Bolton, John Bright, Sidney Buchman, Lester Cole, Isabel Dawn, Boyce DeGaw, Ernst Lubitsch, Walter DeLeon
From a story by Robert Hardy Andrews,
Produced by Louis D. Lighton, Bejamin Glazer, Emmanuel Cohen
Cinematography: Harry Fischbeck, Charles Edgar Schoenbaum, Gilbert Warrenton, Alvin Wyckoff
Film Editing: LeRoy Stone

Cast:
Gary Cooper	Steve Gallagher
Charles Laughton	Phineas V. Lambert
George Raft	Eddie Jackson
Jack Oakie	Private Mulligan
Richard Bennett	John Glidden
Charles Ruggles	Henry Peabody
Mary Boland	Mrs. Peabody
Allison Skipworth	Emily La Rue
W. C. Fields	Rollo La Rue
Roscoe Karns	Private O'Brien
May Robson	Mrs. Mary Walker
Wynne Gibson	Violet Smith
Gene Raymond	John Wallace
Frances Dee	Mary Wallace

Reginald Barlow	Otto Bullwinkle
James Bush	Bowen Wallis
Joyce Compton	Marie
Lucien Littlefield	Zeb
Blanche Friderici	Mrs. Garvey
Tom Kennedy	Joe
Edward LeSaint	Mr. Brown
Charles McMurphy	Mike
William V. Mong	Harry
Fred Santley	Marvin
Edwin Stanley	Galloway
Morgan Wallace	Mike
Irving Bacon	China shop salesman
Fred Holmes	China shop clerk
Bess Flowers	China shop customer
Harry Bradley	Guard
Bob Burns	Marine sergeant
James P. Burtis	Jailer
Byron Murphy	Beds proprieter
Fred Kelsey	jailer
Marc	Lawrence Henchman
Jerry Tucker	Boy with balloon
Clarence Muse	prisoner
Dewey Robinson	cook
Louise Emmons	Margarety Fealy
Harlene Hill	Idylwood resident
Margaret Mann	Idylwood resident
Gertrude Norman	Idylwood resident
Barbara Norton	Idylwood resident
Tempe Pigott	Idylwood resident
Mildred Pitts	Idylwood resident
Cora Shannon	Idylwood resident
Alice Smith	Idylwood resident
Emma Tansley	Idylwood resident
Mai Wells	Idylwood resident
Joy Winthrop	Idylwood resident

Released December 2 1932
Paramount Pictures
Running time: 88 minutes
Black and White

George Raft starred on one of many episodes for If I Had a Million

If I Had a Million is an episodic comedy-drama about a wealthy steel magnate who is dying, but doesn't trust any of his relatives or employees. He comes up with the idea of leaving his fortune to strangers by randomly picking names out of the phone book and then personally delivers a check for one million dollars to each individual. The recipients are shown in separate vignettes reacting to receiving the money.

Henry Peabody (Charlie Ruggles) works in a china shop. He uses his million to cheerfully destroy all of the expensively fragile vases in the store. Violet Smith (Wynne Gibson) is a prostitute whose sudden fortune allows her to sleep in a bed alone. Phineas Lambert (Charles Laughton) is a staid office worker who, upon receiving the million dollars, quietly walks into his employer's office and blows a raspberry at him. Rollo and Emily Larue (W.C. Fields and Alison Skipworth) are an old vaudeville couple who buy a fleet of automobiles and set out to violently eliminate road hogs.

While most of the episodes are amusing or compelling, varying in intensity from slapstick comedy to powerful tragedy (Gene Raymond plays a young man going to the electric chair), nearly all of them work effectively. However, there are some that fall flat. The scene with three army buddies interested in the same woman, then losing her to an old man after he gets the million dollar check, is not quite as interesting or amusing, despite the presence of Gary Cooper, Roscoe Karns, and Jack Oakie. The concluding sequence with May Robson as a rebellious woman in a highly structured old folks home, who transforms it with her million dollars, is an amusing idea that goes on too long.

George Raft's segment casts him as Eddie Jackson, a check forger who has such notoriety, he isn't trusted well enough by anyone to cash a legitimate check. While it was only one vignette among many and was overshadowed by the comedy segments (it was a bridge between the Wynne Gibson and W.C. Fields episodes), it has a significance to this portion of George Raft's screen career. Raft was drawn to the role due to it being so much against type for him. As an actor who liked playing it cool without raising his voice, Raft was intrigued by a role that would have him yelling in desperation within the parameters of its one reel running time.

The film opens showing the forger no longer able to utilize his skills in the area, as his notoriety has taken over the town. He needs money to leave town, however, and can't acquire that. When he is given the million dollars, his inability to cash the check, even with the understanding that he'd deposit the rest, makes him become increasingly more desperate. He agrees to "sell" the check for $100,000. Then only $50,000. Even an attempt to reach his benefactor fails. He finally reaches the end of his rope and trades the entire amount for a bed in a flophouse.

While first maintaining his noted economy of movement, George Raft's ability to reach the audience with nuanced expression is utilized, but much differently than he had so far established in films.

Eddie Jackson isn't tough, anchored, and in control like the characters Raft played in *Quick Millions, Scarface,* or *Night After Night.* Eddie Jackson is nervous, jittery, unable to control his present situation or his destiny. Even when given a million dollars, he remains broke. Raft plays the role quite brilliantly, becoming increasingly more frustrated. He yells desperately at a crook accomplice that the check is good, and he's willing to trade it for only five percent of its worth, but to no avail.

Raft makes the audience feel his desperation. When he finally succeeds in getting a bed after days of no sleep trying to get something for a million dollar check, he laughs maniacally at finally "getting something for it." The flop house proprietor (Byron Murphy) calls the police because he believes that man is "off his nut" and then giggles while burning the check that he believes is phony. Because it would remain a very different role for Raft, his segment in *If I Had a Million* and its significance to this period in his career is notable.

While the immediate attraction of this movie was that it featured so many of Paramount studios' top stars, *If I Had a Million* also has a significance for having been produced and released during the height of the Great Depression. At a time when so many Americans were struggling, a movie about suddenly getting a million dollars was a wild fantasy. As uneven as the film's random episodes might be, *If I Had a Million* is often a fascinating film, and it features George Raft in one of his most emotionally charged performances.

UNDER-COVER MAN

Directed by James Flood
Screenplay by Francis Faragoh and Garrett Fort from a story by
    John Wilstach adapted by Thomson Burtis.
Cinematography by Victor Milner

Cast:
George Raft	Nick Darrow
Nancy Carroll	Lora Madigan
Roscoe Karns	Dannie
Lew Cody	Kenneth Mason
Gregory Ratoff	H.L. Martoff
Noel Francis	Connie
David Landau	Inspector Conklin
Paul Porcasi	Sam Dorse
William Janney	Jimmy Madigan
George Davis	Bernie
Leyland Hodgson	Bill Gillespie
Robert Homans	Flannagan
Jack Kennedy	Pat Kilbane
Kent Taylor	Russ
Hal Price	Detective
Frances Moffett	Secretary at Shooting Scene

Released December 2, 1932
Paramount Pictures
Running Time: 74 minutes
Black and White

   While George Raft was exploring what he could do with his screen character while remaining true to the essence of its presentation, the studio was also wondering what different roles in which he could

George Raft and Nancy Carroll in Under-Cover Man

comfortably fit. *Under-Cover Man* is a typically aggressive B-level drama, but it allowed the bad guy Raft plays to also be a good guy, adding another layer to his established screen persona.

George Raft plays Nick Darrow, a hood with successful rackets in the Ohio area, who travels to New York and meets with Inspector Conklin (David Landau) in an attempt to join the police force undercover to find the man who killed his father in a bond selling scheme. He teams up with Lora (Nancy Carroll) who wants to avenge the death of her brother by the same racketeers. Nick takes up the alias of an imprisoned crook named Oliver Snell, and gets connected with the mob by posing as a fence for stolen bonds. Nick passes a test involving a dictaphone recording and a phony cop in order to prove to the mob he isn't an undercover man. Nick's knowledge and understanding of criminal schemes gives him the special insight to do so. Lora pretends to be interested in the older

Kenneth Mason (Lew Cody), a respected businessman who, secretly, is deeply involved with the bond schemes. Nick gets in close with the boss, Martoff (Gregory Ratoff), and eventually discovers he is the man who murdered his father. Nick kills Martoff, and with the help of Dannie, a career undercover man who has also infiltrated the mob (Roscoe Karns), brings the others to justice.

A consistently tense crime drama with a few interesting twists along the way, *Under-Cover Man* does its best with the talented cast, while Raft firmly anchors every scene he is in. Nick Darrow is a hood, but carrying a feeling of angry vengeance that is discernible in Raft's expression. While he always keeps a calm demeanor, Nick Darrow is always thinking, his eyes darting around the room.

One interesting tangential scene has Mason's girl Connie (Noel Francis) attempting to seduce Nick, but he'll have none of it. He maintains character, stating that he wouldn't help her cheat on Mason. When she cries, he tosses her a handkerchief to wipe her eyes. Connie had lied to Mason over the phone, and does not realize he has come to the apartment to spy on her and Nick. Mason overhears Connie falling for Nick, and starting to tell him things he shouldn't know, and Nick refusing to succumb. This causes him to respect Nick and become angry with Connie. She avoids danger when Mason finds the handkerchief left behind. It has an N monogram, which doesn't match Oliver Snell. When he is later confronted, Nick says, "You think I would use my real initial and get caught by the cops?" He then tells them they must be amateurs and threatens to end the whole deal. Throughout the film, Nick outsmarts the others while allowing them to believe they are controlling him effectively.

George Raft maintains the delicate balance between good guy and bad guy. Although a hood, the death of his father is significant enough for him to never waver from his focus. When he first connects with Lora and she thinks he's trying to get to know her on another level, he is offended and proceeds to angrily leave her apartment. She calls him back. Nancy Carroll is effective as the wide-eyed girl who wants to help capture her brother's killers but, unlike Nick, does not have the experience of working with criminals.

Roscoe Karns had played George's loyal friend and supporter in *Night After Night* and scores again here as the supposed hood who turns out to be an actual undercover man for the law in a neat twist. Gregory Ratoff is volatile and sinister as the evil Martoff. A busy character actor during the first part of the 1930s, Ratoff soon became a successful director, helming such films as *Intermezzo* (1939), *The Corsican Brothers* (1941), and the Mae West comeback vehicle *The Heat's On* (1943). Lew Cody had been a silent film actor, and was one of the few who made a successful transition to sound films. Married to Mabel Normand until her death in 1930, Cody died of a sudden heart attack in 1934. Noel Francis had appeared with James Cagney in *Smart Money* (also starring Edward G. Robinson), and *Blonde Crazy* (both 1931). The same year she appeared *Under-Cover Man*, Francis appeared with Paul Muni in the classic *I Am a Fugitive From a Chain Gang* (1932). She also enjoyed success on Broadway.

When it was first released, a special screening of *Under-Cover Man* was shown to journalism students in Louisiana:

> Students of the department of Journalism at Centenary college as part of their study will attend the showing of *Under-Cover Man*, thrilling film drama based on crime material gathered by a police reporter in New York city. The Journalism class will study different phases of the story as a regular assignment from the instructor. *Under-Cover Man*, in which the featured roles are filled by George Raft and Nancy Carroll with support from such other notables of the screen as Roscoe Karns, Lew Cody, and Gregory Ratoff, is a story set in the upper crust of the underworld. Raft is a film sensation who gained much fame in *Scarface*, and added largely to it in *Night After Night*." The story of *Under-Cover Man* was written by John Wikatach who gathered the material while a reporter on the *New York Sun* and later doing special newspaper work. In that capacity he made personal studies of various rackets including the bond stealing racket which figures prominently in this story. The newspaper man he says gets the low-down on crime adding: "The reason a reporter is

let in on so much Is that he can be trusted and simply will not divulge stuff."[10]

Under-Cover Man was well received and George Raft's momentum as a film star continued. Newspaper accounts indicated that upon completing *Under-Cover Man*, George Raft would then star in a film about a bullfighter entitled *The Trumpet Blows*. Raft did star in that film, but not for a couple more years. Because of his success in crime dramas, Paramount chose for him appear in one that, like *Under-Cover Man*, challenged aspects of the formula. In *Pick Up*, George Raft would co-star with Carole Lombard in a crime drama with more romance than usual. However, before filming even began, some significant changes were made.

---

10 Under-Cover Man Will Be Studied By Journalism Students. *The Shreveport Journal*. December 7, 1932

PICK-UP

Directed by Marion Gering
Screenplay by S.K Lauren and Agnes Brand Leahy, from a story by Viña Delmar adapted by Sidney Lazurus.
Produced by B.P. Schulberg
Cinematography by David Abel

Cast:
Sylvia Sidney	Mary Richards
George Raft	Harry Glynn
Lilian Bond	Muriel Stevens
William Harrigan	Jim Richards
Clarence Wilson	Sam Foster
Brooks Benedict	Tony
Robert McWade	Turner
Purnell Pratt	Prosecuting Attorney
Charles Middleton	Mr. Brewster
Oscar Apfel	The Warden
Alice Adair	Sally
Louise Beavers	Magnolia
Eddie Clayton	Don
Florence Dudley	Freda
Patricia Farley	Sadie
Al Hill	Johnson--Reporter
Dorothy Layton	Peggy
George Meeker	Artie Logan
Eleanor Lawson	Matron
Lona Andre	Party Girl
Dave O'Brien	Party Boy
Gail Patrick	Party Girl
Harry Semels	Movie Theater Patron
Ted Billings	Prison Inmate
Jimmie Dundee	Court Clerk

Released March 24, 1933
Paramount Pictures
Running Time: 76 minutes
Black and White

Just as George Raft had been signed to do *Pick Up*, reporter Elizabeth Yeaman of the *Los Angeles Daily*, caught up with George Raft who appeared to be pleasantly surprised by his recent success:
"I'm not an actor I don't know what acting Is all about" protests George Raft with unmistakable candor: "If people think I can act that's all right too but I know I just do what the director says." Raft is one of the sensations at Paramount right now. He has patent leather hair and wears pointed shoes. He might have been a double for Rudolph Valentino but he doesn't like the comparison "This business of being a movie actor and getting lots of publicity leaves me in a daze," he confessed. "I never thought of being an actor and if I am one it's an accident" But being a movie actor is lot of fun" Who wouldn't enjoy holding these beautiful movie actresses in his arms? Five years from now when Hollywood has forgotten all about me I'll go to the theater with my friends and when a glamorous lady appears on the screen, I'll nudge my pals and say, "See that beautiful woman up there? Well I held her In my arms one time."' Raft has been cast for the romantic lead in half a dozen big pictures soon to be made at Paramount. But the picture he is most looking forward to is *Pick Up* in which he will play with Carole Lombard. There's a girl to hold in your arms," he said. "Isn't she beautiful? But aside from that, Miss Lombard is a regular scout. Nothing high-hat about her. Why, you'd never know she was a star when she's working on the set. She is just friend with everybody and makes working a pleasure. Yes, I am going to enjoy making *Pick Up*.[11]

---

11 Raft Credits Director for Acting Fame. *Los Angeles Evening Citizen*. July 5, 1932

George Raft in Pick Up

It is both fortunate and unfortunate that Carole Lombard ended up not appearing in *Pick Up*. After refusing to be loaned to Warner Brothers for a movie opposite James Cagney, Lombard was suspended by Paramount and replaced by Sylvia Sidney in *Pick Up*. Raft's part was then recast with Gary Cooper, but when Cooper took longer than expected on another project, Raft was returned to the role.

Pick-Up showed the studio, and George Raft, further exploring what he could do with his established screen persona. This is a much more romantic crime drama, and it gives Raft the opportunity not only for tenderness in romantic scenes, but also to succumb to the emotions of falling in love and the anguish that often goes along with it.

George Raft plays Harry Glynn, a taxi driver who finds a woman in his cab who has just gone in to get out of the rain. When he discovers she has no place to stay, he invites her to his place, but soon realizes she wasn't a professional lady of the evening, although they do have a genuine attraction to each other. The woman is Mary Richards, who was arrested and sent to prison along with her husband Jim (William

Sylvia Sidney and George Raft in Pick Up

Harrigan). But while Mary has been released, her husband is still in jail, and she wants nothing to do with him. Their friendship develops into a relationship, and Harry proposes, but Mary confesses she is married. Harry respects her honesty. Harry gets Mary a job at the switchboard of the cab company where he works but she becomes restless, believing they can do better, while Harry is satisfied. She fakes that her flirtatious boss (Clarence Wilson) pinches her, causing Harry to react and both of them to get fired. Harry then starts his own business as an auto mechanic, and does very well at it. But he becomes distracted by, and attracted to, a woman named Muriel (Lillian Bond); a rich lady who is merely toying with him. Harry falls for Muriel and tells Mary the truth, right as she has arranged to get her marriage annulled. Muriel reveals that she has no further interest in Harry, that he was just a dalliance, even to the point of laughing out loud at his proposal. Mary's now ex-husband escapes prison and, unaware of the annulment, intends to kill Harry. Mary pretends to still be interested in Jim to protect Harry. Mary calls the police and both are sent to prison as Mary's past makes her seem to be a willing accomplice. Harry goes to a lawyer friend and

George Raft and Purnell Pratt in Pick Up

tearfully pleads for his help. During a trial, the lawyer tricks Jim by handing him a loaded gun, realizing he would take advantage and try to shoot Harry. Mary runs to protect Harry, and it is revealed the gun was filled with blanks. Mary is acquitted and she meets Harry outside the courtroom where they playfully re-enact their first meeting.

George Raft's acting is expanded a bit in *Pick-Up*, even though he is still maintaining the screen character he had created. With each new film, Raft explores what more he can do with the character, and the studio obliged with scripts that were conducive to his interest. In *Pick-Up*, Raft not only plays a romantic figure who is an honest working man, he gets the opportunity to show real emotion when he tearfully begs the lawyer for help. While it sometimes drags a bit, *Pick-Up* remains an important film in the early portion of Raft's starring career because of the opportunities it provides him as an actor.

Sylvia Sidney was fairly well established by the time she replaced Carole Lombard for this movie. She scored in such hit films as *Street Scene* (1931) and *Merrily We Go To Hell* (1932) before appearing in *Pick-Up*. And, despite not being able to co-star with Carole Lombard, Raft ended up connecting well with Sylvia Sidney and would appear in two more movies with her.

The supporting cast is strong. Clarence Wilson was better known for playing comic foils for the likes of W.C. Fields and the Our Gang kids, so his performance as an old, creepy employer making flirtatious advances was a departure for him, and he plays it well. Lillian Bond is exceptionally good at playing the frivolous rich girl who uses the earnest cabby like a throwaway toy. William Harrigan is pure menace as Jim. And Louise Beavers is an always welcome presence, here playing Harry and Mary's maid after the mechanic business makes enough money for them to hire domestic help.

Pick-Up was a box office hit and was given great reviews by the critics. *The Hollywood Reporter* stated in their review:

> *Pick-Up* is a program picture so far above the average that your cash-registers should click a merry tune, even in these sorry times. The picture is packed with down-to-earth speech and sentiment and is of the human interest variety that has been plenty scarce for a long time. The charm of the film lies for the most part in its simple, straightforward story and the utterly natural and sincere performances of Sylvia Sidney (who has never looked better) and George Raft in the leading roles. Too, *Pick-Up* moves along at a good pace under the direction of Marion Gering, and though its wind-up is melodramatic, the entire piece is well to the "light" side. The screenplay and dialogue by S.K. Lauren and Agnes Brand Leahy are really something to rave about, and the photography by David Abel is beautiful. William Harrigan is excellent as the gun-toting husband, Charles Middleton, Robert McWade, Louise Beavers (never forget that gal) and Lilian Bond, O.K. in support. You should have lots of smiles for this one. Sidney and Raft at their best in a yarn with great general appeal and a swell box office title are a combination that looks like dollars to us.[12]

Both George Raft and Paramount liked the idea of his playing characters that were complex enough to retain the essence of his noted persona, but also had layers of personality that added depth to his performances.

---

12 Pick-Up review. *The Hollywood Reporter*. March 13, 1933.

Raft was next to be cast in the film *The Story of Temple Drake*, but it notoriously became the first of many roles he would turn down in his career. While this activity would have a much stronger impact later on, Raft's instincts for *The Story of Temple Drake* might have been right. The character he was to play, called Trigger in the movie, was so sadistic, Raft told the press, "It will kill any man who plays it." Paramount suspended Raft, and hired Jack LaRue to play the part. LaRue stated, "it will make any man who plays it," and was signed to a contract by the studio. LaRue had originally been considered for the role Raft ended up playing in *Scarface* – the role that resulted in his current leading man status.

One of the edgier pre-code movies that aroused the ire of the culture warriors when first released in 1933, *The Story of Temple Drake* deals with a sexually active young woman who leads men on but never connects. She becomes friendly with a lawyer, but ends up in the throes of a controlling gangster. The film is very brutal and frightening, with Temple and a wealthy, drunken boyfriend getting into a car accident in the woods and being held hostage in a rustic cabin filled with backwoods bootleggers under the control of a gangster. The scenes are darkly lit, with the rumblings of a thunderstorm backing up the soundtrack. Rape, sexual slavery, and murder are all elements of the story. Raft felt it was just too despicable. LaRue specialized in such roles and offers a chilling presence in all of his scenes. It is unlikely that had Raft taken the role it would have either hurt or advanced his career at any level.

In his next film, *Midnight Club*, Raft plays another good guy posing as a bad guy to catch some crooks. And this time the movie is set in England.

MIDNIGHT CLUB

Directed by Alexander Hall, George Somnes
Screenplay by Leslie Charteris and Seton I. Miller from a story by
    E. Phillips Oppenheim
Produced by Bayard Veiller
Cinematography by Theodor Sparkuhl
Film Editing by Eda Warren

Cast:
Clive Brook	Colin Grant
George Raft	Nick Mason
Helen Vinson	Iris Whitney
Alison Skipworth	Lady Barrett-Smythe
Sir Guy Standing	Commissioner Hope
Alan Mowbray	Arthur Bradley
Ferdinand Gottschalk	George Rubens
Forrester Harvey	Thomas Roberts
Ethel Griffies	Duchess
Charles Coleman	Carstairs
Teru Shimada	Nishi
Charles McNaughton	Detective
Billy Bevan	Detective
Rita Carlyle	Nick's landlady
Jean De Briac	Headwaiter
Leo White	Waiter
Dennis O'Keefe	Dance Extra
Jeffrey Sayre	Dance Extra
Elinor Fair	Bit Role
Julanne Johnston	Bit Role
Mary MacLaren	Bit Role

Released July 29, 1933
Paramount Pictures
Running time: 64 minutes
Black and White

The influential Louella Parsons announced in her column that George Raft's next film would feature him as a good guy:
> George Raft has reformed. He is fed up playing crooks on the screen and he has told Paramount that he wants to go straight. Perhaps that is why in his next picture, *Midnight Club*, he will play the hunter instead of the hunted. Clive Brook and Sir Guy Standing are also in this romantic melodrama. Young Raft is exceedingly popular, and he is wise enough not to make any mistakes in his choice of vehicles although his crook roles have really been responsible for his screen following.[13]

When word got out that Clive Brook and George Raft were appearing in a film together, although not in their usual roles, the press reacted further:
> George Raft has gone straight and Clive Brook has gone wrong. These two phenomena take place in *Midnight Club*, the romantic drama in which Raft and Brook are co-featured. Brook, who has played "righteous" roles from Sherlock Holmes on down, is now cast as the head of a ring of London jewel thieves, and Raft, who has played many types of underworld characters in his various films, is cast as an American detective brought over by Scotland Yard to break up Brook's gang.[14]

Of course, Raft played an honest working man in his most recent film, but the press reaction shows how he was generally identified as a movie badman. Playing a lawman was indeed something new, as far as his fans were concerned.

Clive Brook liked being cast as the villain, but was dissatisfied with the script. He quarreled with the studio heads until his part

---

13 Louella Parsons column. Syndicated. Universal Service. April 19, 1933
14 Brook Goes Bad, Raft Straight. *The San Francisco Examiner.* September 17, 1933

George Raft, Helen Vinson, and Clive Brook surround Alison Skipworth in Midnight Club

was rewritten to his specifications. Alison Skipworth appears again, having already appeared in several films featuring Raft, including *Madame Racketeer, If I Had a Million,* and *Night After Night.*

Midnight Club features George Raft as Nick Mason, an American detective who is summoned to Scotland Yard to investigate a series a jewel thefts led by Colin Grant (Clive Brook). Pretending to be a jewel thief himself, he infiltrates the gang to figure out how the supposedly guilty parties always seem to have an alibi when a robbery is committed. It is discovered that, while they are under surveillance, the crooks have lookalikes in masks to represent them in a nightclub, while they sneak off and commit a robbery.

While the film has an intriguing plot, *Midnight Club* is not as good as Raft's other starring vehicles thus far. In fact, it really isn't a starring film for Raft, but is more of an ensemble piece. However, George Raft enjoyed the experience of playing a detective and also liked the London setting as something different. Raft's leading lady in this is Helen Vinson, who had made her film debut opposite William Powell in *Jewel Robbery* (1932), and had already appeared in such films as *I Am a Fugitive From a Chain Gang* (1932), and the Edward G. Robinson vehicle *Little Giant* (1933). Thus, she was quite well established in crime dramas. Vinson and Raft had little chemistry, so the scenes where she becomes interested in Nick despite being connected to Colin are not as believable.

Although a weaker film, *Midnight Club* was still fairly well received on the strength of Raft's name and the rest of the notable cast. It has some sense of foreshadowing regarding Raft's movie career in that he would settle into a niche of playing detectives or investigators in crime dramas as he settled into middle-age.

George Raft's next movie was a significant improvement over *Midnight Club*. Raft was allowed to work against type and expand his abilities much further with a character that was far more layered and complex. Rising to the challenge, Raft responded with one of the finest performances from this period in his career.

THE BOWERY

Directed by Raoul Walsh
Screenplay by Howard Estabrook and James Gleason from the novel by Michael Simmons and Bessie Roth Solomon
Produced by Darryl F. Zanuck
Cinematography by Barney McGill
Film Editing by Allen McNeil

Cast:
Wallace Beery	Chuck Connors
George Raft	Steve Brodie
Jackie Cooper	Swipes McGurk
Fay Wray	Lucy Calhoun
Pert Kelton	Odbray
Herman Bing	Max Herman
Oscar Apfel	Ivan Rummel
Ferdinand Munier	Honest Mike
George Walsh	John L. Sullivan
Lillian Harmer	Carrie A. Nation
Fletcher Norton	Googy Cochran
John Bleifer	Mumbo the Mute
John Kelly	Lumpy Hogan
Fred Kelsey	Detective Kelsey
Charles Middleton	Detective
James Burke	Recruiting Sergeant
Harold Huber	Slick
Irving Bacon	Hick
Wong Chung	Chinese Man
Jimmy Conlin	Enlistee
Bobby Dunn	Violinist
Lester Dorr	Cynic
John Ince	Crony

Leonard Kibrick	Older boy on the pier
Sidney Kibrick	Little boy on pier
Charles Lane	Doctor
Charles McAvoy	Waiter
William Irving	Fireman
Frank Moran	Bettor
Hal Price	Editor
Harry Semels	Artist
Phil Tead	Tout
Andrew Tombes	Shill
Dorothy Vernon	Carrie Nation Follower
Rose Plumer	Carrie Nation Follower
Frank Mills	Fireman
Pat Harmon	Fireman
Harry Tenbrook	Fireman
Tammany Young	Fireman
Bull Anderson	Pug
Phil Bloom	Pug
Kid Broad	Pug
Pueblo Jim Flynn	Pug
Joseph Glick	Pug
Sailor Vincent	Pug
W.C. Robinson	Pug
Mack Gray	Pug
Kit Guard	Pug
Jack Herrick	Pug
Joseph Herrick	Pug
Heinie Conklin	Pug
Paulette Goddard	Blonde
Lucille Ball	Blonde

Released October 7, 1933
20th Century Pictures
Running time: 92 minutes
Black and White

In April of 1933, Darryl Zanuck left Warner Brothers and formed a new studio with Joseph Schenck. They called it 20th Century Pictures. Their first planned film was to be the story of Chuck Connors, a bowery figure from the 19th century, and his rival, Steve Brodie, who was known for jumping off the Brooklyn Bridge, and surviving, as part of a wager.

Daryl Zanuck had been given Michael Simmons and Bessie Roth Solomon's unpublished novel while still production head at Warner Brothers. Zanuck was intrigued with the idea, but others at the studio thought it wasn't worth pursuing. Former silent movie comedian Raymond Griffith was then an associate producer at Warner Brothers, and sent a memo to Zanuck which stated:

> This is the life story of Chuck Connors. Why it was written I don't know because he was of no importance. He was merely an illiterate fool that wore a ridiculous costume and was a guide through Chinatown. He was connected with nothing of importance in his period; he wasn't even an important hoodlum of the day. I do not see anything of consequence in this at all.[15]

When Zanuck formed his own studio with Schneck, one of the people he hired as an associate producer was Raymond Griffith, who, ironically, was active in that capacity on this project, the studio's first release.

Zanuck wanted to cast Wallace Beery as Connors and George Raft as Brodie. It was announced in the press, but then Paramount indicated that Raft would be unable to play the role due to a scheduling conflict. Zanuck then considered Clark Gable for the role. According to Wood Soanes' syndicated column:

> Clark Gable is going to impersonate Steve Brodie, the man who took a chance and jumped off the Brooklyn Bridge. Twentieth Century Pictures, that new studio with Darryl F. Zanuck at the helm, has borrowed him to appear with Wallace Beery in *The Bowery*. Beery has also been

---

15 Twentieth Century-Fox Produced Scripts Collection at the UCLA Theater Arts Library

George Raft, Jackie Cooper, and Wallace Beery in The Bowery

borrowed from M-G-M. and Raoul Walsh from Fox to direct the film.[16]

However, things worked out, and George Raft was soon returned to the production not long afterward and Gable was out. According to columnist Edward Schallert:

> Mere talk, perhaps, but it indicates that George Raft may after all enact that role in *The Bowery* for which he was originally announced. That would mean his teaming with Wallace Beery, provided Beery does play the other part, though there has been some argument about that, too. Anyway, it doesn't look right now to us if Clark Gable would go into the picture. There is an expressed opinion that the way the role is shaping up it will be much more of a Raft character than a Gable. Seems all in all that first

---

16 Soanes, Ward. In The World of Stage and Screen. *Oakland Tribune*. June 2, 1933

Jackie Cooper and George Raft in The Bowery

choice may have been the best in this case. Arrangements will naturally have to be made for the borrowing of Raft from Paramount by the Twentieth Century organization. It would be quite a striking bit of teaming, that combining of Beery and Raft.[17]

The cast would be rounded out by Jackie Cooper, Fay Wray, and Pert Kelton, and would go into production by August of 1933. There were some early reports that Clara Bow would also appear in the film, but when Howard Estabrook and James Gleason adapted the novel into a screenplay, the character she was to play was written out.

Jackie Cooper had been a member of Hal Roach's Our Gang in a series of shorts from 1929-1931, and had been the star of the

---

17 Schallert, Edwin. Raft May Do Bowery. *Los Angeles Times*. June 17, 1933

ensemble. Thus, once he left the gang, he secured a leading role in the film *Skippy* (1931) which became a bit hit. But later that year he was teamed with Wallace Beery in *The Champ*, which became a sensation. The idea to put him in another movie with Beery was a shrewd move by Zanuck, ensuring box office for his new studio's first feature release.

Wallace Beery is one of the few major stars of his era (which covered the teens, twenties, thirties, and forties), where nobody has written a biography. The conventional wisdom is because nobody liked him. Back in the 1970s, when such biographies were highly sought during a nostalgia boom for vintage Hollywood movies, and actors from that period were alive and able to be interviewed, any project on Wallace Beery was met with disdain from his former co-stars.. Beery was an insecure performer, and jealous of any other actor's attention, especially children. Jackie Cooper recalled in his autobiography: "As a young boy I was demonstrative -- that trait had been encouraged by most grownups I had met – I liked to hug and kiss people. Beery brushed me off." Cooper also said that Beery tried to upstage him during their scenes in *The Champ* and, "I never did actually hate him, although I never liked him."[18]

Fay Wray had scored the previous year in the massive hit *King Kong* for RKO Radio Pictures. It was a role that would continue to define her career, although she remained active in movies for nearly 50 more years. Director Raoul Walsh was already a veteran filmmaker and a visual stylist who knew how to frame a scene and properly display his actors. The package Darryl Zanuck put together for his new studio's first project was very promising.

Regarding George Raft, *The Bowery* was yet another film that allowed him to stretch beyond his established screen persona. Steve Brodie was a happy, boisterous, gregarious type who relished his rivalry with Chuck Connors and delighted in playing practical jokes. Raft extends beyond his more stoic screen persona and plays Brodie as written, with impressive results.

The story has Chuck Connors, a saloon owner, and happy-go-lucky Steve Brodie as rivals who first compete when their respective

---

18 Cooper, Jackie. *Please Don't Shoot My Dog, Mister.* NY: William Morrow. 1981

George Raft and Fay Wray in The Bowery

volunteer fire brigades try to be the first to arrive at a fire in Chinatown. Swipes McGurk (Jackie Cooper) is a young orphan boy who Connors has taken in as his own. He sits on a hydrant, preventing Brodie from using it, which allows Connors' brigade to be first, winning $100 from Brodie. Brodie then challenges Connors' fighter Bloody Butch to battle a fighter he calls the Masked Marvel. Connors accepts and the two fighters square off. The Marvel knocks out Butch with one punch. Brodie then removes his mask and reveals him to be John L. Sullivan (George Walsh, brother of the director). Connors takes in a naïve, innocent homeless girl named Lucy (Fay Wray) whom he pays to take care of the house where he and Swipes live, and to cook for them. Swipes is jealous of her and leaves. Brodie finds Swipes sleeping in a hallway and invites him to stay at his apartment. He goes to check out Lucy, believing her to be a mistress, tries to seduce her. When she rebuffs him and when he realizes her true identity, he apologizes and eventually they start seeing each other. Brodie wants to open a saloon bigger than Connors' and a couple of brewers agree to sponsor him, but first he needs to make a name for himself. Brodie plans a stunt where he jumps off the Brooklyn Bridge, and Connors bets his saloon he won't survive. Brodie plans to use a dummy and has one made, but it is stolen at the last minute so he must actually jump. Meanwhile, Carrie Nation and her Temperance union arrive at Chuck Connors' saloon with plans to tear it down as "evil." Connors stops her, but when he sees Brodie having survived the jump, being triumphantly carried through town by citizens, he steps aside and lets the women tear up the saloon that he has lost to Brodie. Brodie reopens the refurbished saloon when war is declared against Spain. A despondent Connors, no longer an important bowery figure, enlists in the army. The men who stole the Brodie dummy show it to Connors and insist it was used in the stunt. Connors confronts Brodie, demands his bar be returned, and the two fight. Connors wins but is arrested for assault and battery. Brodie refuses to implicate him. Connors appreciates it, and visits Brodie in the hospital, and they almost fight again. Swipes stops them and the two shake hands. Both enlist in the army together, with Swipes hiding on the supply wagon as they all go off to war.

While there are many films throughout cinema's history that have unsettling elements when viewed in more enlightened times, *The Bowery* is one that is so filled with racial slurs and other such offensive content, it is rarely revived. This is unfortunate, because it features another successful pairing of Wallace Beery and Jackie Cooper, some strong acting by Fay Wray, and one of George Raft's finest performances. While it wasn't the likely intent of the filmmakers to be offensive, when Swipes refers to Asians and Italians with derogatory terms, talking about his delight in swindling or throwing rocks at them, it is difficult to accept even as a cultural artifact. The very first shot of *The Bowery* is the front of a bar that repugnantly features an offensive word for an African American as part of its name, which was, remarkably, the actual name of a bar on The Bowery during this time.

Other than the Fay Wray role, women don't fare any better. When a lady accosts Connor at the bar, hugging and kissing him

George Raft and Wallace Beery in The Bowery

while making reference to a recent tryst they had, he hits her with a blackjack and has her dragged out of the bar.

While these incidents are not a focal point of the film, and are likely representative of the way people talked and acted on the bowery in the 19th century, they are offensive enough to merit some discussion in the 21st century. But it is important in any study of history to have a film like this available for examination and discussion, even when some of its content is quite repugnant in more enlightened times.

Wallace Beery and George Raft didn't get along during the shooting, mostly due to Beery's insolence and insecurity. During one of the fight scenes, Beery asked Raft to let him throw the first punch. Raft agreed, and Beery actually hit him, knocking him out. The fight nearly resumed for real. According to Jackie Cooper in his autobiography:

> Beery continued his upstaging tricks, not only with me, but also with Raft. George was not about to take that and, being an old pro, countered tit for tat. So the two old pros waged an upstaging battle that forced the director, Raoul Walsh, to call for retake after retake. Consequently, the film began falling behind schedule. Dozens of takes would be ruined because of the jockeying for position between Beery and Raft or because while one was speaking, the other would be scratching his head or rubbing his chin or one of the other time-tested tactics for stealing a scene. Walsh would blow up and Zanuck would come down to the set.[19]

Despite the conflict with Beery, Raft got through his part successfully, maintaining the lighthearted Brodie persona effectively without wavering. It is so markedly different than what moviegoers were used to, but also a successful departure from the norm. *The Bowery* broke attendance records and futher solidified George Raft's star status.

The movie's Los Angeles premiere was lavish, because it was the first film from a new studio. According to *The Los Angeles Times*:

> It was a spirited premiere, with stars and executives present to greet the first offering here by the new Twentieth Century Pictures, youngest of the larger producing

---

19 Cooper, Jackie. *Please Don't Shoot My Dog, Mister.* NY: William Morrow. 1981

organizations, which offered a production destined popularly to afford plenty of entertainment. Bows were taken and speeches were made to flash up the event. George Raft, Jackie Cooper, Fay Wray, Pert Kelton and Raoul Walsh the director of The Bowery, as well as Joseph M. Schenck and Darryl Zanuck as heads of the organization, were introduced before the picture showing. *The Bowery* is a brisk, laughable, down-to-earth affair. It bangs its way along with many a good blow struck with blackjack, bottle, cane, fist, and even garbage pail. Walsh's talents are at work full force in devising riotous happenings that take place in an environment which offers great possibilities. He doesn't miss any of those that help to spell turbulent excitement. *The Bowery* moves along.

However, in a more recent review published in *The New Yorker*, Richard Brody looks at the films from a 21st century perspective:

The director Raoul Walsh infused this rowdy comedy, from 1933, with his memories of roughhouse New York of the Gay Nineties and inflated it with legends of earlier times…the casual and constant violence, the drunkenness and gambling, the punished and unkempt bodies, and the mercurial swings between gutter and glory lend Walsh's raw, raunchy film a pungent authenticity. He caught the chewy, gimcrack accents, the grotesquely atavistic manners, and the ugly, unquestioned racism, which is repellently prominent from the film's first shot onward.[20]

Whatever animosity Beery and Raft shared off-screen translated well on-screen, and it's fun to watch their characters engage. The heart-tugging moments in the relationship between Beery and Cooper in are similarly effective here as they had been in *The Champ*. And as slimy as Brodie occasionally is, Raft brings him some charm and charisma that makes him ultimately pretty likeable—the same can be said for Beery.

With his next film, George Raft was back to playing hoods, but once again was allowed to explore different aspects of the character. Unfortunately, it was not a particularly good movie.

---

20 The Bowery review. *The New Yorker*. 2011

ALL OF ME

Directed by James Flood
Screenplay by Sidney Buchman and Thomas Mitchell based on the play by Rose Albert Porter.
Produced by Louis Lighton
Cinematography by Victor Milner
Film Editing by Otho Lovering

Cast:
Fredric March	Don Ellis
Miriam Hopkins	Lydia Darrow
George Raft	Honey Rogers
Helen Mack	Eve Haron
Nella Walker	Mrs. Darrow
William Collier Sr.	Jerry Helman
Gilbert Emery	The Dean
Blanche Friderici	Miss Haskell
Kitty Kelly	Lorraine
Astrid Allwyn	Ray
Eleanor Bullen	Woman in Speakeasy
James Burke	Welfare Island Guard
Jill Dennett	Molly
Helena Evans	Mrs. Haron
Patricia Farley	Bee
Lillian West	Jennie
Al Hill	Mickey
Laura La Marr	Lil
John Marston	Nat Davis
Leslie Palmer	Paul
Dennis O'Keefe	Policeman
Edgar Kennedy	Guard
Mack Gray	Tough Guy

Barton MacLane	First Cop
Bruce Mitchell	Second Cop
Jason Robards Sr.	Man in Speakeasy
Harry Stubbs	Second Man in Speakeasy
Guy Usher	District Attorney

Released February 1, 1934
Running Time: 70 minutes
Paramount Pictures
Black and White

Although *All of Me* allowed Raft to play a gangster with a bit more substance, he didn't like the script or the fact that he would be playing a third-billed supporting character. Raft was sent the script while he was working on *The Bowery* and told Paramount that he refused to make the film. Paramount and Raft had been in conflict since before *The Bowery* started shooting in the summer of 1933. Pleased with his work in *The Bowery*, Raft was offered, by Joseph Schenck and Darryl Zanuck, a contract to continue making movies for their new Twentieth Century Pictures studio, and even discussed buying out his Paramount contract to do so. Paramount, however, wasn't interested in releasing him. According to Phillip K. Scheuer in *The Los Angeles Times:*

> Final settlement of the George Raft - Paramount difficulties seem to have been attained. There have been slight after-rumblings and post-grumblings of the row ever since Raft returned to Hollywood, and much talk about his switching over to Twentieth Century Pictures in the last week or two. He was, however, definitely contracted for by Paramount, according to announcement made yesterday.[21]

The film was originally to be called *Chrysalis* but the title was changed to *All of Me* by November of 1933.

Fredric March stars as college professor Don Ellis who falls in love with Lyda Darrow (Miriam Hopkins), one of his students. He wants to marry her but she is hesitant. He is offered a job in another state and she is reticent about going with him. George

---

21 Raft's Services Retained. *The Los Angeles Times.* June 24, 1933

George Raft and Helen Mack in All of Me

Raft stars as Honey Rogers, a gangster who is trying to go straight and leave his criminal life behind. He and his girl, Eva (Helen Mack), star in a subplot that only occasionally meets with the main plot. George Raft is in the first third and final third of the movie, while the entire midsection concentrates on March and Hopkins. What the film attempts to do is present the type of social drama that Warner Brothers was beginning to become noted for producing. Lyda perceives Honey and Eva not as gangsters, but as victims of society, even though Honey kills a guard (Edgar Kennedy) in a prison escape and the two jump to their death when their hotel is surrounded by police.

Despite a good cast, *All of Me* was not a film that did anything for the careers of its actors. George Raft's momentum as a starring actor didn't stall, but it was the first of his films since achieving stardom that got consistently bad reviews and flopped at the box office. This was the first film director James Flood had helmed in two years, his previous one being another Raft movie, *Under-Cover Man*, which was much more successful, both aesthetically and at the box office. Flood worked from the late silent movie era into the early television period before his death in 1955, but none of his movies could be considered enduring classics.

Frederic March was a serious and skilled actor whose stardom would steadily increase from this point and would later include such classics as *The Best Years of Our Lives*, *Les Miserables*, and the 1937 version of *A Star is Born*.

While he was consistently dissatisfied with the project from the outset, George Raft was pleased on two counts when told that for his next assignment he'd not only be finally co-starring with Carole Lombard, he would have the opportunity to show off his dancing skills.

BOLERO

Directed by Wesley Ruggles
Screenplay by Horace Jackson from a story by Carey Wilson and
 Kubec Glasmon based on an idea by Ruth Ridenour
Produced by Benjamin Glaser
Cinematography by Leo Tover
Film Editing by Hugh Bennett

Cast:
George Raft	Raoul De Baere
Carole Lombard	Helen Hathaway
Sally Rand	Annette
Frances Drake	Leona
William Frawley	Mike DeBaere
Gertrude Michael	Lady D'Argon
Ray Milland	Lord Robert Coray
Gloria Shea	Lucy
Fred Warren	Doc - Vaudeville Theater Pianist
Phillips Smalley	Leona's Angel
Paul Panzer	Bailiff
Ann Shaw	Young Matron
Martha Bamattre	Belgian Landlady
Frank Dunn	Hotel Manager
Dell Henderson	Theatre Manager
Gregory Golubeff	Orchestra Leader
Elinor Fair	Dancer
William Irving	Violinist
Dutch Hendrian	Burlesque Brawler
John Irwin	Porter
Adolph Milar	Beer Garden Manager
Heinie Conklin	Beer Garden Waiter
Jacques Vanaire	Headwaiter

William Wagner	Waiter
Max Barwyn	Waiter
William H. O'Brien	Waiter
Ann Sheridan	Chez Raoul Patron
Eugene Borden	Chez Raoul Patron
Constant Franke	Chez Raoul Patron
Julanne Johnston	Chez Raoul Patron
Jean Perry	Chez Raoul Patron
Ellinor Vanderveer	Chez Raoul Patron
Mack Gray	Club Patron
Larry Steers	Cafe Patron
Frederick Sullivan	Cafe Patron
Jack Chefe	Nightclub Patron

Released February 23, 1934
Running Time: 85 minutes
Paramount Pictures
Black and White

By the Fall of 1933, it was already announced that George Raft's next movie would be *Bolero* and he would be supported by Carole Lombard as his co-star. Raft was tiring of the tough guy roles he had been playing, even though he was allowed to add more layers to each character and occasionally explore other aspects to the roles. But he wanted to do a musical, while Paramount hoped to capitalize on the moviegoers', and columnists', comparisons to Rudolph Valentino. Raft didn't like the comparison, he wanted to be his own personality, but Valentino, who had died in 1926, was a major superstar and his status as a screen icon continues into the next century. So, back in 1933, when his passing was a short seven years earlier, Paramount felt that Raft's being able to capitalize on the name would be beneficial.

Bolero appears to be a compromise of sorts. The character Raft plays has aspects reminiscent of Valentino, while it is a musical drama, allowing him to show off his formidable dancing skills. Raft was comfortable with the director, Wesley Ruggles, despite never having worked with him before. Raft was also eager to work with

George Raft and Carole Lombard in Bolero

Carole Lombard, a personal friend. It seemed to be a good project for all involved.

It is 1910, and George Raft plays Raoul De Baere, a coal miner who wants to be a dancer. He works in the mines with his brother Mike (William Frawley) who is shrewd enough and enterprising enough so that Raoul wants him to be his manager. He has some success with Lucy (Gloria Shea) in New Jersey beer gardens, but Raoul loftily believes his skills deserve better. Traveling to Paris, Raoul makes a decent amount of money dancing with older women in the clubs, until he notices Leona (Frances Drake) a dancer with whom he believes he'll achieve greater success. She has romantic feelings for him, which he does not have for her, but Mike persuades him to pretend that he does for the sake of the act. Leona is very volatile, frequently refusing to go on or threatening to quit if her needs are not met. Raoul is approached by Helen Hathaway (Carole Lombard) a chorus girl from the Ziegfeld Follies who believes she is a better dancer than Leona and wants to team with Raoul. This is just as Leona is having yet another outburst, complete with ultimatum. Raoul has had enough, and agrees to team up with Helen once he realizes her skills are so good, she can sense what he's about to do next during a dance and match him. He and Helen travel to England. Raoul is attracted to Helen but avoids mixing business with pleasure so it doesn't hurt the act. However, when Annette, a fan dancer friend (Sally Rand), tells Raoul that Lord Coray (Ray Milland) is interested in Helen, a jealous Raoul starts an affair with her so as not to lose her from his act. After Raoul starts his own club in Paris, he and Helen devise a dance routine for Ravel's Boléro and are set to perform it, when World War One breaks out, distracting the audience. To attract their attention, Raoul announces he is going to enlist. Believing the war will be a skirmish that might last a week or two, he enlists for the publicity but quickly learns the horrors of war when he is wounded in action. Meanwhile, Helen leaves show business, becomes a nurse, and marries Lord Coray. She is so satisfied with her life, that when Raoul returns after Armistice, teams with Annette, and returns to the stage, Helen is happy for him. However, the wounds Raoul suffered have affected his heart, but he ignores the doctors who caution him to not exert himself. Raoul plans to re-introduce the Boléro dance with Annette as his partner, but just before they are to go on, she's drunk and can't perform. Mike finds Helen in the audience and convinces her to dance with Raoul. She does so, and it is a huge success. The applause is so strong, Raoul insists on doing an encore despite Mike desperately trying to talk him out of it due to his health. Just before he's about to go out on stage, Raoul collapses and dies. When Helen and Mike discover him, they see his lifeless body has a smirk of satisfaction.

Bolero was loosely based on the life of dancer Maurice Mouvet (1889-1927) who was said to have had romantic relationships with his female dance partners, and who died young of tuberculosis. Raft knew Maurice personally, so he insisted some changes be made in the screenplay. The studio refused, Raft refused to work, so he was put on suspension. The impasse was brief before the studio agreed to his demands. However, there was another scene in which Raoul kneels over his deceased mother's grave, that Raft outright refused to do, and he made this known to producer

Benjamin Glaser. Glaser, tired of Raft's demands, said, "You'll do it because I say so!" Raft then allegedly punched Glaser, but in later news reports the producer said George merely shoved him, apologized, and it was a closed issue.

Carole Lombard was not originally cast in *Bolero*. It was originally supposed to be Miriam Hopkins, but she had to bow out due to illness, and was replaced by Lombard, who had never danced before. She learned well, and keeps up with Raft satisfactorily, but ballroom dancers Veloz and Yolanda are said to have acted as dance doubles in some of the long shots. Shortly after completing this film, which was shot in December of 1933 and January of 1934, Lombard would appear in *Twentieth Century* (1934). Its success would result in a series of screwball comedies including such films as *My Man Godfrey* (1936) and *Nothing Sacred* (1937) which caused Lombard to be dubbed "the screwball girl," a name that continues to this day, despite her making comparatively few romantic comedies in her career. Carole Lombard is great in this film, and she and Raft have strong chemistry. One of the film's highlights is when they first dance together, Lombard taking off her dress and then matching Raft's moves step for step. Raft's dancing skills at their best in *Bolero* Of his co-star, George Raft told Lewis Yablonsky:

> I truly loved Carole Lombard. She was the greatest girl that ever lived and we were the best of pals. Completely honest and outspoken, always seeing to it that people she knew or felt sorry for worked as extras. If they didn't work, she wouldn't go on the set.[22]

Fan dancer Sally Rand was a bit controversial for movies, especially now that the Hayes Office was enforcing censorship restrictions more carefully. They objected to her appearing in a film, but Paramount recalled the last time this happened, with Mae West, also in a George Raft movie, it resulted in a successful new star on their roster. Sally Rand was hired. Rand was no newcomer to movies, having had small parts in films dating back about ten years, well into the silent era. While her performance in *Bolero* is competent, she does not light up the screen like Mae West did, and only made two more movies, in 1936, and in 1938. Sally kept doing her fan

---

22 Yablonsky, Lewis. *George Raft*. NY: McGraw-Hill, 1974

dance onstage until 1978 when illness forced her to retire. She died a year later.

William Frawley hadn't made ten movie appearances when he appeared in *Bolero,* and was 17 years away from the role that would define his career for all time and generations, Fred Mertz on TV's iconic early sitcom *I Love Lucy*. He plays Mike not unlike the Fred Mertz character, with the same sardonic gruffness as Fred Mertz. Even his dialog delivery is about the same, suggesting that Frawley had honed his skills as a character actor quite early.

Despite the fact that the Boléro dance is one of the film's focal points, it takes place as the war is about to break out in 1914. Ravel did not compose the piece until 1928. This glaring historical error did not affect the film. Critics were pleased, and so were moviegoers. *Bolero* was a big hit, and audiences got to see George Raft dance.

It seemed that with each new film, George Raft added more nuance to his acting skills. For the character of Raoul, he had the opportunity, at the end of the film, to exhibit the effects of the war on his heart. This is especially evident when he comes back stage after the successful Boléro dance and starts happily pacing while the applause continues. Talking, he starts to run out of breath easily; a portent to his collapsing and dying only moments later. Raft plays it subtly as his character excitedly chooses to ignore his own symptoms. It really is some of the best acting Raft had done.

Raft, however, although he liked the film overall, was not too appreciative of his character's traits, telling Lewis Yablonsky:

Bolero was good but I didn't particularly like it because they made me unsympathetic. Someone too conceited, only interested in dancing and success. I only talk about rehearsals, making the act better, or shout about how important my career is to me.[23]

Raft wanted Raoul to, at some point, indicate that Helen was more important to him than his career, but the studio refused, and for once Raft decided to do it their way.

For his next film, George Raft was cast in the unlikely role of a bullfighter. *The Trumpet Blows* had been a project that the studio had planned for a while, a pretty obvious attempt to capitalize on

---

23 Yablonsky, Lewis. *George Raft*. NY: McGraw-Hill, 1974

the Rudolph Valentino comparisons in the press; Valentino having scored big in the silent era with the classic *Blood and Sand*. Raft once again walked out on the project, demanding script changes, and was once again suspended.

THE TRUMPET BLOWS

Directed by Stephen Roberts
Screenplay by Bartlett Cormack and Wallace Smith
Produced by Benjamin Glaser
Cinematography by Harry Fishbeck
Film Editing by Ellsworth Hogland

Cast:
George Raft	Manuel Montes
Adolphe Menjou	Pancho Montes
Frances Drake	Chulita
Sidney Toler	Pepi Sancho
Edward Ellis	Chato
Nydia Westman	Carmela Ramirez
Douglas Wood	Senor Ramirez
Lillian Elliott	Senora Ramirez
Katherine DeMille	Lupe the Maid
Francis McDonald	Vega
Charles Stevens	Sheriff Mejias
Gertrude Norman	Grandma Albrentez
Morgan Wallace	Police Inspector
Hooper Atchley	Detective
Al Bridge	Policeman
Mischa Auer	Bullfighter
Howard Brooks	Priest
E. Alyn Warren	Stationmaster
Joyce Compton	Blonde on Train
Aleth Hansen	Singing Beggar

Released April 14, 1934
Running time: 72 minutes
Paramount Pictures
Black and White

The idea to place George Raft in *The Trumpet Blows*, to capitalize on the Rudolph Valentino comparison, goes back to late 1932 when it was first considered by Paramount. However, at the time, Raft's success in crime dramas was something with which the studio did not want to tamper, so they put him in a few more such films. It was the beginning of 1933 when *The Trumpet Blows* was first announced in the press:

> The first definite move to set George Raft in the Latin lover footsteps of Rudolph Valentino is about to be made. Paramount will star Raft in a picture called *The Trumpet Blows*, in which he will have the role of a Spanish matador. Miriam Hopkins and Wynne Gibson are set for the principal feminine roles although several other featured la femme spots will be handed out. Raft's physical likeness to Valentino was the cause of widespread comment when he made his first appearance on the screen. Since that time it has been freely predicted that he would be groomed as a "second Rudy." Hitherto, however, Paramount has kept him far from the type of parts that made Valentino famous. Finally in *The Trumpet Blows* the dark New Yorker will actually do a picture very similar to the kind the fans have been expecting him to play.[24]

However, there were several delays in the production. Raft was supposed to do this film after *Pick Up*, but then the conflict with *The Story of Temple Drake* happened. Not long afterward he was borrowed by Twentieth Century for *The Bowery*. In fact, that film's director, Raoul Walsh was then attached to direct *The Trumpet Blows*.

Paramount continued to pepper the press, and, thus, the public, with the Raft-Valentino connection, even referencing other actors who did similar roles. According to Phillip K. Scheuer's column in *The Los Angeles Times*:

> Thrice has Gaston DuVal, Paramount wardrobe man and keeper of the Valentino trappings, laid out the ornate dress, Montera hat, picador trousers, dress cape, and

---

24 George Raft To Do Valentino Type Film Role. *Los Angeles Record*. February 8, 1933

toreador sword for the actor's successors to wear. Once for Ricardo Cortez. Once for Paul Ellis. And recently for George Raft, in *The Trumpet Blows*.[25]

Miriam Hopkins was announced as the lead actress, but when it finally came time to film the movie, she was in contract negotiations and replaced by Frances Drake. Adrienne Ames and Roscoe Karns were set for supporting roles, but they were eventually replaced by Katherine DeMille and Sidney Toler. It was announced that Jack LaRue would be cast as Raft's brother in the film. When LaRue replaced Raft in *The Story of Temple Drake*, he told *Photoplay*: "I don't look like Raft, I don't act like him, and I certainly don't want to follow in his shoes." Casting them as brothers was an intriguing idea that was jettisoned when Adolphe Menjou was cast in the role. Walsh was then replaced by Stephen Roberts.

Stephen Roberts was a director of short subjects for Jack White's Mermaid Comedies unit at Educational Pictures. He had moved on to features, and was the director of *The Story of Temple Drake*, among others. After a stint at Paramount, Roberts went over to RKO and directed two William Powell mysteries to capitalize on his *Thin Man* fame: *Star of Midnight* (1935) and *The Ex-Mrs Bradford* (1936). Roberts died suddenly of a heart attack at the age of 40, shortly after the release of *The Ex-Mrs. Braford*.

George Raft had known Adolphe Menjou back when Menjou was a successful Broadway actor and Raft was a top dancer. One night after closing time, Menjou insisted Raft be awakened and perform a dance number for him. Raft agreed to do so, and afterward Menjou thanked him profusely and complimented his talents --- but he gave him no tip or gratuity of any kind. Arriving on the set of *The Trumpet Blows* for the first day of rehearsal, Raft reminded Menjou of the incident and said, "You owe me some dough!"

George Raft insisted on some changes to the script for *The Trumpet Blows*. As per usual, Paramount eventually agreed to George Raft's script changes after suspending him. This time, it made no difference. *The Trumpet Blows* remains one of the worst films in George Raft's entire movie career.

---

25 News and Gossip from the Stage and Screen. *Los Angeles Times*. May 7, 1933

George Raft and Adolph Menjou in The Trumpet Blows

Raft plays a Mexican matador named Manuel. To keep the actor from having to sustain a Latino accent throughout the film, the story indicates that he is returning to Mexico from New York, where he was schooled for years. Adolph Menjou plays his brother Pancho, Frances Drake plays his brother's girl Chulita. Manuel falls for Chulita and it is reciprocated. Pancho is secretly a notorious bandito. The cast is rounded out by Sidney Toler, Katherine DeMille, Edward Ellis, and Frances McDonald, all playing Mexicans. There were, of course, Latino actors in Hollywood, but none appear in this movie.

The movie's fleeting highlights include a rhumba danced by Drake (without Raft), and the stock footage of actual bullfights used to add authenticity to the proceedings. But none of this keeps *The Trumpet Blows* from being a wrongheaded project for all involved. Raft tries but he is not successful in this role. *The Trumpet Blows* is

George Raft and Frances Drake in The Trumpet Blows

a very dull and predictable movie. One thing that did please Raft regarding this film – after it became a huge flop at the box office, nobody compared him to Rudolph Valentino again.

LIMEHOUSE BLUES

Directed by Alexander Hall
Screenplay by Arthur Phillips and Cyril Hume
Produced by Arthur Hornblow Jr.
Cinematography by Harry Fishebeck
Film Editing by William Shea

George Raft	Harry Young
Jean Parker	Toni
Anna May Wong	Tu Tuan
Kent Taylor	Eric Benton
Montagu Love	Pug Talbot
Billy Bevan	Herb
John Rogers	Smokey
Robert Loraine	Inspector Sheridan
E. Alyn Warren	Lee
Wyndham Standing	Assistant Commissioner Kenyon
Louis Vincent	Rhama
Forrester Harvey	McDonald
Tempe Pigott	Maggie
Colin Tapley	Man Fighting with Wife
Rita Carlyle	Wife
Eric Blore	Slummer
James May	Taxi Driver
Otto Yamaoka	Chinese Waiter on Boa
Elsie Prescott	Woman Employment Agent
Ted Billings	Passerby at Murder Scene
Richard Loo	Customer at Harry Young's
Eily Malyon	Woman Who Finds Pug
Dora Mayfield	Flower Woman
Jack Perry	Barfly
Desmond Roberts	Constable

Ann Sheridan	A Bit
Keith Hitchcock	Bit
Colin Kenny	Bit

Released December 11, 1934
Running Time: 63 minutes
Paramount Pictures
Black and White

Also known as *East End Chant*

As wrongheaded as it was to cast George Raft as a Latino, it was just as wrong to cast him as half Chinese. Because he is also half American, he makes no attempt to incorporate a stereotypical Chinese accent, so if one can get past the eye makeup, *Limehouse Blues* is a good atmospheric thriller.

George Raft plays Harry Young, a Chinese-American immigrant who owns a club in the Limehouse district of London, The Lily Gardens. The club is basically a front for his smuggling operation. Although he is new to the area, Young has taken over most of the criminal activities, much to the chagrin of his rival, Pug Talbot (Montagu Love). Pug's daughter Toni (Jean Parker) is a pickpocket who is caught by police, but Young intervenes and keeps her from being arrested. Toni is indebted to Young. When her father tries to set him up to be arrested, Toni warns Young who is able to evade police. Pug then beats Toni, and when he hears about it Young summons Pug to his place to negotiate, and has him killed. Young then hires Toni to be his watchdog, keeping an eye on things and warning him as needed. Young's Chinese lover, Tu Tuan (Anna May Wong) is jealous of Toni, and warns Young not to fall for "a white girl." Worried for Toni's safety, he removes her from his organization, but offers her money for living expenses. Toni meets and falls in love with Eric Benton (Kent Taylor), who owns a pet store. They fall in love and Toni gets a job so that she no longer relies on Young. Young does not want Toni to disassociate with him, so an angry Tu Tuan leaves Young because of his love for the white woman. Toni admits her past to Benton, who visits The Lily

Jean Parker and George Raft in Limehouse Blues

Gardens to meet with Young, who makes arrangements for Benton to later be killed in the same manner as Pug. Young then goes on a smuggling caper escorted by Toni. Tu Tuan tells the police, and then kills herself. Toni finds out Young's plan to have Benton killed and her reaction causes Young to realize her love is genuine. He decides to do the right thing and call off his assassins, and does so in time, but is shot while evading police and dies.

Sylvia Sidney was originally planned for the role of Toni, but turned it down. Heather Angel was also considered before Jean Parker was cast. *Limehouse Blues* was originally called *Limehouse Nights* but the title was changed during production. It was retitled *East End Chant* for most TV showings. The film was shot in October of 1934 on

Anna May Wong and George Raft in Limehouse Blues

location at the port of San Pedro in Los Angeles, much of it directed by second unit director William Shea.

George Raft never seems stiff or ill-at-ease in playing a Chinese American complete with eye makeup to make him look Asian. He comfortably fits into the role as a gangster in a crime drama, and plays it the way he had played other such roles. Harry Young is complex, being both a hero and a villain, a criminal and a businessman, a killer and one who rescues. He overlooks whatever racial boundaries society might impose on his interest in a non-Asian girl, and despite the misgiving of Tu Tuan. Raft's performance is good, the story is compelling, the characters are well-drawn, and the dark visual atmosphere is effective. Raft and Anna May Wong also get to perform a dance, that is one of the highlights of the film, and is organic to the narrative. That is what Harry is doing while Pug is being killed, giving him an alibi.

The fact that this was similar to roles Raft had previously played is a big reason why he doesn't appear uncomfortable, although his makeup and any acknowledgment of his Chinese heritage can be distracting. It was also disappointing to see the one principal Asian actor in the cast, Anna May Wong, sacrifice herself because of him.

The review in the *New York Daily News* was pretty typical of the reaction from critics, as it stated:

> There is hardly any single item that is new or original, although it must be admitted that to watch George Raft perform even in a fair to middlin' opus is to get your money's worth. As in the past, George is called upon in his last scene, to fade out via the death-route. At this piece of histrionics he is rapidly approaching a position which puts him in a class by himself. As regards the script, the dancing man Raft (he briefly tossed around Anna May Wong in this photoplay) is a "half American, half Chinese" who has come to London to plague the police of that city with his Yankee gangland methods. He is in this respect quite successful until, as has been pointed out already, he gets rubbed out by a tommy gun especially imported for that purpose. All this happens only after George has maintained a fruitless love for a cockney waif who is personified by an all-American girl named Jean Parker. Miss Parker is, however, lovely whether she drops her "h's" or hangs onto them according to the best American manner of speaking English.[26]

Limehouse Blues was another box office disappointment, as the previous *The Trumpet Blows* had been, although this is a much better film. Paramount then decided to capitalize on the success of *Bolero* by re-teaming Carole Lombard and George Raft in another musical drama.

---

26 Limehouse Blues review. *The New York Daily News.* December 12, 1934

RUMBA

Directed by Marion Gehring
Screenplay by Howard Green, Harry Ruskin, and Frank Partos
    from a story by Guy Endore and Seena Owen
Produced by William LeBaron
Cinematography by Ted Tetzlaff
Film Editing by Hugh Bennett

Cast:
George Raft	Joe Martin
Carole Lombard	Diana Harrison
Lynne Overman	Flash
Margo	Carmelita
Gail Patrick	Patsy Fletcher
Iris Adrian	Goldie Allen
Monroe Owsley	Hobart Fletcher
Jameson Thomas	Jack Solanger
Soledad Jiménez	Tia Maria
Paul Porcasi	Carlos
Samuel S. Hinds	Henry B. Harrison
Virginia Hammond	Mrs. Harrison
Donald Gray	Watkins
Craig Reynolds	Bromley
Akim Tamiroff	Tony
Bruce Warren	Dean
E.H. Calvert	Police Captain
Frank O'Connor	Police Sergeant
Dick Rush	Policeman
Richard Alexander	Policeman
Hooper Atchley	Doctor
James Burke	Reporter
James P. Burtis	Reporter
Mason N. Litson	Stage Manager

Alfred P. James	Stage Doorman
Robert 'Buddy' Shaw	Ticket Taker
Rafael Alcayde Alfredo	- Cashier
Mack Gray	Assistant Dance Director
Hallene Hill	Wardrobe Woman
Frank Mills	Bouncer
Carlie Taylor	Steward on Yacht
Victor Sabini	Waiter
Charles Stevens	Counterfeit Lottery Ticket Vendor
Ellinor Vanderveer	Member of Audience
Paul Ellis	Waiter at Cafe Elefante
Brooks Benedict	Man in Audience at Cafe
Philo McCullough	Man in Audience at Cafe
Don Brodie	Man in Audience at Theatre
Charles Sullivan	Man in Audience at Theatre
Jack Raymond	Man in Audience at Theatre
Dave O'Brien	Man in Audience at Theatre
Dennis O'Keefe	Man in Diana's Party at Theatre
Peggy Watts	Girl in Diana's Party
Raymond McKee	Dance Director
Laura Puente	Rumba Dancer
Luis Barrancos	Rumba Dancer
Olga Barrancos	Rumba Dancer
Dorothy White	Chorus Girl
Jane Wyman J	Chorus Girl
Alma Ross	Chorus Girl
Jean Ross	Chorus Girl
Ann Sheridan	Chorus Girl
Helen Curtis	Chorus Girl
Dorothy Dayton	Chorus Girl
Jeanette Dickson	Chorus Girl
Bonita Barker	Chorus Girl
Nora Gale	Chorus Girl
Patsy King	Chorus Girl
Lora Lane	Chorus Girl
De Don Blunier	Chorus Girl
Zora	Specialty Dancer
Frank Leyva	Minor Role

Released February 8, 1935
Running Time: 71 minutes
Paramount Pictures
Black and White

The success of *Bolero* prompted Paramount to once again team Carole Lombard and George Raft in another dance-related drama. And while *Rumba* is not as strong of a film as *Bolero* had been, it is redeemed by some great dance numbers, good acting, and some tense moments. The narrative is a bit meandering, but there are some good, creative choices by the director to sustain the film's structure.

George Raft plays Joe Martin, an American dancer in Cuba who is pleased to discover he has a winning lottery ticket worth $5000. When he goes to collect, he finds out that the prize is being claimed by Diana Harrison (Carole Lombard), and that the ticket he bought was counterfeit. Joe vows to get even with the crook that sold him the phony ticket. Later that night, Diana and her party, including her boyfriend Hobart Fletcher (Monroe Owsley), end up in the audience at a club where Joe dances. Diana comes from wealth and doesn't need the money, so she tries to give it to Joe but he has too much pride. She also offers to back him in his own nightclub, but he then tries to seduce her. Offended, she walks out on him. Joe goes to a fiesta with Carmelita (Margo) and sees a performance of the native dance the rumba, and plans for the two of them to learn it, believing it will be a success in the clubs. Joe hires a reporter buddy, Flash (Lynne Overman), to manage, and Flash finds a wealthy Texan willing to back a new club venture. The club is a success after Joe and Carmelita perform the rumba on opening night. Diana and her party are there, and Joe later dances with her. They fall in love and start spending a great deal of time together. Joe even teaches Diana the rumba. Diana's family summons her back to New York to marry Hobart, a man of breeding from a good family, but Diana writes back that she is staying with Joe. Joe, however, believes Diana is going to break up with him, so he arranges for Carmelita to show up at a planned meeting. In the confusion, Diana angrily leaves Joe and returns to New York. Upon her return, Diana discovers something about Joe's past. Joe was also from New York, but had left years ago because he had evidence that

Carole Lombard and George Raft in Rumba

could put a notorious gangster behind bars, so his life was in danger. A Broadway producer tries to hire Joe, but he refuses, not telling the producer, or Flash, the reason why. Joe reads in the papers that Diana has broken her engagement to Hobart, so he agrees to go to New York and join the Broadway show, taking Carmelita with him as his dance partner. While there, Joe receives a telegram warning him to return to Cuba and not go on stage. He defiantly refuses, but Carmelita faints. Diana rushes back stage and goes on with Joe, performing the rumba. They reconnect, and it is discovered that the death threat was a publicity stunt that Flash arranged in order to draw a big crowd to the club, which it did.

The reaction to *Rumba* by both critics and moviegoers was a real mixed bag. Some exhibitors reported to the trades that the film was a big hit in their theater. Others complained it bombed and resulted in walk-outs. Still others reported a 50-50 reaction.

One interesting comment believed the film was a "women's picture" and it would especially have femme appeal. This certainly goes against the review offered by the Women's University Club of Los Angeles, who stated:

> In this melodramatic and exceedingly distasteful musical extravaganza, George Raft impersonates a lowbred cabaret dancer in Havana. Through peculiar and improbable circumstances, the spoiled heiress of many millions meets him, is infatuated with him, and becomes his dancing partner. Though he behaves despicably to her, she seems to thrive on insults, and the picture ends with the course of true love running smoothly. The whole idea is repugnant in the extreme. It is based on false standards, unconventionality, and sordid motives, and the glamourous personality of the heroine, the good acting, and the smooth direction only add to the demoralizing influence of the production.[27]

Interestingly enough, this negative review admits to good acting and smooth direction, so the reviewer appreciated the film as cinema, she just disliked the content.

Today *Rumba* holds up due to its stars, the musical numbers, and some neat camera shots by cinematographer Ted Tetzlaff. George Raft was said to complain to Tetzlaff during shooting because he felt the camera was favoring Lombard over himself. Interestingly, Tetzlaff would later become a director, and would direct Raft in more than one movie.

George Raft and Lombard have very good chemistry in this movie, as they did in *Bolero*, but the story and writing aren't as strong so it doesn't come across so well. Curiously, many moviegoers reacted negatively to *Rumba* because they felt George Raft was miscast. They saw him as a movie tough guy, and wanted to see more examples of that character. Audiences didn't realize, or perhaps didn't care, that Raft had been a dancer before he was an actor. Their checkpoint was his breakthrough role in *Scarface*. Raft does play the same type of tough guy in *Rumba* that he played in other films, but it appeared moviegoers also wanted the crime drama setting, not a series of club dates and dance performances.

Rumba was the last time Carole Lombard and George Raft acted together in a film. From this point, Raft's career continued to progress, but so did Lombard's and in another direction.

---

27 Motion Picture Reviews. Women's University Club. March, 1935

STOLEN HARMONY

Directed by Alfred Werker
Screenplay by Claude Binyon, Lewis R. Foster, and Leon Gordon
    from a story by Gordon
Produced by Albert Lewis
Cinematography by Harry Fischbeck
Film Editing by Otho Lovering

Cast:
George Raft	Ray Angelo, alias Ray Ferraro
Ben Bernie	Jack Conrad
Grace Bradley	Jean Loring
Iris Adrian	Verne
Lloyd Nolan	Chesty Burrage
Goodee Montgomery	Lil Davis
Charles Arnt	Walters
Leslie Fenton	Joe Harris
William Cagney	'Schoolboy' Howe
Paul Gerrits	Ted Webb
Ralf Harolde	Dude Williams
John Kelly	Bates
James T. Mack	Pop
Jack Norton	Phillips
William Pawley	Turk Connors
Cully Richards	Pete
Fred 'Snowflake' Toones	Henry
Duke York	Duke
Christian Rub	Mathew Huxley
Robert Emmett O'Connor	Warden Clark
Arthur Millett	Deputy Sheriff
Billy Wilson	Sheriff
Stanley Andrews	Patrol Chief

Earl Askam	State Trooper
Edgar Dearing	Motorcycle Cop
Ben Taggart	Sergeant / Cop at Motel
Jack Hill	Cop
Ted Oliver	Cop
Jack Herrick	Prisoner
Eddie Magill	Prisoner
Jack Perry	Prisoner
Oscar Smith	Prison Chimist
Kit Guard	Convict in Orchestra
Jack Burnette	Pianist
Constantine Romanoff	Piccolo Player
Eddie Sturgis	Musician
John 'Dusty' King	Fagin in Skit
Fred Lawrence	Hero in Skit / Vocalist
Manny Prager	Nell's Father in Skit
Purv Pullen	Little Nell in Skit
Mickey Garlock	Working Girl in Skit
Carol Holloway	Six Kids Member
Ada Ince	Girl in Sextette
Lois January	Girl in Sextette
Adele Cutler Jerome	Girl in Sextette
Margaret Nearing	Sextette Girl
Jane Wyman	Chorine
Jack Judge	Photographer
Ernest Shields	Elevator Operator
Harry Bernard	Peanut Vendor
Ruth Clifford	Nurse
Eddie Dunn	Hotel Clerk
Dick Stabile	Minister
Al Goering	Bit

Released April 20, 1935
Running Time: 80 minutes
Paramount Pictures
Black and White

George Raft on the set of Stolen Harmony

George Raft movies seemed to be settling into a formula in which he played a man with a nefarious past who wanted to shift his life in another direction and separate himself from his former life. In *Stolen Harmony*, George plays Ray, a saxophonist in the prison band who, upon release, is hired to join an actual jazz outfit led by Jack Conrad, played by actual bandleader Ben Bernie. Ray hooks up with Jean Loring (Grace Bradley) and the two become a dance act when he replaces her drunken partner Ted (Paul Gerrits), extending his life in the music and entertainment world and moving further away from his crime-ridden past. However, when one of Ray's acquaintances from his past robs the band's tour bus, Ray is suspected and must clear his name.

There are a few nuances to Raft's character. First, his name is Ray Ferrera but he tours as Ray Angelo in order to further bury his past. He re-invents himself in attitude and manner. The music world, with its nightclub gigs, naturally rubs up against underworld characters pretty regularly, and Ray's streetwise manner is helpful in situations because of his past. He uses the negative and finds a way to make it positive. The tour bus that Jack Conrad's band uses for their cross-country tour is a massive airplane-shaped vehicle. It shows the noisy power that big band jazz outfits enjoyed as early as the mid 1930s (this would extend well into the war years, but gradually fizzle in the post-war era). Thus, *Stolen Harmony* is an interesting film despite being very standard and formulaic.

It is interesting to see Grace Bradley in a lead role the same year her future husband William Boyd debuted in movies as western hero Hopalong Cassidy. Bradley would marry Boyd two years later, in 1937, and would remain wed until Boyd's 1972 death. William Boyd notably used all of his savings to buy the rights to the character, and successfully marketed it during the 1950s, making a fortune. To the end of her life, on her 97th birthday in 2010, Bradley carefully maintained the legacy of her husband's work.

Ben Bernie was the composer of the song "Sweet Georgia Brown" and this is one of only about a half dozen film appearances he made before his death in 1943.

Some newspaper accounts at the time claimed this to be Lloyd Nolan's film debut, stating that he was brought to movies from the stage with this project. In fact, Nolan had already debuted in the Warner Brothers feature *G-Men* starring James Cagney, which was released earlier the same year.

During the filming of *A Stolen Harmony*, George Raft sustained a minor injury that was reported in the press:

> George Raft dipped from the edge of a studio set, raised three feet from the floor, and suffered a serious muscle strain and a sprained ligament in his left leg yesterday

morning. He was taken to his dressing room at the Paramount studios, where an examination by Dr. H. J. Stratheara, studio physician, revealed that the star must stay off his feet for at least one week. He was removed to his home later. Raft was working with Ben Bernie and Grace Bradley in a scene in a new film, *Stolen Harmony*, when the accident occurred. Schedule has been arranged to work around the star.

Despite this mishap, director Alfred Werker brought the film in on time and it did not go over budget.

Even though Raft is in his element, it contains a car chase as its climax, and there is a lot of comedy peppering the narrative, *Stolen Harmony* is disappointing on many levels. It is very much a by-the-numbers formula picture that does little with the talent involved. Even George Raft's dancing is limited to a few close-up shots and otherwise done by a double who doesn't even resemble his form.

Stolen Harmony is not a terrible movie, but it isn't a good one either. It is merely a throwaway that merits little attention. Raft would fare much better in his next film.

THE GLASS KEY

Directed by Frank Tuttle
Screenplay by Kathryn Scola and Kubec Glasmon from a story by
 Dashiell Hammett
Produced by E. Lloyd Sheldon
Cinematography by Henry Sharp
Film Editing by Hugh Bennett

Cast:
George Raft	Ed Beaumont
Edward Arnold	Paul Madvig
Claire Dodd	Janet Henry
Rosalind Culli	Opal Madvig
Charles Richman	Senator John T. Henry
Robert Gleckler	Shad O'Rory
Guinn 'Big Boy' Williams	Jeff
Ray Milland	Taylor Henry
Tammany Young	Clarkie
Harry Tyler	Henry Sloss
Charles C. Wilson	District Attorney Edward J. Farr
Emma Dunn	'Mom' Madvig
Matt McHugh	Puggy
Pat Moriarity	Mulrooney
Mack Gray	Duke
Ann Sheridan	Nurse
Michael Mark	Swartz
Henry Roquemore	Hinkle
George Reed	Midnight
Frank Marlowe	Walter Ivans
Frank O'Connor	Frank McLaughlin
Richard Kipling	Dice Player
Jack Perry	Pool Player

Ernie Adams	Bettor
Christian J. Frank	Pool Player
Carlton Griffin	Dice Player
Paddy O'Flynn	Reporter
Alfred Delcambre	Reporter
Jack Raymond	Reporter
Veda Buckland	Landlady
Herbert Evans	Senator Henry's Butler
Frank Fanning	Bus Conductor
Carl Faulkner	Policeman
Budd Fine	Street Worker
Oscar 'Dutch' Hendrian	Bodyguard
Mike Tellegen	Bodyguard
John Ince	Politician
Irving Bacon	Waiter
George Lloyd	Hood
Walter McGrail	Madvig Supporter
Bruce Mitchell	Drunk
Percy Morris	Bartender
Harry Semels	Street Speaker
Phillips Smalley	Man in Barber Chair
Harry Stafford	Guest
George Ernest	Boy
Nick Thompson	Street Worker
Kathrin Clare Ward	Gossip

Released June 15, 1935
Running time: 80 minutes
Paramount Pictures
Black and White

Back to doing gangster dramas, and this time with a political background, George Raft scored big with *The Glass Key*, which remains one of the best films of his career. Paramount originally bought the rights to Dashiell Hammett's book for $25,000 back in 1930 with the intention of featuring Gary Cooper in the lead. The working title of this project was *Graft*. However, no film was made.

George Raft and Edward Arnold in The Glass Key

In the summer of 1934, it was taken from the shelf and dusted off for George Raft, with Frank Tuttle hired as director. Elissa Landi was originally cast as the female lead, but was replaced by Claire Dodd before filming began in February of 1935.

George Raft plays Ed Beaumont, who supports city big shot Paul Madvig (Edward Arnold), who runs the city with connections in both the criminal and political world Paul has plans to marry Janet Henry (Claire Dodd) and uses his political influence to support the senatorial campaign of her father (Charles Richman). Janet's brother Taylor (Ray Milland) has a gambling problem and soon becomes heavily indebted to gangster Shad O'Rory (Robert Gleckler), a rival of Madvig's whom he wants to put out

George Raft in The Glass Key

of business. When Beaumont finds Taylor dead in the alley, Madvig is suspected. In order to get information, Beaumont goes to O'Rory pretending to double-cross Madvig, but is badly beaten by Jeff (Guinn Williams), Paul's brutal henchman. It falls to Janet to tell what she knows and clear Paul's name, but it means implicating her guilty father.

The Glass Key is a taut, compelling, exciting drama featuring Hammett at his best, and with the screenplay adaption co-written by Kubec Glasmon, who had come over to Paramount from Warner Brothers after having penned the script for such gangster classics as *The Public Enemy* (with John Bright, from their book), *Smart Money,* and *Taxi,* all featuring James Cagney (Raft had a brief cameo in the latter film). Sadly, Glasmon's successful career was cut short by his early death at the age of 40 in 1938 when he suffered

George Raft and Ray Milland in The Glass Key

a fatal heart attack. His co-writer, Kathryn Scola, had written the screenplays for *Baby Face*, *Midnight Mary*, and *Female* so the two scenarists were already very successful in penning scripts for crime dramas. This was their only collaboration.

George Raft is again given a more complex character to play, and he rises to the occasion as one who is both at the forefront and on the sidelines. Beaumont maintains a supportive presence with Madvig, but it is his suggestions that guide the process. Edward Arnold is perfectly cast as the blustery Madvig with his confident manner punctuated by deep laughter. He lets Beaumont do the worrying for him. However, Beaumont's concerns do not so much rise to the level of worry, as he has his own confidence. He believes that, while it is a challenge at times, he can effectively control the impulsivity of the powerful Madvig, who always appreciates his loyalty and support. Guinn Williams eventually settled into playing more comically based roles, but here he shines as a frightening violent thug who nearly beats Beaumont to death.

Claire Dodd is another who came over from Warner Brothers, after having appeared in films with James Cagney, Joe E. Brown, and William Powell. As Janet Tracy, Dodd has a pivotal role and successfully conveys the conflicting emotions her character must confront. British born Ray Milland was still doing smaller parts at this time (he had also appeared in *Bolero* with Raft), but his brief role as the ill-fated gambler makes an impact, and it is not difficult to understand why he'd be a leading man in another two years.

Reviews of *The Glass Key* were mixed, but the public loved it. It is one of George Raft's most successful films of the 1930s. One of the most positive reviews came from Andre Sennwald of *The New York Times*, who stated:[28]

> Dashiell Hammett and the cinema continue their beautiful friendship in *The Glass Key*. A salty tale of violence and secret murder, it has been excellently produced in the Paramount studios, and it becomes as crisply exciting a melodrama as Broadway has seen lately. You may recall that when the murder films seemed in danger of being too grave in their study of the amiable art of mass slaughter, Mr. Hammett's *The Thin Man* began the cycle of what may be called the hilarious homicide school of crime fiction. Now, just when we were beginning to fear that the imitators of *The Thin Man* were becoming overly jocose on the subject of assassination, Mr. Hammett comes along with proof that murder isn't necessarily funny. And what, you may want to know, is a glass key? It seems to be an underworld figure of speech for an invitation which is motivated by expediency rather than genuine friendliness. It is one of the particular charms of the mystery that the underworld is as anxious as the upperworld to trap the killer. Every one suspects his neighbor, and as far as motive and circumstance go they might all be right. Thus, when Mr. Raft invades the hoodlum's territory, hoping to absolve his boss from a threatened murder indictment, he is captured and cruelly tortured by his enemies, who are convinced that his employer is the murderer. Nothing quite so realistically

---

28 The Glass Key review. *The New York Times*. June 15, 1935.

savage has reached the screen lately as the description in *The Glass Key* of the punishment to which the captive is subjected during his imprisonment in the hoodlum's hideout. Mr. Arnold is characteristically good as the honest ward-heeler who cannot believe that he is actually being accused of murder. Mr. Raft, happily cast in a role which allows him to be sinister and suave, gives the most effective of his recent performances. The photoplay presents that excellent actor, Guinn Williams, in another of his surprisingly versatile performances.

It is interesting that this review points out how the brutality of gangster films were starting to become a bit intense by 1934, and the lighthearted *Thin Man* from MGM allowed moviegoers a chance to relax a bit. But after a few more similar type movies, audiences were ready to welcome another serious crime drama.

By the time *The Glass Key* was made, the production code was now fully enforced, and that limited the screenwriters, both of whom did some of their best work during the pre-code era. However, *The Glass Key* still emerged as a hard-hitting crime drama that was great for George Raft's career.

Because of his interest in playing different types of roles, George Raft was pleased when told that his next film would be a musical comedy. He was further pleased when he found that Raoul Walsh, who directed him in the hit movie *The Bowery* was assigned to direct *Every Night at Eight*.

EVERY NIGHT AT EIGHT

Directed by Raoul Walsh
Screenplay by Gene Towne and Graham Baker from the story
   Three on a Mike by Stanley Garvey
Produced by Walter Wanger
Cinematography by James van Trees
Film Editing by W. Donn Hayes

Songs:
Take It Easy
Music by Jimmy McHugh
Lyrics by Dorothy Fields and George Oppenheimer

Don't Say Good-Night
Music by Harry Warren
Lyrics by Al Dubin

I Feel a Song Coming On
Music by Jimmy McHugh
Lyrics by Dorothy Fields and George Oppenheimer

Speaking Confidentially
Music by Jimmy McHugh
Lyrics by Dorothy Fields

Then You've Never Been Blue
Music by Ted Fio Rito
Lyrics by Joe Young and Frances Langford and Sam Lewis

Take It Easy
Music by Jimmy McHugh
Lyrics by Dorothy Fields and George Oppenheimer

Every Night at Eight
Music by Jimmy McHugh
Lyrics by Dorothy Fields and George Oppenheimer

I Feel a Song Coming On
Music by Jimmy McHugh
Lyrics by Dorothy Fields and George Oppenheimer

I'm in the Mood for Love
Music by Jimmy McHugh
Lyrics by Dorothy Fields and George Oppenheimer
Sung by Frances Langford

Cast:
George Raft	Tops Cardona
Alice Faye	Dixie
Frances Langford	Susan Moore
Patsy Kelly	Daphne O'Connor
Harry Barris	Harry
Herman Bing	Joe Schmidt
Boothe Howard	Martin
John Dilson	Huxley
Louise Carver	Mrs. Snyder
Henry Taylor	Radio Rogue
Jimmy Hollywood	Radio Rogue
Eddie Bartell	Radio Rogue
Walter Catlett	Master of Ceremonies
Claud Allister	Mr. Vernon
Alyce Ardell	Fifi
Stephen Chase	Mr. Graham
Claudia Coleman	Mrs. Reginald Herring-Smythe
Harry Holman	Col. Ratchfield
Florence Roberts	Mrs. Murgatroyd
Herbert Ashley	Piano Remover
Lynton Brent	Mail Sorter
Eddie Conrad	Italian Singer
Phyllis Crane	Phone Operator

Gertie Green	Phone Operator
Ted Fio Rito	Orchestra Leader
James Miller	Band Singer
Dillon Ober	Band Drummer
Charles Forsythe	Sound Effects Man
Nina Gilbert	Chief Operator
Eddie Fetherston	Gold Strike Cigarettes Ad Man
Florence Gill	Chicken Lady Singer
Tom Hanlon	Radio Announcer
Isabel La Mal	Socialite at Party
Louise Larabee	New Employee
Dennis O'Keefe	Huxley Employee
Richard Powell	Motorist
Libby Taylor	Maid

Released August 2, 1935
Running Time: 82 minutes
Paramount Pictures
Black and White

Every Night at Eight is an unusual film for director Raoul Walsh, whose work is notably action drama not musical comedy. And it is also offbeat for George Raft. Unlike his other recent musicals – such as the recent *Bolero* or *Rumba* – there is no underworld or crime element to *Every Night at Eight*. It is light and amusing in the movie musical tradition. In fact, this isn't essentially a George Raft movie at all. While he gets top billing and is the male lead, the story mostly involves the exploits of a singing trio of young ladies who are trying to get a break, and hook up with a bandleader, played by Raft, who helps build and promote their career as his band's singers.

George Raft is Tops Cardona, a bandleader who is struggling despite having a talented outfit. He performs on an amateur radio show for Huxley Mint Julep, and is securing the bulk of audience votes, until three girls come up and do a vocal act. The girls are Dixie, Susan, and Daphne (Alice Faye, Frances Langford, and Patsy Kelly) who had once worked in the Huxley offices, but got

George Raft with Patsy Kelly, Alice Faye, and Frances Langford in Every Night at Eight

fired after being overheard insulting him. The girls are set to win the contest, but Susan collapses from hunger and the prize goes to Tops and his band. Feeling sorry for the girls, Tops uses some of the winnings to buy them food, and then hires him as his singers, christening them The Swanee Sisters to play up a southern angle that attracts Huxley. After Huxley sings a contract with the band, he meets the popular singers and realizes it is the girls he had fired. Several conflicts arise, including Susan's attraction to Tops, who is all business, and the fact that while they are well paid, they don't have any time to enjoy their money. The stage a rebellion and leave the act, attending a society party. But when they hear Tops over the radio talking about how much he misses them, they rush to the studio and join him.

The most immediate elements of *Every Night at Eight* is how it has become, in the 21st century, very much a cultural representative of its era. While talent contests on the airwaves continue, their genesis is depicted here. Even though, for instance, nobody can see his band, Tops throws in some dance moves as he conducts, purely for the sake of the studio audience, realizing their audible response means something. Votes are cast by phone, and there are dozens of operators frantically collecting them.

The popularity of such programs was so strong, the press made mention of this film's exploring them. An article in *The Los Angeles Times* stated:

> Just as madly as they flung themselves into the making of government investigator films a month or two ago, producers are now taking the headfirst leap into films exploiting the amateur programs idea. This is following in the wake of a new theatrical and radio development. Walter Wanger has scheduled the picture *Every Night at Eight*. The studio has also purchased a story called *Talent Night* by Sig Herrig, which is to be produced by Hal Hurley, with Joe Morrison and Rosalind Keith. Miss Keith has just finished opposite George Raft in *The Glass Key* (billed as Rosalind Culli), and Raft, oddly enough, got the lead role in the Wanger feature. All kinds of rivalry that![29]

Notably, neither Joe Morrison (who appeared in only 7 movies his entire career) nor Rosalind Keith appear in such a movie, and were instead cast together by Paramount in director Eddie Cline's Depression drama *It's a Great Life* (1935).

The big band music, and equally jazzy vocal songs by the girls, also nicely represent what was popular in the mid 1930s, and would continue into the 1940s through the war years. By the post war era, a cultural shift eventually led to the rock and roll that would take over by the middle of the 1950s. But during the 1930s, as Americans slowly climbed out of the depths of the Depression, the happy orchestral sounds were what entertained them.

Along with these elements that make the film a special production for the more modern era, George Raft's offbeat role explores another dynamic to his acting ability. He is focused and driven, but also bright and clever. Any romantic feelings are suppressed by his drive.

While he doesn't command the entire film, sharing the spotlight with three actresses, Raft did not balk upon reading the script. He welcomed the part as a strong change of pace for both him and

---

29 Amateur Show Latest Rage. *Los Angeles Times*. May 6, 1935.

Walsh. Raft seems both comfortable and committed throughout the film. In fact, producer Walter Wanger wanted George Raft so badly to play Tops, he was willing to hold production until Raft returned from a vacation.

Alice Faye was borrowed from Fox to play the role of Dixie. She was cast in the film in April and filming began in May. Paramount wanted to change her hair color from blonde to brunette for the film so that she looked more like Frances Langford and Patsy Kelly, but Daryl Zanuck of Fox, who was grooming Faye for stardom, refused. As a result, there is a scene in the film in which the girls dye her hair brunette, Tops doesn't like it, and insists they change her back to a blonde.

Frances Langford was a popular radio star making her film debut in this movie. Her acting is good and her singing is great. In this film she introduces the song "I'm in the Mood For Love," which became a pop standard and Langford's signature song for the remainder of her long career (she worked into the 1950s and lived into the 2000s). It is she who gets to play the romantic interest with Raft, not higher billed Alice Faye.

Patsy Kelly was starring opposite Thelma Todd in a series of popular short comedies for Hal Roach productions. Whenever the studio would take a break, the actors were encouraged to find work elsewhere, and Patsy Kelly's wisecracking presence was quite popular and it is most delightful here. This film wrapped in June of 1935 and, sadly six months later Thelma Todd died under mysterious circumstances. Roach tried to keep the series going, teaming Patsy with Pert Kelton (who didn't work out), and Lyda Roberti (who died in 1937).

Every Night at Eight was a box office hit and further proved that audiences would accept Raft in roles other than crime dramas. *The New York Daily News* stated:

> With George Raft in the role of a jazz orchestra leader and Alice Faye borrowed from Fox for this Walter Wanger production; Frances Langford, who is a well-known radio singer, and the inimitably funny Patsy Kelly. It runs true to form in that it follows the prescribed line for backstage romances but its lack if originality is offset by Raoul

Walsh's light and smooth touch in the handling of the players and by Patsy Kelly's ease in putting over the cracks and with telling effect.[30]

For his next film, George Raft was loaned to Columbia studios who were interested in capitalizing on their recent success with *It Happened One Night* (1934). Raft was intrigued at the idea of playing in a comedy and looked forward to the role, and the film.

---

30 Every Night at Eight review. *New York Daily News.* August 3, 1935

SHE COULDN'T TAKE IT

Directed by Tay Garnett
Screenplay by Oliver H.P. Garrett from a story by Gene Towne and Graham Baker
Produced by B.P. Schulberg
Cinematography by Lee Shamroy
Film Editing by Gene Havlick

Cast:
George Raft	Joseph 'Spot' Ricardi
Joan Bennett	Carol Van Dyke
Walter Connolly	Daniel Van Dyke
Billie Burke	Mrs. Daniel Van Dyke
Lloyd Nolan	Tex
Wallace Ford	'Fingers' Boston
James Blakeley	Tony Van Dyke
Alan Mowbray	Alan Bartlett
William Tannen	Cesar
Donald Meek	Uncle Wyndersham
Stanley Andrews	Attorney Wyndersham
Wyrley Birch	Dr. Schaeffer
Frank Conroy	Attorney Henry Raleigh
Peppino Dallalic	Don
Mack Gray	Ike
Harrison Greene	Spieler
Maynard Holmes	Edgar
George McKay	Red
Huey White	Eddie Gore
Tom Kennedy	Slugs
Walter Brennan	Peddler
Nadine Dore	Girl
Donald Kerr	Sailor

Ivan Lebedeff	Count
Maxine Lewis	Crooner
Franklin Pangborn	Spot's Secretary
Heinie Conklin	Waiter
Phillip Ronalde	Waiter
Frank Austin	Railroad Attendant
Irving Bacon	Man at Toll Gate
Olaf Hytten	Van Dyke Butler
Thomas E. Jackson	Spieler at Car Exhibition
Joseph North	Butler
Henry Sylvester	Manager
Ray Turner	Janitor
Frank Rice	Milkman
Loren Riebe	Human Fly
John Quillan	Bellboy
Jack Duffy	Farmer
'Pop' Kenton	Farmer
Victor Potel	Farmer
Lee Phelps	Bailiff
Lon Poff	Judge
Robert Middlemass	Desk Sergeant
Charles Sullivan	State Trooper
James P. Burtis	Motorcycle Cop
Ted Oliver	Motorcycle Cop
Ky Robinson	Motorcycle Cop
C.A. Beckman	Traffic Cop
Walter Walker	Judge
Jack Daley	District Attorney's Man
Eddie Gribbon	Detective
Gene Morgan	Policeman - Precinct 5
Edgar Dearing	Policeman - Precinct 5
Frank Fanning	Warden
Jack Holmes	Prison Doctor
John Ince	Prison Official
George Lloyd	Prison Turnkey
Kernan Cripps	Guard
Frank Marlowe	Prisoner

Al Ferguson	Prisoner
Stark Bishop	Prisoner
John Webb Dillion	Prisoner
Frank LaRue	Prisoner
Paul Power	Prisoner
Walter Perry	Prisoner
Robert Wilber	Prisoner
Mike Lally	Photographer
W.E. Lawrence	Photographer
George Webb	Editor
Antrim Short	Reporter
Emmett Vogan	Reporter
Billy West	Reporter
Tom Costello	Reporter
Joc Clive	Reporter
Jack Gardner	Reporter
James Harrison	Reporter
Stanley Mack	Reporter
Charles Sherlock	Reporter
Oscar Rudolph	Newsboy
Carrie Daumery	Dowager Party Guest
Bess Flowers	Party Guest at Car Exhibition
Arthur Stuart Hull	Party Guest at Car Exhibition
Raymond Walburn	Party Guest
Lois Lindsay	Party Guest
Edith Kingdon	Party Guest
Gladys Gale	Party Guest
Grace Goodall	Party Guest
Thurston Hall	Party Guest
Emily Fitzroy	Party Guest
Arthur Rankin	Party Guest
Henry Roquemore	Party Guest

Released October 8, 1935
Columbia Pictures
Running Time: 77 minutes
Black and White

Movie ad for She Couldn't Take It

She Couldn't Take It was made for Columbia Pictures, which had been considered a poverty row studio that was only good for second-features until director Frank Capra began making films there. Movies like *The Miracle Woman* (1931), *Platinum Blonde* (1931), *The Bitter Tea of General Yen* (1932), and *Lady for a Day* (1933) were popular and commanded the top bill of a double feature program, putting Columbia on the map. When Capra's movie *It Happened One Night* (1934) became a sensation and won all of the major

Academy Awards, Columbia was now a studio that deserved notice. That same year, studio head Harry Cohn wanted his company to begin producing short subjects, so he hired Jules White to begin a comedy shorts unit, that eventually attracted The Three Stooges, Buster Keaton, Charley Chase, Andy Clyde, and Harry Langdon.

The success of *It Happened One Night* was such that Columbia wanted to explore producing more romantic comedies, one of which was *She Couldn't Take it*. George Raft and Joan Bennett had appeared in *Hush Money* (1931), back when Joan was a star and Raft was a little-known supporting player. Now, in *She Couldn't Take It*, Raft is top billed and Joan is his co-star. In a further attempt to capture the magic of *It Happened One Night*, Columbia hired the patriarch from that film, Walter Connolly, to play the same type of role in *She Couldn't Take It*.

Connolly is Dan Van Dyke, a wealthy man whose family's outrageous behavior and lack of responsibility have him at his wit's end. He gathers the family together, including his wife (Billie Burke), daughter (Joan Bennett), and his son (James Blakely) and tells him he has been arrested for tax evasion and plans to go to prison rather than fight it, just to get away from them. While in prison, Van Dyke's cell mate is a man named Spot Ricardi (George Raft). The two become friends as Van Dyke tells of his wealth, his family's irresponsibility, and various woes. Van Dyke dies in prison, and before he dies, he signs over his interests to Ricardi, who is instructed to take charge of his family and set up some boundaries.

Comedies of the 1930s often took issue with the irresponsible rich and their gaining comeuppance from a working class person. That is the basic concept of *It Happened One Night*. However, with *She Couldn't Take It*, the idea is that a criminal who had served time would be in charge and put these rich people in their place. The film is amusing, but uneven, wavering between lighthearted situations and melodramatics.

There are a few tangents to the central plot. One concerns Riccardi's old gang wanting him to join them in a kidnapping caper, which he refuses. Another has the Van Dyke daughter being engaged to a hammy actor (Alan Mowbray) who is only interested in the family's wealth. Walter Byron had been playing the hammy actor when, after two weeks of shooting, he was replaced by Mowbray. At about the same time, it was decided that Raymond Walburn was not quite working out as Fingers, Riccardi's right hand man in his gang, so George Raft suggested they hire his friend Wallace Ford, with whom he had worked successfully in other films.

In one of the methods of promoting the film, an abridged radio version of the screenplay was created, and Raft, Bennett, Burke, and Connolly performed it over the airwaves. This plan apparently worked, because *She Couldn't Take It* was quite a big hit at the box office and showed that this type of movie remained popular with audiences.

While he was once again playing a character who had been involved in the underworld, George Raft liked the idea of doing a comedy. He and Joan Bennett were producer B.P. Schulberg's first choices to play the leads. Schulberg had produced films since the silent era, including *Wings* (1927), the first movie to win a Best Picture Oscar. No stranger to comedy, Schulberg had produced the surreal classic *Million Dollar Legs* (1932) and the comic parody *Make Me a Star* that same year. This was the first of a four-picture deal the producer had with Columbia.

An article in the *Los Angeles Times* claimed that the casting of *She Couldn't Take It* was one of its chief assets:

William Perlberg, who was head of Columbia's casting department during the filming of *She Couldn't Take It*, and who is now a production executive, feels that this is one of the few perfectly cast pictures of the season. The film executive says that there may be 10,000 available actors in Hollywood for a certain role, but getting the right player for the job at the right time is no easy matter. George Raft was so suited to the role in *She Couldn't Take It* that he was borrowed from the studio to whom he is under contract, and Joan Bennett was obtained in similar manner. Walter Connolly, who fitted his role ideally, was under contract to Columbia, and still is. But getting him was another matter. He was starring in a New York play, and production was held up until the end of the run. Billie Burke was called back from a vacation for her part. Others in the cast are Lloyd Nolan, Alan Mowbray and Wallace Ford.[31]

While Tay Garnett would later be best known for directing melodramas like *The Postman Always Rings Twice* (1946), and had just finished helming the action-drama *China Seas* at MGM just prior to this film, he maintains the necessary breezy pace for *She Couldn't Take It*. Upon completing work on this film, Garnett went on a cruise around the world.

The film was known as *Rich Man's Daughter* throughout production, but the title was changed to *She Couldn't Take It* just prior to its release. *The Los Angeles Times* proclaimed it as George Raft's best movie, and the actor was pleased that a film in the comedy genre not only became a hit, but resulted in his getting positive critical notices. Biographer Everett Aaker, however, believed that Raft seemed ill at ease in the more comical scenes, and more at home during the dramatic part of the narrative.

Raft comes off more as a straight man thrust into some comedic situations and surrounded by strange individuals like the wealthy family, but he plays that well. There is discernible chemistry between him and Joan Bennett—their back-and-forth dialog sequences as he was trying to deter her from marrying the wrong man, are sharp and well timed. Raft is even better at the dramatic moments though, showing real genuine concern as Dan is passing away in prison, and later for Carol Van Dyke in a sequence when her character is supposedly kidnapped. Sometimes it does feel like bargain bin *It Happened One Night*, especially the scenes where Raft and Bennett become stranded, but the premise is still fun.

Surprisingly, Raft's home studio Paramount still wasn't completely sure which direction they should take their star. They were comfortable with him playing hoods, despite the success of films like *Every Night at Eight* and now *She Couldn't Take It*. Raft told the studio he no longer wanted to play characters with few or no redeeming features and the studio searched for a property that would satisfy the actor, and the front office.

---

31 Executive Says New Film Perfectly Cast. *The Los Angeles Times*. November 6, 1935

For his next film, George Raft was once again loaned out to another studio. This time it was the newly formed 20th Century Fox. It was another breezy comedy, so Raft was pleased with the assignment.

IT HAD TO HAPPEN

Directed by Roy Del Ruth
Screenplay by Howard Ellis Smith and Kathryn Scola from the story *Caravan, The Man Who Had His Way* but Rupert Hughes
Produced by Darryl F. Zanuck
Cinematography by J. Peverell Marley
Film Editing by Allen McNeil

Cast:
George Raft	Enrico Scaffa
Rosalind Russell	Beatrice Newnes
Leo Carrillo	Giuseppe Badjagaloupe
Arline Judge	Miss Sullivan
Alan Dinehart	Rodman Dreke
Andrew Tombes	Dooley
Arthur Hohl	Honest John Pelkey
Pierre Watkin	District Attorney
Stanley Fields	Mug
George Irving	Jury Foreman
Thomas E. Jackson	Mayor's Secretary
Charles Lane	State Examiner
Clay Clement	McCloskey - Scaffa's Attorney
Matt McHugh	Elevator Man
John Sheehan	Pelkey's Secretary
Paul Stanton	Mayor of New York
Harry Stubbs	Bailiff
Ray Turner	Zeke
Jay Novello	Santoro
James Burke	Foreman
George Bookasta	Italian Boy
Tommy Bupp	Shoeshine Boy
Lynn Bari	Secretary

Curtis Benton	Radio Announcer
Wallis Clark	Immigration Officer
Edward Cooper	Butler
John Dilson	Juror
Pauline Garon	French Maid
Herbert Heywood	Trainer
John Hyams	Man in Cafe
Lloyd Whitlock	Man in Cafe
Edward Keane	Politician
John Kelly	Moving Man
Loo Loy	Chinese Man
Ben Taggart	New York Cop
Frank Meredith	Motorcycle Cop
Torben Meyer	Sign Painter
Frank Moran	Moving Man
James C. Morton	Bartender
Inez Palange	Italian Mother
Harry Woods	Workman
Jack Curtis	Workman
Jimmie Dundee	Workman
Paul Hurst	Workman
G. Pat Collins	Workman
Ben Hendricks Jr.	Workman
Franklyn Ardell	Reporter
Sam Ash	Reporter
Cully Richards	Reporter
Emmett Vogan	Reporter
Jack Hatfield	Reporter
J. Anthony Hughes	Reporter

Released February 14, 1936
20th Century Fox
Running Time: 79 minutes
Black and White

George Raft had just finished work on *She Couldn't Take It* when 20th Century Fox requested his services for *It Had to Happen*. 20th

Century Fox was somewhat of a new studio, as Fox and 20th Century had just merged. The first film under the 20th Century Fox banner was *Call of the Wild*, based on the Jack London novel and featuring Clark Gable. There was some tentative talk of Clark Gable playing the lead in *It Had to Happen*, as he was just completing production on *Call of the Wild*, but it was decided that George Raft was better suited to the role.

George Raft was intrigued with playing an easygoing immigrant who is toughened up after some negative incidents, and also that it was another chance to do a comedy. He accepted the role in September 1935, and Roy Del Ruth was named as director right around the same time. Roy Del Ruth had worked with Raft in the past, but it was for the bit part George did in the James Cagney film *Taxi* (1932). Del Ruth had done many strong pre-code crime dramas at Warner Brothers, including other Cagney starrers *Blonde Crazy, Winner Take All* and *Lady Killer*. Constance Bennett was considered for the female lead according to press reports at the time, which also indicated Leo Carrillo was hired:

> Will Constance Bennett play in *It Had to Happen*? It would be a new combination, Raft and herself. Naturally, the Lady Bennett has to have approval of the story. The last production in which Miss Bennett starred was *After Office Hours* six or seven months ago. Leo Carrlllo has been secured from Columbia for the production of *It Had to Happen*, which is very shortly to be filmed.[32]

Rosalind Russell was eventually hired. Shooting began in November of 1935.

The film opens with George Raft and Leo Carrillo playing immigrants from Italy who are trying to make their way in America. Uncharacteristically, Raft's character is pushed around, and rather timidly backs down from any confrontation. His character soon evolves, and becomes more familiar as to his established screen persona, but Raft the actor was intrigued at playing so far against type during the film's opening scenes.

---

32 Constance Bennett May Team With Raft. *The Los Angeles Times*. October 19, 1935

George Raft, Alan Dinehart, and Leo Carillo in It Had To Happen

George Raft is Enrico Scaffa and Leo Carillo plays his friend Giuseppe Badjagaloupe. They are traveling by boat from Italy to America to start a new life. While on board the ship, they run into to the wealthy Beatrice Newnes (Rosalind Russell). Once in America, Enrico and Giuseppe stand in line to get jobs digging ditches, and are pushed around by thuggish blue collar workers with a disdain for immigrants. Enrico is given the job of directing traffic, holding up a red flag to stop cars from driving where there is an accident on the road. He connects with the power this job gives him, and is very specific, keeping back important people who need to get through, including the mayor. Enrico's foreman confronts him for doing so, and, having had enough, Enrico slugs his boss and gets himself and Giuseppe fired. This forcefulness impresses the mayor, who hires Enrico as an assistant. Enrico eventually rises to become a powerbroker who heads many charitable organizations that help the underprivileged. He discovers that one of his charities has books that don't balance, so he contacts the head of that district, and it is Rodman Drake, husband of Beatrice Newnes. Maneuvers happen to implicate Enrico, but a trial reveals the truth.

It is an interesting character trajectory to present George Raft as an immigrant who is timid and picked on by bigger men. But soon this development results in his becoming the same sort of tough guy he usually played. And while there are underworld situations abounding, the character Raft plays is honest throughout, sacrificing himself for others and always striving to do the right thing. Leo Carrillo is an amusing presence throughout the proceedings, Rosalind Russell is fashionable and dazzling, and the appearances of familiar character actors like Arthur Hohl, Alan Dinehart, and Charles Lane are always welcome. But perhaps the most impressive supporting performance comes from Arline Judge as Enrico's secretary, Miss Sullivan. While Russell is classy and glamourous, Judge is spunky and tough. When accosted by a couple of thugs, she punches one of them out. In one of the more amusing scenes in the film, Beatrice comes to see Enrico at the office, he says to send her right in, and Miss Sullivan puckishly makes her wait, claiming that Enrico is busy.

Some viewers have written that they wish Enrico had ended up with Miss Sullivan instead, but we must realize the appeal of a society woman who is somewhat outside of his class. There are charming scenes where Beatrice and Enrico court each other – she is initially reluctant, he's a little pushy but not too much -- before they actually get together.

The New York Daily News agreed, in its review, that Arline Judge was a significant contribution to the movie, stating: Miss Russell, as Beatrice, lacks the sparkle and charm that she brought to her role in *Rendezvous*. Miss Judge, on the other hand, is delightfully engaging as Enrico's pert secretary."[33]

There are, however, some problems with *It Had to Happen*. Leo Carrillo plays his character with a thick accent (the American born Carrillo had no accent at all in real life, but nearly always played a character who had one). Raft, however, who is also supposed to an Italian immigrant right off the boat, has no accent at all. This was noticed in the film's review that appeared in the trade paper *Variety*:

---

33 It Had To Happen review *The New York Daily News* February 15, 1936

This four year triumph of Enrico Scaffa is totally improbable in itself but making it even more incredible is the Raft characterization of a poor immigrant who speaks perfect English before he gets off the boat. As his companion on the way over, and throughout his career on this side, Leo Carrillo does heavy dialect, which tends to pile on more implausibility.[34]

Meanwhile, *The Los Angeles Times*, unimpressed with the movie overall, also pointed out Raft's lack of an accent in their review:

It Had to Happen, is hardly up to standard. In fact, it Is considerably below it in every particular, There is some excellent straight dialogue in the picture, too; sensible, direct and thoughtful. But for some reason the story is peppered with implausibilities and therefore falls to stack up as a believable yarn even though the screen has offered the same essentials often enough to become gospel. In this instance, however, a little more careful observance of realities would have vastly helped. At the outset the character played by Mr. Raft isn't comprehensible. The spectator does not understand why an Italian immigrant, bewildered by the strangeness of New York, should enter the port speaking local English. On second thought one supposes that Mr. Raft must not be able to negotiate any speech but his own or that the dialectic honors must be thrown Mr. Carrlllo's way at all costs. Rosalind Russell does not fare any better as far as characterization goes. Her charm and refinement have fitted her other roles, but here she becomes rather monotonously patrician and disturbingly limited as an actress, again proving, that a player is no better than the material provided by the literary workshops. Once more Arllne Judge proves a lifesaver. Hers is the most stimulating and satisfying contribution to the doubtful entertainment provided by the picture as a whole.[35]

Despite its flaws, the movie was a hit at the box office, and George Raft's career continued to flourish.

---

34 It Had To Happen review. *Variety* February 19, 1936

35 It Had To Happen review. *The Los Angeles Times*. February 23, 1936

Paramount noticed Raft's comfortability in the comedy genre and decided to try their hand at casting him in a more lighthearted project of their own. Originally it was to be *The Princess Comes Across* with Carole Lombard, but its cinematographer was Ted Tetzlaff, whom Raft had accused of favoring Lombard in their previous film together, *Rumba*. Raft believed the same thing was happening on *The Princess Comes Across* and walked off the project, being replaced by Fred MacMurray. He was then cast in another lighter film, purposefully peppering it with surefire comedic supporting players.

YOURS FOR THE ASKING

Directed by Alexander Hall
Screenplay by Eve Greene, Harlan Ware, and Phillip MacDonald
  from a story by William Lipman and William Wright.
Produced by Lewis E. Gensler
Cinematography by Theodor Sparkuhl
Film Editing by James Smith

Cast:
George Raft	Johnny Lamb
Dolores Costello	Lucille Sutton
Ida Lupino	Gert Malloy
Reginald Owen	Dictionary McKinney
James Gleason	Saratoga
Edgar Kennedy	Bicarbonate
Lynne Overman	Honeysuckle
'Skeets' Gallagher	Perry Barnes
Walter Walker	Mr. Crenshaw
Robert Gleckler	Slick Doran
Richard Powell	Benedict
Betty Blythe	May
Huntley Gordon	Clark Bering
Ralph Remley	O'Rorke
Charles Requa	Mr. Ames
Eddie Becker	Dealer
George Green	Dealer
Dave Harris	Dealer
Jack Barrett	Dealer
Albert Pollet	Headwaiter
Edward Peil Sr.	Waiter
Max Barwyn	Waiter
Francis Sayles	Waiter

Harry C. Bradley	Art Dealer
Jack Byron	Chauffeur
Keith Daniels	Henchman
Louis Natheaux	Henchman
Arthur Stuart Hull	Deaf-mute
Al McDonald	Dealer
Henry Roquemore	Pot-bellied Man
Dennis O'Keefe	Man
Fred Minter	Man
Edmund Mortimer	Man
Phillips Smalley	Man
Thomas A. Curran	Man
Bud Herbert	Man
William Arnold	Man
Olive Tell	Society Woman
Connie Emerald	Woman
Florence Wix	Woman
Jeanne Perkins	Woman
Bess Flowers	Woman
Jean Fowler	Woman
Rosemary Theby	Woman
Marie Wells	Girl
Sally West	Girl

Released July 24, 1936
Paramount Pictures
Running Time: 68 minutes
Black and White

   Paramount finally cast George Raft in a lighthearted movie, and, curiously, he doesn't appear to be the lead in his own starring film. *Yours for the Asking* is carried by the presence of three notorious scene stealers – comedy character actors James Gleason, Richard "Skeets" Gallagher, and Edgar Kennedy.
   George Raft plays Johnny Lamb who runs a casino on a Miami farm. Dolores Costello is Lucille Sutton, a woman who is gambling to win money to pay her mortgage. She offers her jewelry to

Ida Lupino, George Raft, Dolores Costello in Yours For The Asking

Johnny as payment for a bet but he turns her down. Johnny has a run-in with mobsters, resulting in a fistfight, and then offers to take Lucille home. She lives in an impressive mansion, so he tells here he will help with her debts by turning her home into a casino. However his friends Saratoga (James Gleason), Honeysuckle (Skeets Gallagher), and Bicarbonate (Edgar Kennedy) believe he is being duped. They enlist two con artists, Dictionary (Reginald Owen) and Gertie (Ida Lupino) to play wealthy socialites to fool Johnny and lure him away from the situation with Lucille. Johnny falls for the ruse and asks Lucille to help him with his social manners so as to impress Gertie. Lucille, who has feelings for Johnny, realizes the ruse so Gertie pretends to be sick so that she and Dictionary can leave town for a warmer climate as the antidote. Johnny eventually discovers he's been tricked, and turns against Honeysuckle, Bicarbonate, and Saratoga for conspiring against him. They apologize to him, and to Lucille, for getting everything wrong, and Johnny decides to go into a legitimate business.

There are times in *Yours for the Asking* that George Raft seems like the dull straight man in a comedy that involves James Gleason, Edgar Kennedy, and Skeets Gallagher. While the proceedings are fun, albeit unremarkable, they really do nothing to advance George Raft, the star of the movie. Dolores Costello does not register too well, but Ida Lupino does. Tough girl roles were great for Lupino, plus she was funny. She would work with Raft again and the results would be far more significant.

Yours for the Asking explored similar themes to some of Raft's previous crime dramas, in which he played a hood who gets caught up with a society woman who's outside his class, but it was interesting how that was spun into a comedy here. Perhaps, despite his success in comedies at other studios, Paramount was reticent about letting George Raft carry such a film on his own, and added Gleason, Kennedy, and Gallagher for insurance. It is their work that stands out here, and each of them are typically amusing playing characters they had, by now, very firmly established. Edgar Kennedy had been around since the early Keystone comedies.

The film was originally titled *The Duchess* but the title changed just before release. There are some news reports that when some of the film's footage was shot on Catalina Island, Groucho Marx and Charles Ruggles happened to be there and were unbilled extras in the film. Neither can be spotted.

Even though it is of little significant to George Raft's movie career, which had been building and investigating different opportunities, *Yours for the Asking* was well received by critics. *Film Daily* called it:

> A lively comedy-romance with an ace cast and plenty of amusing stuff to please audiences generally. Raft is right in his element and does a swell job as the gambling joint operator. Dolores Costello is appealing and effective. The comedy element is expertly handled by Gleason, Kennedy, and Gallagher, while Owen and Miss Lupino carry off the villainous roles in fine style. A good script job with much

sprightly dialog and breezy direction are also among the film's assets.[36]

Yours for the Asking was a success at the box office and pleased Paramount as to George Raft's ability to handle a role in a comedy.

Paramount next paired George Raft with Gary Cooper for the action-adventure film *Souls at Sea*, which would turn out to be one of the best films in Raft's entire career. And he almost didn't do the film.

---

36 Yours for the Asking review. *Film Daily*. August 26, 1936

SOULS AT SEA

Directed by Henry Hathaway
Screenplay by Grover Jones and Dale Van Every based on a story by Ted Lesser
Produced by Grover Jones
Cinematography by Merritt Gerstad and Charles Lang
Film Editing by Ellsworth Hoagland

Cast:
Gary Cooper	Michael 'Nuggin' Taylor
George Raft	Powdah
Frances Dee	Margaret Tarryton
Henry Wilcoxon	Lieutenant Stanley Tarryton
Harry Carey	Captain of 'William Brown'
Olympe Bradna	Babsie
Robert Cummings	George Martin
Porter Hall	Court Prosecutor
George Zucco	Barton Woodley
Virginia Weidler	Tina
Joseph Schildkraut	Gaston de Bastonet
Gilbert Emery	Captain Martisel
Lucien Littlefield	Toymaker
Paul Fix	Violinist
Tully Marshall	Pecora
Monte Blue	Mate
Stanley Fields	Captain Paul M. Granley
Fay Holden	Mrs. Martin
Luana Walters	Eloise
Eddie Borden	Friend of Gastonet
Rolfe Sedan	Friend of Gastonet
Clyde Cook	Hendry – Coachman
Rollo Lloyd	Parchy

Colin Tapley	Donaldson
Jameson Thomas	Pelton
William Stack	Judge
Paul Stanton	Defense Attorney
Charles Middleton	Foreman
Davison Clark	Bailiff
Harvey Clark	Court Clerk
Lowell Drew	Jury Foreman
Franklyn Farnum	Court Bailiff
Forbes Murray	Associate Justice
Edward Hearn	Courtroom Spectator
Robert Barrat	The Reverend
Arthur Blake	Prime Minister
Norman Ainsley	Taker
Allan Cavan	Dignitary
Phillips Smalley	Dignitary
John M. Sullivan	Dignitary
Wilson Benge	Doctor
Frank Benson	Gardener
Herbert Clifton	Ticket Clerk
David Clyde	Butler
J. Gunnis Davis	Barber
Leslie Francis	Secretary
George MacQuarrie	Doctor
Henry Mowbray	Bus Man
Carlyle O'Rourke	Puppeteer
Phyllis Godfrey	Housemaid
Mary Gordon	Cook
Robert Warwick	Vice Admiral
Ben Taggart	Ship's Officer
Harry Tenbrook	Lifeboat Crewman
Edward Van Sloan	Ship's Officer
Stanley Andrews	First Mate
Lon McCallister	Cabin Boy
Lee Shumway	Mate
G. Pat Collins	Slaver
Blue Washington	Ship Slave

Alan Ladd	Sailor
Jimmy Dime	Sailor / Prisoner
Colin Kenny	Military Guard
Crauford Kent	Navy Clerk
Olaf Hytten	Proprietor
Forrester Harvey	Pub Proprietor
Gertrude Astor	Barmaid
Lina Basquette	Brunette in Saloon
Pauline Haddon	Blonde
Jane Weir	Barmaid
Grayce Hampton	Old Knitting Woman
Paul Walton	Puppeteer
Dorothy Vernon	Passenger
Ethel Clayton	Passenger
Gloria Williams	Passenger

Released September 3, 1937
Paramount Pictures
Running Time: 92 minutes
Black and White

Souls at Sea turned out to be one of the finest films in which George Raft appears, so it is surprising to discover that he initially refused to be in the movie. In fact, his misgivings about the role were so strong, Raft was willing to break his contract with Paramount to avoid being in it. Raft told biographer Lewis Yablonsky:

> We were supposed to go to Catalina for the scene where I was to throw a rock at Frances Dee, but I told them I wouldn't do it. It would be different if Frances was playing a no-good sort of a dame. But she was a real lady in this picture. When I didn't show up in Catalina, they called me at the studio and I went in and told them to tear up my contract."[37]

Once the news of Raft breaking with his studio became known, other producers expressed interest in his services. An article in *The Los Angeles Times* stated:

---
37 Yablonsky, Lewis. George Raft. NY: McGraw-Hill, 1974

The compass points in half a dozen different ways for George Raft, since he secured his release from the Paramount organization, and just what will come first remains to be seen. It is very likely that he will be signed more or less permanently by Darryl Zanuck of Twentieth Century-Fox, for whom he played in *The Bowery* and *It Had to Happen,* but meanwhile Samuel Goldwyn wants him for *Dead End,* and David O. Selznick and Universal are bidding for the actor. Raft, believing that the part in *Souls at Sea* was not for him, sought and obtained his release from a $1000-a-week contract.[38]

The offer to George Raft to play the role of Baby Face Martin in *Dead End* for Goldwyn is intriguing. This was the film that introduced The Dead End Kids, who play a juvenile gang that idolizes the snarling criminal Martin. Raft read Lillian Hellman's screen version of Sidney Kingsley's play, and balked at a scene where Martin shows the kids how to effectively throw a knife. He wanted a scene written into the script where Martin complains about the life of a criminal, being on the run all the time, etc. Of course, this would disrupt the narrative's focus and would be the antithesis of the character as written. But George Raft would not do the role unless it was rewritten to his specifications, no matter how wrongheaded that would be in context. The role instead went to Humphrey Bogart, advancing his career. It would not be the last time that a role George Raft rejected went to Bogart.

While there were reports that Lloyd Nolan had replaced George Raft in *Souls at Sea,* Paramount summoned Raft back to the studio to discuss the role with director Henry Hathaway and co-star Gary Cooper, whom Raft knew as a friend. Raft told Yablonsky: "I told Coop what I thought and why and he agreed with my decision and told Hathaway that he wouldn't do the picture without me. With Coop on my side, Hathaway cut the scene."[39] Soon afterward, *The Los Angeles Times* reported:

All is peace again between George Raft and the Paramount studio. Solution of the problem was reached at

---

38 Zanuck likely to sign Raft. *The Los Angeles Times.* November 16, 1936
39 Yablonsky, Lewis. George Raft. NY: McGraw-Hill, 1974

a dinner, at which William Le Baron, vice-president in charge of production, and the star met Tuesday night. Raft's contract was resumed yesterday afternoon, and he immediately went into *Souls at Sea* with Gary Cooper. When Le Baron and Raft met at the dinner, the conversation-turned in quite a casual manner to the discussion of Raft's own differences with the studio. The star felt he was being forced to do certain things and that this caused the flare-up of a few months ago. The part in *Souls at Sea* was really to the star's liking, and he wanted to play it. The entire teapot tempest came to a quick settlement shortly after noon, so Raft's $4000-a-week contract with Paramount is resumed. Real truth of the matter is that Raft was given assurances, I understand, that the script of *Souls at Sea* would not make him appear to be a "heel" in the plot, which has been the difficulty all along.[40]

While Lloyd Nolan is, himself, a good actor who appeared in some of Raft's films, he was a supporting character actor whereas George Raft is a leading man. Nolan would have been support for Cooper, while Raft is clearly a co-star in *Souls at Sea*. With Nolan, the dynamic would have been much different.

Set in the 1840s, the film opens with Gary Cooper as Michael "Nuggin" Taylor about to go on trial for causing 19 deaths while escaping the ship William Brown after it caught fire and sank. British secret service agent Barton Woodley (George Zucco) recounts Nuggin's story in court. Nuggin and his friend Powdah (George Raft) are put in charge of a slave ship, The Blackbird, by a dying captain who has been attacked by the slaves. They are instructed to bring the slaves to the slave traders and complete the deal. Nuggin, an abolitionist who goes undercover on slave ships, instead, with Powdah's help, sails near shore and releases the slaves so they can swim to safety. When a patrol ship captures The Blackbird, Nuggin and Powdah refuse to tell them what happened to the slaves so they are hung by their thumbs over the ocean. One of the men on the patrol ship is Lieutenant Tarryton, who has a real interest in whether the dying captain of The Blackbird revealed any names of the traders. Docking

---

40 Star Goes Into Souls at Sea. *The Los Angeles Times*. November 20, 1936

George Raft and Gary Cooper in Souls at Sea

in Liverpool, Powdah and Nuggin are absolved of any wrongdoing, and Nuggin is asked to work for British intelligence to trap the slavers, which includes Tarryton, by working undercover. Tarryton and his accomplices purchase the ship William Brown with plans to take the slave trading route that The Blackbird had been taking. Nuggin and Powdah are also passengers. Nuggin falls or Tarryton's sister Margaret (Frances Dee), causing more conflict with the suspicious Lieutenant. Powdah meets and falls in love with Babsie (Olympe Bradne). A little girl, Tina (Virginia Weidler), knocks over an oil lamp causing a fire that spreads to stored gunpowder and causes a series of explosions, destroying the ship. Nuggin tries to rescue people onto a lifeboat, but is attacked by Tarryton who drowns after a struggle. Meanwhile, Powdah discovers Babsie has been injured in the explosion with a heavy beam pinning her. After she dies, Powdah refuses to leave the ship and goes down with it as it sinks, holding Babsie's hand. Nuggin tries to save as many as he can, but there are too many in the lifeboat, and it is sinking, so he

Olympe Bradna and George Raft in Souls at Sea

shoots several people so he can help the others to safety. Once he is on trial, Nuggin is remorseful over the decision he believes he had to make, while the survivors who are alive because of his actions passionately defend him. His guilty verdict is overturned and he gets together with Margaret.

It can be argued that this is more Gary Cooper's movie than George Raft's, because the story is about Nuggin and his exploits that have led to his going to trial. Raft is in support as Powdah who makes the ultimate sacrifice. But Raft's performance is so strong, he commands every scene he is in, and when he's not on screen, his character continues to resonate. Powdah is a series of conflicts. He is not romantic, but he becomes one with his introduction to Babsie. He is tough and rugged but fears water. And although he fears water, he chooses to confront and overcome this phobia by choosing a life on the sea.

But while Powdah has character conflicts, Raft is able to convey him as being layered rather than complicated. He is a simple, forthright man whose presence shows a smoldering charisma while he discovers different traits within his own personality. His relationship with Nuggin, and later his relationship with Babsie, help expand how he'd been defined up to this point.

While the scene throwing the rock at Frances Dee's character was removed at Raft's request, there likely were other rewrites that expanded his character's personality, thus offering the conflicts. There is a romantic heroism to Powdah's choice to go down with the ship after Babsie has died. And his thwarting Nuggin's efforts to save him by punching his friend and knocking him out, then making sure he is securely on a lifeboat, is another act of heroism within its context. The central narrative may be more about Gary Cooper's character, but George Raft turns in what might be his best performance so far, and his best film at this point in his career. So many of his scenes toward the end of the movie, especially the final scene with him where he goes down with the ship holding Babsie's hand, are real tearjerker moments that allow him to demonstrate his emotional range. Raft and Gary Cooper had really great chemistry and their camaraderie was totally convincing, whether they were dangling in peril or getting dressed up.

Variety noticed Raft expanding his talent, when stating in their review: "George Raft is a bit of a surprise as a sympathetic player who meets his dramatic opportunities more than half way."[41] Frank Nugent, critic for *The New York Times* reviewed the movie negatively, then after several letters from moviegoers, Nugent changed his review, stating, "Ever since rereading my review of *Souls at Sea*, I have been suffering recurrent pangs of remorse which have not been alleviated by friendly, but reproachful, letters." Most critics were closer to the breathless praise offered by the *Santa Ana Register* whose critic raved:

> *Souls at Sea* has so much of moving humanness, of spectacle and suspense, such fine performances and forthright direction and sturdy quality generally, as to put it in the big money class unquestionably. Gary Cooper and George Raft., and their joint endeavors in a tale of magnificent friendship put to the ultimate test are so splendidly realized that the honors split memorably for both.[42]

---

41 Souls at Sea review. *Variety*. August 31, 1937
42 Souls at Sea review. *Santa Ana Register*. August 28, 1937

George Raft, Olympe Bradna, Frances Dee, Gary Cooper in Souls at Sea

Along with George Raft's contribution, *Souls at Sea* is a very good adventure film overall. Gary Cooper is typically sturdy and compelling as Nuggin, while Frances Dee and Olympe Bradna offer solid support. Child actress Virginia Weidler's shocking on-screen killing by an explosion has a jarring effect that makes the ensuing violence and action even more powerful. Director Henry Hathaway focuses on narrative and character development effectively, but the rousing climax is exceptionally well filmed, shot mostly on the Paramount lot (some footage was shot on location on the aforementioned Catalina Island). The effects in the climax are really well done, and the moment where Nuggin has to start shooting the people scrambling to get on to the life boat is another shocking moment.

Souls at Sea was a major box office success, and became so well known that Laurel and Hardy parodied the title a few years later with their comedy feature *Saps at Sea* (1940). However, despite Lewis Yablonsky's claim in his biography of George Raft, he did not receive an Oscar nomination for his role as Powdah.

For his next film, George Raft was set to co-star with Carole Lombard in a film to be directed by its screenwriter, Norman Krasna. Raft and Lombard, however, both rejected Krasna as director due to his lack of experience. Lombard left the project and was replaced by Sylvia Sidney. Richard Wallace was assigned to direct. Sidney wanted Fritz Lang as director, having worked with him in the past, so Lang replaced Wallace as director and also produced the film. Its release title was *You and Me*.

YOU AND ME

Directed and Produced by Fritz Lang
Screenplay by Virginia Van Upp from a story by Norman Krasna
Cinematography by Charles Lang Jr
Film Editing by Paul Weatherwax

Cast:
Sylvia Sidney	Helen Roberts
George Raft	Joe Dennis
Barton MacLane	Mickey
Harry Carey	Mr. Morris
Roscoe Karns	Cuffy
George E. Stone	Patsy
Warren Hymer	Gimpy Carter
Robert Cummings	Jim
Adrian Morris	Knucks
Roger Gray	Bath House
Cecil Cunningham	Mrs. Morris
Vera Gordon	Mrs. Levine
Egon Brecher	Mr. Levine
Willard Robertson	Dayton
Guinn Williams	Taxi
Bernadene Hayes	Nellie
Joyce Compton	Curly Blonde
Carol Paige	Torch Singer
Ernie Adams	Nick
Harlan Briggs	Thomas McTavish
William B. Davidson	N. G. Orton - Attorney-at-Law
Joe Gray	Red
Oscar Hendrian	Lucky
Arthur Hoyt	Mr. Klein
Edward Pawley	Dutch

Juanita Quigley	Nasty Little Girl
Fern Emmett	Mother of Nasty Little Girl
Matt McHugh	Newcomer
James McNamara	Big Shot
Paul Newlan	Bouncer at Danceland
Max Barwyn	German Waiter
Herta Lynd	Swedish Waitress
Louise Seidel	Hat-Check Girl
Gwen Kenyon	Hat-Check Girl
Harriette Haddon	Cigarette Girl
Paula DeCardo	Cigarette Girl
Jimmie Dundee	Greyhound Bus Driver
Julia Faye	Secretary
Phil Warren	Secretary
Kit Guard	Prison Inmate
Jack Pennick	Gangster
Ethel Clayton	Employment Agency Clerk
Sheila Darcy	Perfume Clerk
Hal K. Dawson	Information Clerk
Ellen Drew	Cashier
Jack Mulhall	First Floorwalker
Sam Ash	Second Floorwalker
Robert Homans	Security Guard in Store
Margaret Randall	Shoplifter
Ruth Rogers	Blonde Salesgirl
John Hubbard	Salesman
Richard Denning	Salesman
Ray Middleton	Salesman
Archie Twitchell	Salesman
Cheryl Walker	Sales Clerk
Marie Burton	Sales Clerk
Dorothy Dayton	Sales Clerk
Jane Dewey	Sales Clerk
Yvonne Duval	Sales Clerk
Greta Granstedt	Sales Clerk
Lola Jensen	Sales Clerk
Joyce Mathews	Sales Clerk

Helaine Moler	Sales Clerk
Carol Parker	Sales Clerk
Barbara Jackson	Demonstrator
Barbara Salisbury	Demonstrator
Marion Weldon	Demonstrator
Harry Tenbrook	Bartender
Blanca Vischer	Flower Girl
John McCafferty	Policeman

Released June 10, 1938
Paramount Pictures
Running time: 94 minutes
Black and White

George Raft went from one of the finest films of his career to one of the weakest in the transition from *Souls at Sea* to *You and Me*. Despite a strong cast and an excellent director who also produced, *You and Me* is not only generally lacking, it often becomes a confused mess. While Lang's penchant for trying something different is commendable, the result is disappointing on several levels.

While George Raft was working on films as a loan out to other studios, Paramount producer William LeBaron asked Norman Krasna to come up with a story for the actor. Krasna agreed to do so, but with the provision that he be allowed to direct. However, once Carole Lombard became interested in the project, Paramount had misgivings about entrusting a Raft-Lombard project with an inexperienced director. Then the film was further delayed when Raft refused to work with a first time director. Raft was suspended and a portion of his salary was withheld by the studio. But the project ended up being shelved and Raft's suspension was lifted so he could appear in another movie. Later on, while Raft was filming *Souls at Sea*, this idea was resurrected by producer B.P. Schulberg. Carole Lombard was replaced by Sylvia Sidney and John Trent was decided as her co-star, with Richard Wallace directing. Sylvia Sidney, a star who had some control over her projects, insisted that Fritz Lang direct the film. Sidney had scored big in two Lang films – *Fury* and *You Only Live Once*. Lang agreed to direct the film, but

Sylvia Sidney and George Raft in You and Me

only if he could also produce. Lang also wanted George Raft to return to the project, having worked successfully with him in *The Pick Up* (1933). Raft agreed, and the movie was made.

George Raft plays Joe Dennis, who has been hired by Mr. Morris to work in a department store he owns. Morris is noted for hiring people released from prison to help with the rehabilitation and parole. Joe is dating a sweet girl named Helen Roberts (Sylvia Sidney) but believes his nefarious past makes him unworthy of such a nice lady, so he resigns from the store and plans to leave for California. He doesn't realize that Helen is also on parole. As he starts to leave on the bus, Helen says she'd marry him if he'd only ask. Joe jumps off the bus, and they rush to get married quickly. While looking for a towel while Helen is taking a shower, Joe finds some letters which he believes are love letters, but they are actually Helen's parole statement cards. She doesn't want Joe to know she is on parole, and lets him continue to think they are love letters. But he feels jealous and leaves. Joe returns to his criminal past and plans with some old cohorts to rob the department store. Helen finds out and warns Morris. Thus when the robbery is attempted, the police are ready and waiting. They hold the criminals at Morris's request, so Helen can break down the heist and show that the rewards would not meet the effort. Joe is angry with Helen and refuses to make up with her. She then leaves and can't be found, despite efforts to search for her. They finally find her and she and Joe make up and plan to stay together as they are about to have a baby.

You and Me doesn't seem to know if it wants to be a comedy or a crime/social drama, and while these elements can blend cohesively, and have with other movies, this time they clash. Lang admitted he was influenced by the work of Bertolt Brecht and wanted to make a film that had a message but also included humor and music. He brought in Brecht's *Threepenny Opera* collaborator Kurt Weill to do the music. Lang oversaw the screenplay with Norman Krasna's support (the two were friends) but eventually Lang took so long that Krasna went on to other things and screenwriter Virginia Van Upp was brought in. The two worked together, while Lang also continued working with Weill, who didn't like composing music before the script was completed. Pre-production dragged on for so long, Sylvia Sidney took a job in a Broadway play and Weill left Hollywood for a gig in New York. George Raft continued to work on *Souls at Sea*. When *You and Me* was finally in production, Lang's perfectionism and retakes caused friction between him and Raft and it became a difficult shoot.

For all its artistic ambition, *You and Me* lost money at the box office. Fritz Lang recalled: "I wanted to make a didactic picture teaching the audience that crime doesn't pay, which is a lie, because crime pays very well. The message was spelled out at the end by Sylvia Sidney on a blackboard to a classroom of crooks. It was – I think deservedly – my first real flop."[43]

Audiences didn't quite know how to react to the odd presentation. For instance, the scene where the ex-cons gather to pull the department store heist has them recalling prison life wistfully by tapping on the table, rhyming, and chanting while flashback sequences fill the screen. Some critics, however, tapped into Fritz Lang's vision and offered a good review. For instance, *The New York Daily News* stated:

---

43 Lang, Fritz. *Fritz Lang: Interviews*. Univ. Press of Mississippi, 2003

Fritz Lang, who made the powerful picture, *Fury* for Warner Brothers and the gruesome *M* for the Berlin studios, has turned to a less punchful theme in directing *You and Me* for Paramount. The latter picture, starring Sylvia Sidney and George Raft, is based on the story of one of the 50,000 girls in this country forbidden to marry while on parole. There have been numerous pictures built around the men and women who are hounded on their release from prison, but Lang has managed to give this latest one an original twist or two. These clever and unusual turns, combined with the excellent acting of the principals and the supporting cast, lift the film out of the merely mediocre into the provocative class. The director has touched his serious drama with unexpected bits of comedy and has garnished it with an impressionistic rhythm. The picture moves quickly and as it marches along it gets progressively lighter in tone, ending on a farcical note. Sylvia Sidney catches the sympathy of the audience in the very beginning of the story, when, as Helen, she lies her way to happiness. She holds that sympathetic interest through the girl's desperate effort to preserve her marriage to an ex-convict, by keeping him from the knowledge that she, too, has served time in jail.[44]

For all of its problems, some modern day viewers also find *You and Me* better than its box office receipts would have one believe. Many conclude that *You and Me* was perhaps too experimental for Hollywood at the time, but holds up better today. Raft and Sidney do have good chemistry, and their scenes together can be sweet and genuine. Raft plays the tough guy but still effectively showcases his emotional vulnerabilities.

While he didn't like working with Fritz Lang, George Raft seems committed to his character and performance in *You and Me*, and he is supported by some top level character actors, including Warren Hymer, Barton MacLane, Harry Carey, Adrian Morris, and George E. Stone. Raft particularly liked working with Roscoe Karns, who appears in several of his Paramount films, so his presence in the cast

---

44 *You and Me* review. *The New York Daily News*. June 2, 1938

is also welcome. But despite some interesting, offbeat ideas, *You and Me* is generally considered a misfire, although many modern day viewers argue that Lang took a pretty standard message movie and turned it into something wholly unique.

SPAWN OF THE NORTH

Directed by Henry Hathaway
Screenplay by Jules Furthman from a story by Barrett Willoughby
Produced by Albert Lewin
Cinematography Charles Lang Jr
Film Editing by Ellworth Hoaglund

Cast:
George Raft	Tyler Dawson
Henry Fonda	Jim Kimmerlee
Dorothy Lamour	Nicky Duval
Akim Tamiroff	Red Skain
John Barrymore	Windy Turlon
Louise Platt	Dian 'Di' Turlon
Lynne Overman	Jack Jackson
Fuzzy Knight	Lefty Jones
Vladimir Sokoloff	Dimitri
Duncan Renaldo	Ivan
John Wray	Dr. Sparks
Michio Ito	Indian Dancer
Stanley Andrews	Partridge
Richard Ung	Tom
Henry Brandon	Davis
Adia Kuznetzoff	Vashia
Robert Middlemass	Davis
Alex Woloshin	Gregory
Guy Usher	Grant
Egon Brecher	Erickson
Leonid Snegoff	Peter
Harvey Clark	Purser
Edmund Elton	Minister
Irving Bacon	Cannery Official

Monte Blue	Cannery Official
Bob Kortman	Russian Henchman
Eddie Marr	Red's Gang Member #1
Frank Puglia	Red's Gang Member #2
Lee Shumway L	Fisherman
Archie Twitchell	Fisherman
Arthur Aylesworth	Fisherman
Wade Boteler	Fisherman
Rollo Lloyd	Fisherman
Earl Pingree	Fisherman

Released August 26, 1938
Paramount Pictures
Running time: 102 minutes
Black and White

Although working comfortably with a solid contract at a major studio, and bringing in a reasonable amount of revenue with his films, George Raft was dissatisfied. He felt he had gone as far as he could at Paramount, where he had spent nearly his entire film career, and was interested in moving to another studio. Raft's contract with Paramount was due to expire in February of 1939, and he was seriously pondering not renewing with them, and seeking work elsewhere.

Spawn of the North was originally planned to feature Carole Lombard in the lead role when it was first proposed in 1936. The male leads were going to be Cary Grant and Randolph Scott. By the time production was ready to begin in 1938, both Lombard and Scott had moved on to other projects, so the plan was to instead cast Frances Farmer and Fred MacMurray in their roles. There were also plans to shoot the film in color. All of these ideas were eventually jettisoned, and George Rigaud was announced for the lead. However, his French accent seemed to be too strong for the role, so Henry Fonda was cast opposite George Raft, while Dorothy Lamour, who had scored big in John Ford's *The Hurricane*, had the female lead. George Raft was pleased when Henry Hathaway signed on as director, as he worked well with him on *Souls at Sea*,

George Raft and Henry Fonda in Spawn of the North

which was a box office hit that brought greater acclaim to Raft as an actor.

Spawn of the North deals with salmon cannery owner Jim Kimmerlee (Fonda) and his buddy Tyler Dawson (George Raft). When Russian bandit Red (Akim Tamiroff) is stealing from fishing traps, Jim sets out to stop him but Tyler joins up with him. This causes a conflict between the two friends with Tyler making the ultimate sacrifice in the end. There is also a romance between Jim and Dian (Louise Platt) a girl he's known since childhood, but who has gone to college and has trouble dealing with the fishing community after experiencing education and refinement. Tyler's girl is Nicky Duval (Dorothy Lamour) with whom he has a loving but contentious relationship.

George Raft carries Dorothy Lamour in Spawn of the North

Henry Fonda later stated that he made this movie for the money, but became impressed with how well the film turned out. His performance is typically solid and never falters. Dorothy Lamour was allowed to explore a more layered character rather than rely on her beauty. She effectively rises to the occasion. It is great that her character is basically a business owner and she is outwardly fiery, but still expresses a lot of affection for Raft's character. Lamour is also a great contrasting figure to Fonda's more prim and proper love interest. Arguably, Raft's chemistry with Fonda is not as strong as his with Gary Cooper in *Souls at Sea* but the friendship between them still resonates. And George Raft once again plays a character that has many varied elements. His love for the Lamour character, affection for his childhood friend Fonda, and choice to throw in with Tamiroff, all eventually clash. His final scene, when he causes an avalanche to kill both him and the Tamiroff character offers a powerful conclusion that defines the complexities of Raft's character as positive.

It is interesting that Raft played a similarly layered character as when he last was directed by Henry Hathaway. In *Souls at Sea*, Raft also plays a character that balances between good and bad, and concludes by making the ultimate sacrifice. And, also like *Souls at Sea*, Raft rises to the occasion as an actor. He exudes the proper attitude for each of the varying thoughts and feelings that he must convey. It is a powerful performance that owes a great deal to the subtle nuance that George Raft always seemed able to exhibit.

Filling in the supporting roles with such veterans as the great John Barrymore, Fuzzy Knight, and Lynne Overman helps round out the cast with top-level acting. Richard Talmadge was responsible for second unit direction that was shot on location, which provides an impressive opening montage. And the entire production is enhanced by the musical score by Dimitri Tiomkin.

As an amusing novelty, a pet seal is added to the proceedings, and Slicker the seal manages to steal a few scenes along the way. Slicker's owner and trainer was H.W. Winston, who termed Slicker as the smartest seal ever to gulp a fish. Winston had found Slicker tangled up in a fish net off the coast of Monterey. He had been hauled out of the ocean by a fisherman with a catch of halibut. Winston bought him from the fisherman and trained him. *Spawn of the North* has some heavily dramatic scenes, but the inclusion of Slicker never distracts or disrupts the narrative. In fact, Slicker even had his own stand-ins:

> Dorothy Lamour and George Raft were speeding across the country by train to appear in person at a New York movie house and then to be placed on permanent display in the Central park zoo. Not Dorothy Lamour and George Raft, the movie stars, but Dorothy Lamour and George Raft the California sea lions that stood in for Slicker, the sea lion actor featured with the real George Raft, Henry Fonda and Dorothy Lamour In Paramount's. Alaskan salmon saga, *Spawn of the North*. They will appear in person in connection with the engagement.[45]

---

45 Stand-in Seals Off To New York for Personal Appearance. *Los Angeles Daily News*. September 2, 1938

Spawn of the North is a remarkable production, director Hathaway doing a lot with the backlot filming, making it appear like the movie was shot on location. Paramount had built a steel and concrete tank on the studio lot that held 375,000 gallons of water. It was used for fishing boats and power cruisers in closer shots. Much can be said about the brilliant efforts of the film's special effects and production team. Their work was so good, they were given a special Oscar at the 11th Academy Awards. The Oscar was given to special effects artist Gordon Jennings, with assistance from Jan Domela, Dev Jennings, Irmin Roberts and Art Smith; the transparencies artist Farciot Edouart, with assistance from Loyal Griggs and the sound effects artist Loren L. Ryder, with assistance from Harry D. Mills, Louis Mesenkop and Walter Oberst.

Spawn of the North was a major box office hit. It was remade by Paramount in 1954 as *Alaska Seas*, directed by Jerry Hopper and starring Robert Ryan, January Sterling and Brian Keith.

Paramount next wanted George Raft to appear in *St. Louis Blues*, which would reteam him with Dorothy Lamour in a musical directed by Raoul Walsh, a director Raft liked. However, he was tiring of the films he was being offered by the studio, feeling they had little opportunity for him to explore a role like in *Souls at Sea* or *Spawn of the North*. He refused, Lloyd Nolan was cast in his part, and he was once again put on suspension. In October of 1938, Raft started work on the comedy *The Lady's From Kentucky*, a race track story with a script that appealed to him. It would be his final film on his Paramount contract.

THE LADY'S FROM KENTUCKY

Directed by Alexander Hall
Screenplay by Malcolm Stuart Boylan from a story by Rowland Brown
Produced by Jeff Lazarus
Cinematography by Theodor Sparkuhl
Film Editing by Harvey Johnson

Cast:
George Raft	Marty Black
Ellen Drew	Penelope 'Penny' Hollis
Hugh Herbert	Mousey Johnson
Zasu Pitts	Dulcey Lee
Louise Beavers	Aunt Tina
Lew Payton	Sixty
Forrester Harvey	Nonny Watkins
Harry Tyler	Carter
Edward Pawley	Spike Cronin
Gilbert Emery	Pinckney Rodell
Eugene Jackson	Winfield
Jimmy Bristow	Brewster
George Anderson	Lane
Bill Cartledge	Jones
Charles Trowbridge	Charles Butler
Stanley Andrews	Doctor
Hooper Atchley	Surgeon
Fern Emmett	Attending Nurse
Nell Craig	Nurse in Corridor
Carol Holloway	Nurse in Corridor
Paula DeCardo	Nurse
Gloria Williams	Nurse
George Melford	Veterinarian

Carl Stockdale	Veterinarian
Archie Twitchell	Radio Announcer
Hal K. Dawson	Announcer
Tom Hanlon	Announcer
Irving Bacon	Information Clerk
Harry Tenbrook	Longshoreman
George Turner	Longshoreman
Robert Milasch	Big Longshoreman
James Flavin	Policeman
Frankie Van	Taxi Driver
Gus Glassmire G	Pole Judge
Roger Gray	Waiter
Charles C. Wilson	Steward
Bob Perry	Dealer
John Merton	Gambler
Paul Newlan	Gambler
Robert Stephenson	Gambler
Virginia Sale	Cashier
Frank Moran	Customer
Jack Raymond	Customer

Released April 28, 1939
Paramount Pictures
Running time: 67 minutes
Black and White

It is somewhat curious that George Raft would refuse some projects and accept others. He soon became legendary for the movies he turned down, but at this point it appeared Raft was simply being difficult for a studio where he believed he no longer had the opportunity for advancement.

The Lady's From Kentucky started out under the title *Racing Form* and it was announced that the screenplay would be written by Olive Cooper and Cy Bartlett. However, there is no confirmation either worked on the screenplay, which was credited solely to Malcolm Stuart Boylan, who had penned scripts for MGM (*Politics*), Warner Brothers (*Devil Dogs of the Air*) and Paramount (the Three Marines

Ellen Drew and George Raft in The Lady's From Kentucky

segment in *If I Had a Million*). The story was by Rowland Brown, notable for having penned the original story for films like *Hell's Highway* and *Angels With Dirty Faces*.

Frances Dee was set to be George Raft's leading lady, while Raoul Walsh was announced in the press as the film's director. However, by the time shooting commenced in October of 1938, Dee had been replaced by Ellen Drew, and Walsh was replaced by Alexander Hall, who directed Raft in other films, including *Madame Racketeer* and *Midnight Club*.

George Raft plays Marty Black, a bookie and a gambler who wins half interest in Roman Son, a race horse. The chief owner of Roman Son is Penny Hollis (Ellen Drew) who has inherited him as part of a stable. A blue-blood Kentuckian, Penny is concerned with the proper care of her horses, with little regard as to their ability to win races. After Roman Son wins a juvenile stakes competition, Marty wants to continue racing him, but Penny returns with the horse to Kentucky. Finally entering him in another race, Marty discovers that while Roman Son wins, he hasn't been properly trained and falls ill afterward. Feeling guilty, Marty helps nurse the horse back to recovery and sells his interest to Penny. With proper training, Roman Son wins the Kentucky Derby, but is injured and no longer able to race. Penny forgives Marty, they fall in love, and return to Kentucky together.

The Lady's From Kentucky is yet another George Raft movie that is basically average with no real impact on his career. It is significant as being his last film for Paramount, but otherwise it is a very standard comedy drama that is usually predictable. Raft, a real life gambler, was reportedly attracted to the horse race setting and that is why he liked the script. Overall the filming of *The Lady's From Kentucky* was a pleasant, comfortable experience for George Raft, but of no lasting importance to his filmography.

It is not a bad film. The leads are both good, the story is adequate, and welcome veterans like ZaSu Pitts and Hugh Herbert add to the fun. *The Lady From Kentucky* is merely a standard movie with little real merit.

It wasn't already decided that *The Lady's From Kentucky* would be the last film Raft would make under his Paramount contract. The studio was readying other projects to be filmed after this one finished shooting. However, by the time production concluded on *The Lady's From Kentucky* it was already January of 1939, and George Raft had one month left on his contract. He continued to turn down projects, and soon found himself a freelancer.

Warner Brothers was the first studio to express an interest in George Raft. They had a strong stable of tough guy actors, including James Cagney, Edward G. Robinson, and Humphrey Bogart, and were interested in possibly adding Raft. However, they first needed to find the right property as a sort of test run. If the subsequent film was a hit, then Raft would be offered a contract.

The press indicated that among the film projects considered for Raft included a remake of the silent drama *The Patent Leather Kid*, and a remake of the earlier Warner prison drama *20,000*

Years in Sing Sing, which had starred Spencer Tracy. However, Raft informed the studio that he would not appear in remakes of earlier movies. John Garfield ended up being cast in the remake of *20,000 Years in Sing Sing*, under the title *Castle on the Hudson*. Garfield was also considered for the *Patent Leather Kid* remake, but that film was never produced.

Warner Brothers had been considering starring John Garfield opposite James Cagney in *Each Dawn I Die*, another prison drama in which Garfield would play a crusading reporter who is framed into a prison sentence and meets up with gangster Cagney. However, when Garfield was placed in another film, it was decided to revamp *Each Dawn I Die* and cast Cagney as the reporter and George Raft as the gangster. The result was another one of George Raft's finest performances.

EACH DAWN I DIE

Directed by William Keighley
Screenplay by Norman Reilly Raine, Warren Duff, Charles Perry, from a novel by Jerome Odlum.
Produced by Hal Wallis
Cinematography by Arthur Edeson
Film Editing by Thomas Richards

Cast:
James Cagney	Frank Ross
George Raft	Stacey
Jane Bryan	Joyce
George Bancroft	Warden Armstrong
Maxie Rosenbloom	Red
Stanley Ridges	Mueller
Alan Baxter	Carlisle
Victor Jory	Grayce
John Wray	Pete
Edward Pawley	Dale
Willard Robertson	Lang
Emma Dunn	Frank's mother
Paul Hurst	Garsky
Louis Jean Heydt	Lassiter
Joe Downing	Limpy Julien
Thurston Hall	Hanley
William B Davidson	Bill Mason
Clay Clement	Stacey's attorney
Charles Trowbridge	Judge
Harry Cording	Temple
Abner Biberman	Shake Edwards
Mack Gray	Joe
Al Hill	Johnny

Bob Perry	Bud
John Harron	Jerry
Jack Perry	Hood
John Ridgely	Reporter
Selmer Jackson	Patterson
James Flavin	Policeman
Stuart Holmes	Witness
Cliff Saum	Witness
Jack Goodrich	Witness
Walter Miller	Turnkey
Wilfred Lucas	Bailiff
Emmet Vogan	Prosecutor
Lew Murphy	Trial Warden
Chuck Hamilton	Court Officer
Wedgwood Nowell	Parole Board
Art Howard	Parole Board
John Dilson	Parole Board
Leo White	Cabbie
Martin Cichy	Convict
James P Spencer	Convict
Charles Sullivan	Convict
Elliot Sullivan	Convict
Harry Tenbrook	Convict
Jack Wise	Convict
Hector Sarno	Convict
Paul Panzer	Convict
Sammy Finn	Convict
John Irwin	Convict
Max Hoffman	Guard
Eddie Hart	Guard
Fred Graham	Guard
Frank O' Connor	Guard
Henry Otho	Guard
Lee Phelps	Guard
Dick Rich	Guard
Jack Smith	Guard
Maris Wrixon	Girl in Car

Garland Smith   Man in Car
Arthur Garnder   Man in car
John Conte   narrator

Released July 22, 1939
Warner Bros
Running Time: 92 minutes
Black and White

For his first movie as a free-lancer after ending his association with Paramount, George Raft accepted yet another convict role in the Warner Brothers production of *Each Dawn I Die*. George insisted that his agreeing to play another hood was because the character had redeeming values, while Cagney, who had been friends with Raft since each man's New York beginnings, told biographer John McCabe:

> Curious thing about George. He was one of the underworld yet not in the underworld. From Al Capone down, he knew them all the worst hoods you could imagine, yet George had no part of lawbreaking. An amazing man, a superb dancer, and I didn't mind a bit his stealing *Each Dawn I Die* from me.[46]

Prison dramas were already rather cliché by the time *Each Dawn I Die* was in production, some of the more significant examples of the sub-genre being early talkies like *The Big House* (1930) and *Hell's Highway* (1932). What sets this movie apart is the acting by James Cagney, George Raft and a strong supporting cast, as well as excellent direction by William Keighley. *Each Dawn I Die* was originally going to be directed by Michael Curtiz but he was replaced by Keighley who probably did better with this material. Keighley zeroes in on the underlying tension of the situation, making the film highly effective as one of the finest prison dramas of its kind.

George Raft had misgivings about playing hoods, wanting to break free from that role once he left Paramount, but seeing how the character he is playing has redeeming values, and makes an ultimate sacrifice for the greater good, he accepted the role. He also

---

46 McCabe, John. *Cagney* NY: Carroll & Graf. 1999

George Raft and James Cagney in Each Dawn I Die

liked the idea of appearing in a movie with Cagney, who was a longtime friend. Raft had cameos in a couple of earlier Cagney films, so to be a co-star in this film showed how far Raft had gone in the past few years.

James Cagney plays Frank Ross, a crusading reporter who has been investigating the nefarious dealings of Jesse Hanley (Thurston Hall) who is running for governor. Ross spies on Hanley and his accomplice, Grayce (Victor Jory) and sees them burning papers that could lead to further investigation. The D.A. is also corrupt and Ross is framed into a drunk driving accident where innocent people are killed, and ends up in prison. While there he meets up with Stacey (George Raft), a career criminal who is serving yet another prison sentence, this time for life. Ross and Stacey form a bond and it is arranged that Frank implicate him in a prison stabbing so Stacey can escape at the subsequent trial and find the men

James Cagney and George Raft in Each Dawn I Die

who framed Ross. Stacey, however, is merely taking advantage of the situation to escape his life sentence. Frank's girl (Jane Bryan) goes to see Stacey and convinces him to find the information as promised. He discovers that the man who knows all is serving a sentence at the prison. Stacey turns himself in and, during a prison break, forces a confession out of the culprit while the Warden listens. This clears Ross before Stacey is killed during the prison revolt.

James Cagney is the star of this film, and most of the narrative deals with Frank Ross's emotional breakdown while enduring prison life. George Raft's contribution is as the narrative anchor, the hardened criminal who has seen so much, he has resigned himself to believing that one must pay people to cooperate. The idea that Frank Ross made sacrifices to expose the criminal element among politicians, who are also Stacey's enemy, is hard for the gangster to grasp.

It's quite far-fetched to think that a criminal facing a life sentence would voluntarily return to prison to help another man out, but the film tries to convey that Ross's sacrifice goes above and beyond, and thus it is only right that he does the same.

Along with the unbelievable idea of Stacey returning to prison voluntarily, Ross is also a bit too naïve and trusting of Stacey, a racketeer that the savvy reporter should understand more clearly. And yet, somehow it works. The actors are strong and effective, and William Keighley's direction expertly dwells on the tension in the prison scenes and the layers of the two men's relationship. There are some tangents. Maxie Rosenbloom adds an element of humor as a dopey inmate, and there is a sub-plot involving a sadistic guard terrorizing a weak inmate who dies. The inmate's friend brutally kills the guard in such a violent manner (offscreen) that Ross has to look away.

It is Stacey's actions that free Ross, and while it might be considered hokum that as Ross leaves prison he is given a note Stacey left behind ("To Ross, I found a square guy"), somehow it works in context.

There was some real life drama during the filming of *Each Dawn I Die*. Willie Bioff, a labor racketeer, had arranged that one of his men, who was a gaffer on the film, drop a heavy klieg light on Cagney, which would have seriously injured or perhaps even killed him. The action was stopped when it was discovered that the connected George Raft was in the movie. Raft was so angry upon finding this out, he personally confronted Bioff, letting him know that Cagney was a longtime friend.

Critics were generally impressed with the taut suspense, the compelling narrative, and the fine acting in *Each Dawn I Die*, overlooking the more far-fetched elements. *The New York Journal-American* stated:

> If it weren't close to heresy to say so, indeed, one might even go so far as to aver that it is Mr. Raft who comes nearest to stealing the entire picture, even in the face of the usual masterful playing of Brother Cagney in *Each Dawn I Die*. Mr. Raft is once again back in his own element, the role of a tough guy with a heart of gold, a con-

vict with a stretch of 199 years before him, and taking his time about playing it out. In such parts as these Mr. Raft literally shines, the sinister shadow of his playing dominating every scene in which he appears, and most of the rest in which he isn't seen at all. If that isn't picture stealing, I don't know what it is.[47]

Variety said essentially the same thing, singling out George Raft as one of the main reasons the film was a success:

Raft shoulders up, inspirationally, to equal level (with Cagney) in a role of difficult transitions as a tough repeater convict who makes himself the instrument for the unjustly convicted reporter's vindication through voluntary reprisonment and heroism in the surging battle of the cons with machine gunning militia. A fiery, wholly pervasive and telling enactment.[48]

Warner Brothers was pleased with George Raft's performance and cooperation during the filming of *Each Dawn I Die*, but did not offer him a contract. Raft continued to freelance until *Each Dawn I Die* was released. When it became a huge box office hit, he was then offered a contract.

Until that happened, George Raft continued to be in demand as a freelance actor, as his name continued to mean good box office. For his next film, Raft went to Universal to appear in *I Stole a Million*.

---

47 Each Dawn I Die review. *The New York Journal-American*. July 20, 1939
48 Each Dawn I Die review. *Variety* July 18, 1939

I STOLE A MILLION

Directed by Frank Tuttle
Screenplay by Nathaniel West from a story by Lester Cole
Produced by Burt Kelly
Cinematography by Milton Krasner
Film Editing by Edward Curtiss

Cast:
George Raft	Joe Lourik
Claire Trevor	Laura Benson
Dick Foran	Paul Carver
Henry Armetta	Nick
Victor Jory	Patian
George Chandler	Herbert
Irving Bacon	Simpson
Tom Fadden	Verne
Robert Elliott	Peterson
Joe Sawyer	Billings
John Hamilton	Atty. Wilson
Harry C. Bradley	Sexton
Wallis Clark	Jenkins - Mgr. of Cab Installment Sales
Hobart Cavanaugh	Jenkins' Bespectacled Asst.
Mira McKinney	Mrs. Loomis - Laura's Landlady
Phil Tead	Charlie
Ernie Adams	The Mooch
John Butler	Logan - Cab Manager
Raymond Bailey	Cabby
John Berkes	Hobo
Virginia Brissac	Nurse
Arthur Q. Bryan	Cafe Mgr. Forbidding Dancing
Mary Foy	Prison Matron
Jack Gardner	Reporter

Al Hill	Post Office Guard
Harold Hoff	Garage Attendant
J. Anthony Hughes	Bank Robber
Lloyd Ingraham	Sympathetic Man
Charles Irwin	Theater Manager
Mike Lally	Croupier
Dick Elliott	Small-Town Doctor
Fern Emmett	Visitor in Hospital
Billy Engle	Bookkeeper
Eddy Chandler	Baggage Car Guard
Jim Farley	Doorman
Sam Finn	Cabby
Mary Forbes	Customer in Flower Shop
Lee Ford	Theatre Usher
Edmund MacDonald	First Cop
Dick Wessel	2nd Cop
Mary MacLaren	Nurse
Jerry Marlowe	Photographer
Larry McGrath	Gas Station Attendant
Bud McTaggart	Reporter
Margaret McWade	Matron
Harold Minjir	Jewelry Salesman
Frances Morris	Prisoner
Lee Murray	Jockey
Drew Demorest	Reporter
Eddie Dunn	Trucking Superintendent
Ralph Dunn	Bartender
Jimmy O'Gatty	Mug
Sarah Padden	Lady in Post Office
Emory Parnell	Friendly Cop at Flower Shop
Edward Peil Sr.	Doorman
Russ Powell	Watchman
Joey Ray	Clerk
Stanley Ridges	Downs - Crooked Atty.
Betty Roadman	Matron
Jason Robards Sr.	Bank Teller
Frances Robinson	Elsie - Movie Cashier

Constantine Romanoff   Wrestler
Henry Roquemore   Manager of Acme Cab Company
William Ruhl   Detective
David Sharpe   Cabby
Tom Steele   Cop
Landers Stevens   Businessman
Charles Sullivan   Gas Station Helper
Ben Taggart   Police Guard at Hospital
Harry Tyler   Kibitzer at Dice Game
Emmett Vogan   Movie Theater Mgr.
Billy Wayne   Mild Cabbie
Claire Whitney   Hospital Matron
Arthur Yeoman   Telegrapher
Dot Farley   Bit
Mack Gray   Bit

Released August 1, 1939
Universal Pictures
Running Time: 81 minutes
Black and White

   According to the press, Edward G. Robinson was in negotiation to star in this film for Universal, but when negotiations broke down, George Raft was offered the role. Raft liked the script despite it being a crime drama, because the character was an honest working man who falls into crimes through desperation and unfortunate circumstances, and wasn't a mere hood. And despite his wanting to expand his range, Raft realized that while freelancing, before he landed a contract with one of the major studios, it was best that he work in crime dramas because that's what his audience generally wanted from him. He needed to keep his box office status intact in order to secure a contract, and *Each Dawn I Die* had not yet been released.
   For his leading lady, Universal considered many strong actresses, including Joan Blondell and Frances Dee, before Claire Trevor was cast in the role. The cast is rounded out with several top-drawer

Clare Trevor and George Raft in I Stole a Million

character actors, even Arthur Q. Bryan, voice of cartoon character Elmer Fudd, who amusingly uses the Fudd voice for his small part.

An article in *Hollywood Citizen News* announced director Frank Tuttle being hired for this project, and being quite happy about it:

> The film will mark a reversion to his favorite medium for Frank Tuttle— namely melodrama. Known In recent years for his work in such frothy musicals as *Waikiki Wedding, College Holiday, Doctor Rhythm* and *Paris Honeymoon,* Tuttle was happier when he was directing William Powell in Van Dine mysteries at Paramount and Gary Cooper in *Only the Brave.* The Raft picture will be in a vein similar to that of these older films.[49]

Raft is Joe Lourik, a cab driver working hard to make ends meet. He gets into a conflict with the finance company that own his cab, believing he has made enough payments to own the vehicle. This leads to his arrest for robbery, but he escapes from custody while still wearing handcuffs. He hops a train and meets a tramp who tells him about a hood named Patian (Victor Jory) who can arrange

---

49 Leading Ladies in Demand. *Hollywood Citizen News.* April 18, 1939

to remove the handcuffs. Joe makes his way to Patian in San Francisco, and gets his cuffs removed, but only after he agrees to drive a getaway car for a bank robbery. Joe is then sent to Sacramento to wait for his portion of the money, but eventually discovers he's never going to be paid. He considers robbing a flower shop, but meets Laura (Claire Trevor) and falls in love with her. Joe wins enough money gambling to open his own garage and settle down, but soon the police catch up with him so he runs off back to San Diego. He confronts Patian for his money from the past robbery, and is forced to commit another crime, so he runs off again. After seeing a picture of his newborn baby in the newspaper, Joe returns to Laura who begs him to turn himself in, serve his time, and get on with his life. The police close in, Joe runs, and Laura is arrested as an accomplice. Joe goes on a crime spree while Laura is in jail, and becomes known as The Million Dollar Bandit, as his goal is to steal enough to set Laura and his daughter up for life. Laura meets with Joe upon being released from prison and again begs him to give himself up. With the police closing in once again, Joe is tired of running, and does so.

George Raft was cooperative on this project except when the time came for his character to rob a post office. Raft insisted that his character would not do such a thing, because the post office is a government office, and such a move would be a federal rap. Once the film was released and Raft was talking to the press to promote it, he addressed questions about playing another hood role by insisting his character is not a hood, and joking that he is a rugged individualist.

Universal was enthusiastic about the project and sent out press releases that were carried in most newspapers:

With George Raft and Claire Trevor both on the job, *I Stole Million* went before the cameras last week at Universal. A powerful story of a man who ruined not only his own, but also his wife's life, because he refused pay the penalty for his first slip, *I Stole a Million* will be one of Universal's top offerings for the coming year. Frank Tutile, for years one of Hollywood's leading megaphonists is directing. Burt Kelly is the producer.[50]

I Stole a Million was a box office disappointment, but *Each Dawn I Die*, released only weeks earlier, was a huge hit, and overshadowed this movie's lack of success. *Each Dawn I Die* was also strong enough for Warner Brothers to offer George Raft a contract. The actor had some conditions. He didn't want to play exclusively in crime dramas, or to play hoods with no redeeming values. He also wanted it in his contract that he didn't have to act in movie remakes. The studio agreed to these demands, and George Raft was now under contract with Warner Brothers. His first film as a contracted actor with the studio was *Invisible Stripes* with Humphrey Bogart and William Holden. It was yet another crime drama, with George Raft opening the film being released from jail. Raft would later quip that he was in prison so often during this period of his movie career, he had a specially made prison outfit in his closet to wear for such roles. It likely came in handy, because George Raft's next two films would have him in prison.

---

50   George Raft is Cast as Criminal. *The Times*. Hammond, Indiana. June 9, 1939

INVISIBLE STRIPES

Directed by Lloyd Bacon
Screenplay by Warren Duff from a story by Jonathan Finn based
   on the book by Lewis Lawes.
Produced by Lewis Edelman
Cinematography by Ernest Haller
Film Editing by James Gibbon

Cast:
George Raft	Cliff Taylor
Jane Bryan	Peggy
William Holden	Tim Taylor
Humphrey Bogart	Chuck Martin
Flora Robson	Mrs Taylor
Paul Kelly	Ed Kruger
Lee Patrick	Molly
Henry O'Neill	Parole Officer Masters
Frankie Thomas	Tommy
Moroni Olsen M	Prison Warden
Margot Stevenson	Sue
Marc Lawrence	Lefty
Joe Downing	Johnny
Leo Gorcey	Jimmy
William Haade	Shrank
Tully Marshall	Old Peter
William B. Davidson	Montgomery
John Hamilton	Captain Johnson
Frank Bruno	Pauly
Frank Faylen	Steve - Henchman on Bank Job
G. Pat Collins	Alec - New 'Fish'
Ray Cooke	Pinky - Tim's
Bert Hanlon	Shorty - Mug at Party

Ralph Dunn	Doorman
Robert Elliott	Arresting Officer
Sam Finn	Spotter
Pat Flaherty	Worker
Jane Gilbert	Young Society Lady
Jack Gordon	Convict
Mack Gray	Henchman Seated at Party
Raymond Bailey	Bookie
Al Hill	Getaway Driver at Bank Job
Charles C. Wilson	Arresting Officer
Harry Wilson	Worker
Claude Wisberg	Older Boy
Dorothea Wolbert	Flower Woman
George Taylor	Smitty - Returning 'Fish'
Jack Mower	Detective Escorting Convicts
Pat O'Malley	Jailhouse Lieutenant with Capt. Johnson
Emory Parnell	Policeman Outside Bank
Allen Pomeroy	Guard
Tom Quinn	Handcuffed Prisoner
John Ridgely	Employment Clerk
Harry Strang	Party Bartender
Maude Allen	Seated Lady at Dance
Bruce Bennett	Rich Man
Wade Boteler	Policeman Outside Garage
Sidney Bracey	Bank Guard
Eddy Chandler	Driver
Lane Chandler	Detective
Cliff Clark	Police Sergeant
Ethan Laidlaw	Cop Outside Police Station
Mike Lally	Henchman Driver
Marion Martin	Blonde
Frank Mayo	Prison Gate Guard
Stan Meyers	Dance Band Leader
John Irwin	Prisoner
Selmer Jackson	Police Lieutenant
Walter James	Worker
Victor Kilian	Loading Dock Foreman

Richard Clayton	Hired Stockboy
Joseph Crehan	Garage Owner
Joe Devlin	Mug Who Brings Drink to Chuck
Lew Harvey	Betting Room Door Guard
Al Hill Jr.	Stockboy
Max Hoffman Jr.	Chauffeur Showing Off Car
J. Anthony Hughes	Chauffeur #2
William Hopper	Society Gent in Top Hat

Released December 30, 1939
Warner Bros.
Running Time: 81 minutes
Black and White

Because of the success Warners had with *Each Dawn I Die*, the plan was to reteam George Raft and James Cagney for *Invisible Stripes*, a drama about two friends released from prison, one going straight and trying to settle into society, the other maintaining his criminal ways. An article in the press stated:

> For their stronger melodramas the Warner Bros are establishing two surefire teams a James Cagney-George Raft team and a James Cagney-Pat O'Brien team. Cagney and Raft are getting rave notices for their work in *Each Dawn I Die* and are pretty well decided upon for a follow up in *Invisible Stripes*. But before *Invisible Stripes*, Cagney will team again with Pat O'Brien (as he did successfully in *Angels With Dirty Faces* and others) in *Two Sons*, an original story by John Fante and Ross Wills. The Warners are convinced that *Two Sons* has the greatest moral lesson of any of the stern social dramas which they have made a specialty.[51]

Only a month later, there were press reports indicating all of these plans had changed, the announced Cagney-O'Brien film never being made, and the cast of *Invisible Stripes* changing:

> Too bad that the combination of James Cagney and George Raft is to be broken up in *Invisible Stripes* for

---
51 Cagney and O'Brien Again. *Los Angeles Evening News*. July 27, 1949

which the two were named, following *Each Dawn I Die*. But Warner Bros has plans for producing this picture at the same time as *The Fighting 69th*, and Cagney is needed for that film with Pat O'Brien. So in *Invisible Stripes* it will be Raft, and Humphrey Bogart who will have the leads. Cagney and Raft proved quite a team In *Each Dawn I Die*, which witnesses excellent performances by both, despite the somewhat conventional attributes of the story.[52]

John Garfield, who was fairly new to the studio, had scored big in films like *Four Daughters* (1938) and *They Made Me a Criminal* (1939), was planned for the juvenile lead in *Invisible Stipes* but he turned the assignment down. He was replaced by William Holden. Ironically, Holden had just made his screen debut at Columbia in *Golden Boy*, based on the play written by Clifford Odets. Odets wrote the lead with Garfield in mind, but Warners wouldn't lend their up-and-coming star to Columbia for the role, hence the hiring of William Holden. So, when Warners offered *Invisible Stripes* to Garfield, he quipped, "why don't you hire William Holden instead." They did.

Casting continued for the female lead, and, according to the press, Ruby Keeler, known for musicals, was considered for the role:

> Ruby Keeler, who made her screen debut for Warner Brothers in *42d Street*, will return to that studio for a role in *Invisible Stripes*, if negotiations now under way are consummated. Her *Invisible Stripes* assignment would be the role originally scheduled for Jane Bryan, whose present crowded schedule eliminates her from consideration. Miss Bryan is appearing opposite Paul Muni in *We Are Not Alone* and is scheduled for four other roles In quick succession. The leading masculine roles in *Invisible Stripes* will be played by George Raft. Humphrey Bogart and William Holden.[53]

---

52 Bogart New Choice for Invisible Stripes. *The Los Angeles Times*. August 26, 1939

53 Casting for Invisible Stripes. *The Brooklyn Daily Eagle*. September 6, 1939

William Holden, George Raft, and Humphrey Bogart in Invisible Stripes

Jane Bryan ended up taking the role after finishing work on *We Are Not Alone*, but made only one more movie (*Brother Rat and a Baby*), then got married, broke her contract with the studio, and left movies forever. She and her husband, Justin Dart remained married from 1939 until his death in 1984. Jane lived to be 90, dying in 2009. Throughout her long life, she never once discussed her film career.

George Raft plays Cliff Taylor who longs to go straight and leave his criminal past behind, once he is released from prison. Due to his past, Cliff has trouble securing a job. He has a younger brother, Tim (William Holden) who is also struggling to make enough money to get married to Peggy (Jane Bryan). Cliff is concerned Tim might fall into a life of crime, so, to protect his brother, he lies and says he has a job as a traveling salesman, but has actually reunited with criminal friend Charles Martin (Humphrey Bogart). On the train home from prison, career criminal Martin told Cliff that even though they are now wearing civilian clothes, the stripes never go

Jane Bryan, William Holden, George Raft, Flora Robson in Invisible Stripes

away. "You can't see 'em, but they're there!" This is the film's reference to its title. Martin appears to be proven right when Cliff can't successfully maintain an honest man's life. But he is not returning to criminal life permanently. The money he makes for his crimes is given to Tim, who opens his own garage. Once this is accomplished, Cliff plans to quit the gang. When a robbery attempt goes awry and people are killed, an injured Martin and his gang seek refuge in Tim's garage, telling him Cliff will be implemented if he doesn't cooperate. Tim is arrested as an accomplice, and Cliff agrees to testify against Martin and his gang so that his brother can go free. He warns Cliff ahead of time to leave town and avoid capture and likely execution. The result is a shoot-out that involves police.

Now a contract player at Warner Brothers, George Raft immediately settles into a starring role that allows him to mine the different levels of the screen persona he had firmly established. Cliff Taylor does not have particularly big ideas other than a genuine belief that he can go back to being an honest citizen once paroled. He just wants to go back to the home of his mother (Flora Robson), where his younger brother also lives, get an honest job, and return to his girlfriend (Margot Stevenson), whom he believes is waiting for him. He is beset with a succession of disappointments. His girl is no longer interested, not because there is another man, but simply because she can't marry an ex-con. He tries his hand at various jobs, works hard, but keeps getting fired for a myriad of different reasons because the employers aren't comfortable with an ex-con, and his co-workers have the same misgivings. One man wants to hire him as the office stool-pigeon, resulting in Cliff hitting him and risking a return to prison. At one point, Cliff is brought in after a robbery even though he has an alibi. He spends two nights in prison while they check it out, and although they clear him, this inconvenience is yet another addition to his mounting frustration.

We can see these mounting frustrations gradually take their toll on Cliff over the course of the film through Raft's performance. We see the disappointment in his eyes when his girl rejects him, and he's more outwardly gruff toward the officers when he is released from prison after being mistakenly arrested. William Holden also does a good job teetering just on the edge of indulging in criminal activity like his brother, especially when Tim has just purchased flowers for girlfriend Peggy from a street woman selling them, and afterward a well-dressed man on the street mistakes Peggy for a flower seller. Even though William Holden is in support of Raft, the film does a nice job showing his frustrations that he and Peggy can't have all the nice things they want.

Invisible Stripes is the quintessential Warner Brothers crime drama from this time, filled with action, tough drama, social commentary, romance, and sentiment. It might be a bit predictable, but it still has all of the elements that make this type of movie a rewarding viewing experience. The lead character is an ex-con, but his returning to crime is due to desperation that plays like necessity. Raft conveys a lot of strength in the character of Cliff, doing everything he can to maintain an honest life, but being powerless against the forces that keep him from achieving any level of success. Humphrey Bogart had not yet become a star (Raft would be instrumental in making that happen), so he is billed even beneath William Holden, who is appearing in only his second movie. Holden would later recall,

George Raft and Humphrey Bogart in Invisible Stripes

on a *Tonight Show* TV appearance, that during a fight scene he has with Raft, he brought up his head quickly and hit George, causing a gash. Rather than get upset, Raft exhibited patience and understanding. Holden never forgot Raft's kindness and support.

The rest of the cast includes several actors worth noting. Flora Robson, a distinguished actress of stage and screen, plays Raft's and Holden's mother, even though she is actually a year younger than George Raft. Paul Kelly, who plays one of Bogart's henchmen, actually did serve time in prison for manslaughter. Lee Patrick, who plays Bogart's girl, would be even more effective with him a couple years later in *The Maltese Falcon* in a part originally offered to George Raft. And it is fun to spot cameos of Leo Gorcey (Dead End Kids), Frankie Thomas (*Boys Town*), and John Hamilton (Perry Mason on TV's *The Adventures of Superman*). In one scene, when Bogart and Lee Patrick are leaving a theater, the film playing there is *You Can't Get Away With Murder* in which Bogart starred.

While George Raft had left Paramount because he was tired of the roles he was getting, the Warner Brothers approach to the same material was much better. Cliff really is an honest man who wants to leave his criminal past behind. He does the right thing in the end. He makes sacrifices for his family. It was a well-drawn, layered character, the type of which Raft excelled at playing. The actor realized that this would be a good film to begin his contract with a new studio. His instincts were correct. *Invisible Stripes* was a box office success.

However, for his next film, George Raft was loaned by Warner Brothers to producer Walter Wanger for *The House Across The Bay*. Raft didn't want to do the film, because he was again playing a criminal who serves time in prison, and he felt it was the sort of one-dimensional role he was trying to carefully avoid.

THE HOUSE ACROSS THE BAY

Directed by Archie Mayo
Screenplay by Kathryn Scola from a story by Myles Connolly
Produced by Walter Wanger
Cinematography by Merritt Gerstad
Film Editing by Dorothy Spencer

Cast
George Raft	Steve Larwitt
Joan Bennett	Brenda Bentley
Lloyd Nolan	Slant Kolma
Walter Pidgeon	Tim Nolan
Gladys George	Mary Bogale
Peggy Shannon	Alice
June Knight	Babe
Joe Sawyer	Charley
Cy Kendall	Crawley
Billy Wayne	Barney
Max Wagner	Jim
Frank Bruno	Jerry - Slant's Henchman
Etta McDaniel	Lydia
Sam Wren	Wally
Georges Renavent	French Official
Joseph Crehan	Federal Man
Edward Fielding	Judge
Virginia Brissac	Landlady
Sam Ash	Broker
Elsa Peterson	Mrs. Hanson
Herbert Ashley	Man in Park
John Bohn	Reporter
Peter Camlin	French Pilot
Tom Coleman	Café Patron

Marcelle Corday	French Maid
Gino Corrado	Nightclub Waiter
Sam Finn	Headwaiter
Mack Gray	Doorman / Lookout
Lew Hicks	Bailiff
Jack Lubell	Brenda's Friend
James Craig	Brenda's Friend
Jean Del Val	French Official
Harrison Greene	Irate Customer
Charles Griffin	Federal Agent
Kit Guard	Taresca's Gunman
Harry Harvey	Man in Club
Max Hoffman Jr.	Driver
Donald Kerr	Driver
Kenner G. Kemp	Bar Patron
Herman Marks	Gambler
Eddie Marr	Taresca's Henchman / Driver
Major McBride	Roulette Croupier
Miki Morita	Japanese Houseboy
Frances Morris	Slant's Secretary
Paul Phillips	Reporter
Armand Wright	Barber
Tom Quinn	2nd Bartender
Cyril Ring	Dancer
Dick Rush	Bailiff
Harry Tyler	Fur Peddler
Emmett Vogan	U.S. Official
Norman Willis	Henchman
Isabel Withers	Woman in Club
Allen Wood	Newsboy
Bob Kortman	Prison Guard
Pat O'Malley	Prison Guard
Martin Cichy	Prison Guard
Jim Farley	Prison Guard
Franklyn Farnum	Prison Guard
Al Ferguson	Prison Guard
Dorothy Vaughan	Prisoner's Wife on Ferry

Maxine Leslie	Prisoner's Wife
Kitty McHugh	Prisoner's Wife
Helen Shipman	Prisoner's Wife
Ruth Warren	Prisoner's Wife
Kay Gordon	Chorus Girl
Edith Haskins	Chorus Girl
Carol Adams	Chorus Girl
Pearlie Norton	Chorus Girl
Jean O'Donnell	Chorus Girl
Mitzie Uehlien	Chorus Girl
Victoria Vinton	Chorus Girl

Released March 1, 1940
United Artists
Running Time: 88 minutes
Black and White

When George Raft finally agreed to accept the role of a gangster who dies at the end, Warner agreed to loan him out to producer Walter Wanger, but were miffed that he was willing to play this role, and not similar ones for his home studio. The press announced the signing as early as the fall of 1939:

> George Raft and Lloyd Nolan yesterday were acquired for *House Across the Bay*, with Joan Bennett, to be produced by Walter Wanger. Raft quits the picture he was to have made at Warners, *It All Came True*, and will be the leading man in the Wanger opus.[54]

Notably, Raft was replaced in *It All Came True* with Humphrey Bogart, who had also replaced him in *Dead End* for Samuel Goldwyn a few years earlier.

Interestingly, Warner Brothers had once been interested in buying the original story by Myles Connolly as a vehicle for James Cagney, with the possibility of Marlene Dietrich as his leading lady. Walter Wanger bought the rights when Warners couldn't come to an agreement. Wanger had a deal to make six films for United Artists release, but waited to film *The House Across The Bay* until he

---

54 Concentrates of the News. *The Los Angeles Times* October 24, 1939

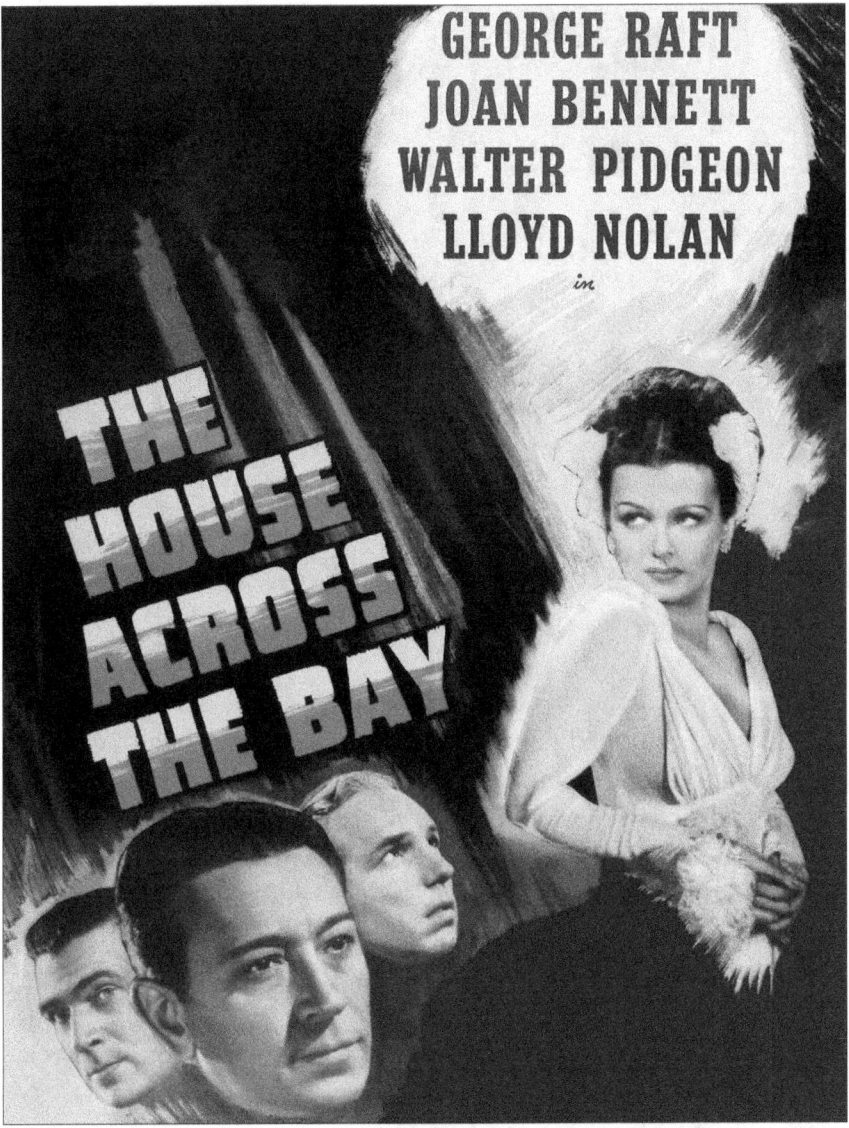

Movie ad for The House Across The Bay

finished work producing *Foreign Correspondent,* which was being directed by Alfred Hitchcock.

George Raft plays Steve Larwitt, a gangster who owns a nightclub where there is a conflict with a couple of the girls in his chorus. One, whom he has been seeing, is in conflict with a new girl, Brenda Bartley (Joan Bennett). Larwitt is attracted to Brenda's

George Raft and Joan Bennett in The House Across The Bay

dark beauty and the two begin seeing each other. After the two marry, Steve's crooked lawyer Slant Kolma (Lloyd Nolan), who has designs on Brenda, frames Steve and he gets a ten year prison sentence in Alcatraz for racketeering. While taking the boat across the bay to the prison, Brenda meets other prison wives and befriends Mary (Gladys George). They connect and start doing things together, eventually running into Tim Nolan (Walter Pidgeon), who is attracted to Brenda. Tim pursues her, she resists, but finally wins her over with the help of his friendly dog. However, because she is still married, and still cares about her husband, Brenda's relationship with Tim remains platonic despite their attraction to each other. When Slant sees the two of them together he attempts to blackmail Brenda, and when that doesn't work, he goes to see Steve in prison and tells him his wife is having an affair. Steve escapes from prison and swims to safety. He is going to kill Brenda, but Tim stops him and tells him about Slant blackmailing her and selling all of her jewelry. Steve finds Slant, kills him, and returns to the bay, where he is shot to death by police, proclaiming his love to Brenda as he dies.

George Raft, Walter Pigeon, Joan Bennett in The House Across The Bay

While a bit far-fetched, with Raft's character escaping Alcatraz by swimming, which is probably impossible and certainly improbable, the real problem with *The House Across The Bay* is that George Raft spends little time in the movie despite being the star. While his character's presence is always looming, he is sent to prison early on, and the film continues without him. There are a couple of scenes where he's visited in prison, but the narrative is commanded by Joan Bennett and Walter Pidgeon with support from Lloyd Nolan and Gladys George.

Filming began in October of 1939. Along with Raft being loaned from Warner Brothers, Walter Pidgeon's appearance was arranged with MGM and director Archie Mayo came over from Samuel Goldwyn's studio. Joan Bennett was under contract with Walter Wanger already, and married him not long after filming completed on this project.

The House Across The Bay is not a bad movie, despite star George Raft not being in it as much (although continuing to be the focal point of the narrative). Joan Bennett is striking and radiant as the chorus girl whose mood and manner changes as she ventures further from that life and takes up with the more sophisticated character played by Walter Pidgeon. Pidgeon, in his usual relaxed, confident manner, anchors the narrative effectively. Lloyd Nolan is delightfully wily and underhanded, and Gladys George is consistently amusing. The story reminds us that Raft is in the movie during the visits to the prison that pop up as the story goes on without him, but this peripheral presence makes it hard to determine *The House Across The Bay* as a George Raft movie.

It seems especially strange that Raft disappears so much in the second half because he dominates so much of the first half. Joan Bennett actually ends up being the real star and the center of the narrative. This was one of the first movies she made after darkening her hair and transitioning from primarily screwball comedies to crime movies/noir, and the role suits her.

Interestingly enough, the scenes in which Joan Bennett and Walter Pidgeon are in an airplane were said to be directed by Alfred Hitchcock as a favor to Wanger for having worked on Hitchcock's film *Foreign Correspondent*.

Apparently, moviegoers, expecting a George Raft film, were disappointed by his limited presence in *The House Across The Bay*. Some exhibitors dismissed it as just another program picture, while others referred to it as a Joan Bennett film in which George Raft was mentioned as support alongside Walter Pidgeon. It suffered a loss of over $100,000 at the box office.

Moving past this film, and getting back to what was now his home studio of Warner Brothers, George Raft was next scheduled to star opposite Humphrey Bogart once again due to the success of *Invisible Stripes*. And *They Drive By Night* became one of the best films in the careers of either man, as well as one of Ida Lupino's finest screen appearances.

THEY DRIVE BY NIGHT

Directed by Raoul Walsh
Screenplay by Jerry Wald and Richard Macaulay from a novel by
  A.I. Bezzerides
Produced by Mark Hellinger
Cinematography by Arthur Edeson
Film Editing by Thomas Richards

Cast:
George Raft	Joe Fabrini
Ann Sheridan	Cassie Hartley
Ida Lupino	Lana Carlsen
Humphrey Bogart	Paul Fabrini
Gale Page	Pearl Fabrini
Alan Hale	Ed Carlsen
Roscoe Karns	Irish McGurn
John Litel	Harry McNamara
Pedro Regas	Harry's Partner
George Tobias	Rondolos
Joyce Compton	Sue Carter
Joe Devlin	Fatso
Jesse Graves	Charles Culpepper
Mack Gray	Mike
Norman Willis	Neves
Charles C. Wilson	Mike Williams
Jack Wise	Jake
Lillian Yarbo	Chloe
Charles Halton	Farnsworth
Chet Brandenburg	Man Griping at Farnsworth
Mike Lally	Man Griping at Farnsworth
Sol Gorss	Truck Driver Warning about Farnsworth
Jack Mower	Deputy with Farnsworth

Paul Hurst	Pete Haig
Dorothea Kent	Sue
George Lloyd	Barney
John Ridgely	Hank Dawson
Harry Semels	Leo
Max Wagner	Sweeney
Marie Blake	Waitress
Demetris Emanuel	Waiter
Brenda Fowler	Prison Matron
Ned Glass	Prison Door Repairman
George Haywood	Policeman at Accident
Frank Mayo	Motorist at Accident Scene
Howard Hickman	The Judge
John Hamilton	Defense Attorney
Henry O'Neill	District Attorney
Wilfred Lucas	Bailiff
Edmund Mortimer	Extra in Courtroom
Dorothy Vaughan	Courtroom Matron
Phyllis Hamilton	Stenographer
Frank Wilcox	Reporter
J. Anthony Hughes	Reporter
Vera Lewis	Landlady
William Bendix	Truck Driver Watching Pinball Game
Harry Levette	Butler
Howard Washington	Garage attendant
Billy Wayne	Repairman
Matt McHugh	Repairman
Carl Harbaugh	Mechanic
Cliff Saum	Man Outside Barney's
Claire James	Party Guest
Bess Flowers	Party Guest
Michael Jeffers	Trucker
William Haade	Tough Driver
Dick Wessel	Driver in Café
Charles Sherlock	Driver in Café
Charles Sullivan	Driver in Café
Ralph Sanford	Driver in Café

Al Hill	Driver in Cafe
Eddie Acuff	Driver in Café
Frank Faylen	Driver in Café
Eddie Fetherston	Driver in Café
Pat Flaherty	Driver in Café
Eddy Chandler	Driver
Alan Davis	Driver
Dutch Hendrian	Driver
Don Turner	Driver
Tom Wilson	Man Outside Barney's
Richard Clayton	Young Man

Released August 3, 1940
Warner Bros
Running Time: 95 minutes
Black and White

It was March of 1940 when George Raft was announced for a drama about truck drivers called *The Long Haul* which was retitled, *They Drive By Night* by the following month. Raft was quite pleased with this assignment from his home studio, because he is undeniably the lead, has a great supporting cast, and a director he respects. *They Drive By Night* also has Raft playing an honest working man, not a hood or former prisoner. The character of Joe Fabrini is exceedingly moral; he never takes a drink, won't succumb to the flirtations of a married woman, and only wants to work honestly and successfully away from the corruption in the trucking field. While it allows Raft to exhibit the nuances of his usual screen persona, it is far from the hoods and former hoods he felt he played too often. Interestingly, Raft essentially displays the same sort of persona here that he does when he's playing crooks, but at the same time it's very clear that his character in this film is not a crook. He's able to adapt to different characters and situations without straying from the personality that made him such a popular star.

George Raft liked Humphrey Bogart and worked well with him in *Invisible Stripes*, so he was pleased that Bogie was cast as his brother. He also connected positively with Ida Lupino at Para-

Humphrey Bogart, Ann Sheridan, George Raft in They Drive By Night

mount when she worked with him in *Yours For The Asking*. Finally, Raoul Walsh, one of Raft's favorite directors, was at the helm. The result is one of George Raft's finest movies, some studies even claiming it to be the best film in which he appears.

George Raft plays Joe Fabrini, a truck driver who works with his brother Paul (Humphrey Bogart) transporting goods for various companies. They make little money, owe on their truck, and are rarely home. This is especially hard for Paul, who has a wife at home (Gale Page). They pick up a hitchhiker in the rain and discover it is Cassie (Ann Sheridan) a wise cracking girl they met at a diner earlier. She quit, due to the owner's physical advances, but has nowhere to go, so decides to remain with the Fabrinis as they drive to Los Angeles. On the way, they see a trucker friend go off the road and crash to his death, having fallen asleep at the wheel. This haunts Paul once he gets home and his wife tries talking him into quitting and taking a regular office job. Meanwhile Joe and Cassie get acquainted. Ed Carlsen (Alan Hale) a former trucker who has become an executive, offers to hire Joe, but he wants to work independently. Meanwhile his wife Lana (Ida Lupino) has long had designs on Joe, making things more awkward and uncomfortable. Ed has always liked Joe, and gives him a tip on a load where he and Paul make enough money to pay off their truck and have some left over. However, on the way back, Paul falls asleep, which results in an accident where he loses his arm. Thereafter, Joe gets a job as traffic manager of Ed's company and Paul is hired as dispatcher. Lana keeps coming around and flirting with Joe, who avoids her advances and even introduces her to Casey whom he plans to marry. Lana becomes more and more unglued until she finally drives a drunken Ed home from a party and leaves him in the closed garage with the car running, resulting in his death. Lana is now free to marry Joe, but he has no interest in her and plans to marry Cassie. Lana goes to the police and insists Joe talked her into killing Ed. However, during the trial, Lana breaks down and confesses, maniacally laughing and claiming the temptation of the automatic garage doors made her commit the crime. She is declared insane, Joe becomes manager of the trucking company and engaged to Cassie. Paul is traffic manager and proudly announces he and his wife are having a baby.

They Drive By Night has two rather distinct halves – the first deals with the Fabrini Brothers as hardworking truckers who make little as freelancers, because the companies for whom they do jobs keep most of the money and offer meager funds to their workers. Both Raft and Bogart excel and playing tough, even menacing. So, when they leave gangster roles and play equally tough working men, they are effective when confronting a businessman who ignores their report of having a busted wheel and not only sends another driver to take their load, he also sends financers to repossess their truck.

Most of the different narrative levels in the film's first half deal with each man's place in life. Bogart's character, Paul Fabrini, is married, grounded, happy, but torn between loyalty to his brother and to his wife. She wants him to quit and get an office job that keeps him near home and, especially, out of danger. His brother has a dream for the two of them to make real money by going into business for themselves. Meanwhile, Raft's character, Joe Fabrini, romances Ann Sheridan's character (Cassie), allowing both actors romantic footage as well as the tough wisecracking element that helps define the complexities of their roles. Each settle very comfortably in their parts and play them with authenticity.

Ann Sheridan, Ida Lupino, George Raft in They Drive By Night

While the first half of the film follows two distinct personalities, their respective portions never conflict or distract. Their underlying connection is always present. The two brothers spend most of their time together, their scenes supplemented by Raft's frequent supporting player Roscoe Karns as a fellow trucker who is distracted by pinball machines at the various eateries.

The scene where two truckers (John Litel, Pedro Regas) flip over the edge of a highway cliff and are killed when their truck catches fire, reveals the danger of the road; the very thing that Paul's wife fears. It is eye-opening for Cassie as a hitchhiking passenger in the Fabrini truck, but both brothers react like this is not the first tragedy they witnessed. Walsh films it by showing the men struggling to escape while the vehicle is on fire, but only for a few seconds before an explosion makes it impossible for them to have survived.

The second half of the film switches gears, as it were, grounding the trucking brothers with stationary jobs. For Paul it is by necessity after he loses an arm, although the film spends some time exhibiting his frustration at being unable to find work once disabled. It is Joe who arranges for his employment, after Ed hires him.

While George Raft holds his own as the center of the narrative, and Humphrey Bogart lends able support, Ida Lupino (Lana) manages to steal the second half of *They Drive By Night* with her remarkable performance as an unfulfilled wife who has married for money, but has become bored with this convenience. Her boorishly happy husband does not have what she perceives as necessary couth for a man with money, and she is annoyed by his nuzzling, tickling, and other signs of playful affection. She has a very pure sexual attraction to Joe, who is clear that he never had much interest in her, and that is especially so since she is married to a friend, and he is in love with Cassie. Lana is consistently obvious in her attraction to everyone except clueless Ed, and she becomes increasingly more desperate and unglued. She actually demands that Joe not marry Cassie, stating that she feels entitled to him. Once she arranges her husband's death in the closed garage, she eventually sees it as a way to trap Joe into a relationship. He is too tough, even for her, and takes his chances at a jury trial.

Ida Lupino ensured her career with her uninhibited performance on the witness stand. Jittery, blubbering, and eventually exploding into maniacal laughter, it is a real tour-de-force and led to a career that would eventually include directing that was as effective as her acting.

Despite Lupino's bravura performance, George Raft is somewhere near his best in *They Drive By Night*. The film features Raft as a good guy, with heroic traits, and the actor commands the screen nicely in a role that is pretty much exactly the type he wanted to play. While in a supporting role, Bogart's deft ability to snarl fast-paced tough dialog with elements of sarcasm would help to more clearly define the iconic character he'd eventually hone throughout the 1940s. Ann Sheridan's striking beauty is matched by her acting prowess. She is at once tough and no-nonsense, and then will appear delicate and romantic, responding effectively to what the scene demands. Raft and Sheridan both have fantastic chemistry, particularly in their innuendo-laden exchange when they first meet

George Raft, Ida Lupino, Alan Hale in They Drive By Night

when she's behind the counter at the diner. And Raft and Bogart are pretty believable as brothers even though they don't look alike; they seem very at ease with each other.

Both critics and moviegoers responded favorably to *They Drive By Night* making it one of George Raft's career-best films and performances. However it is usually Ida Lupino and the earthy screenplay that were singled out in reviews. *Motion Picture Daily* stated:

> *They Drive By Night* is a vigorously, sometimes bawdily told story of the trucking business, which takes in a panorama of rough and reading action, romance, and an adventure in growing insanity. Many of the lines of dialog in the Jerry Wald-Richard Macaulay adaption of A.I. Bezzerides' novel of California trucking are decidedly off-color and have double meanings. Standout in the cast is Ida Lupino, whose portrayal is a fine etched performance.[55]

The studio was pleased with the final film, even before it was released and became a major box office hit. As a result, their next

---

55 They Drive By Night review. *Motion Picture Daily.* July 15, 1940.

project for George Raft was for him to once again play an honest-but-tough working man, this time co-starring with Edward G. Robinson.

MANPOWER

Directed by Raoul Walsh
Screenplay by Richard Macaulay and Jerry Wald
Produced by Mark Hellinger
Cinematography by Ernest Haller
Film Editing by Ralph Dawson

Cast:
Edward G. Robinson	Hank McHenry
Marlene Dietrich	Fay Duval
George Raft	Johnny Marshall
Alan Hale	Jumbo Wells
Frank McHugh	Omaha
Eve Arden	Dolly
Barton MacLane	Smiley Quinn
Ward Bond	Eddie Adams
Walter Catlett	Sidney Whipple
Joyce Compton	Scarlett
Lucia Carroll	Flo
Egon Brecher	Pop Duval
Cliff Clark	Cully
Joseph Crehan	Sweeney
Ben Welden	Al Hurst
Barbara Pepper	Polly
Dorothy Appleby	Wilma
Jean Ames	Thelma
Leah Baird	Mrs. Taylor
Joyce Bryant	Mrs. Brewster
Brenda Fowler	Mrs. Calkin
John Harmon	Benny
Herbert Heywood	Charlie
Barbara Land	Marilyn

Harry Strang	Tommy
Dorothy Vaughan	Mrs. Boyle
William Gould	Freeman
Carl Harbaugh	Noisy Nash
Cliff Saum	Man to Call Substation
Chester Clute	Drug Store Clerk
Harry Holman	Justice of the Peace
Vera Lewis	Wife of the Justice of the Peace
Nella Walker	FloorLady
Billy Wayne	Taxi Driver
Joan Winfield	Nurse Holding Baby
Faye Emerson	Nurse Who Lost Draw
Audra Lindley	Nurse
Isabel Withers	Nurse
Georgia Caine	Head Nurse
James Flavin	Orderly About to Give Bath
Roland Drew	Citizen Reporting Power Outage
Charles Sherlock	Power Company Telephone Operator
Jeffrey Sayre	Power Company Telephone Operator
Al Herman	Power Company Telephone Operator
William Hopper	Power Company Telephone Operator
Eddie Fetherston	Power Company Telephone Operator
Ralph Dunn	Man Calling Sweeney
William Royle	Policeman in Raid
Lee Phelps	Detective in Raid
Eddy Chandler	Detective in Raid
John Dilson	Jail Clerk
Robert Strange	Bailsman
Sailor Vincent	Lineman
Murray Alper	Lineman
Fred Graham Fred	Lineman at Cafe Counter
William Newell	Lineman at Cafe Counter
Charles Sullivan	Lineman at Cafe Counter
Elliott Sullivan	Lineman at Cafe Counter
Dick Wessel	Lineman at Cafe Counter
Frank Mayo	Midnight Club Doorman
Pat McKee	Midnight Club Bouncer

Jack 'Tiny' Lipson	Midnight Club Bartender
John J. Richardson	Midnight Club Waiter
Harry Tenbrook	Midnight Club Waiter
Harry Tenbrook	Midnight Club Waiter
Glen Cavender	Drunk Bounced from Midnight Club
Sam Ash	Extra at Midnight Club
Al Lloyd	Extra at Midnight Club
Nat Carr	28 Club Waiter
Stuart Holmes	28 Club Bartender
John Kelly	28 Club Bouncer
Charles Fogel	Club Patron
Paul King	Club Patron
Paul Panzer	28 Club Bartender
Spencer Chan	Club Patron
Joe Devlin	Bartender
Jane Randolph	Hat Check Girl
Virginia Hill	Hat Check Girl
Dick Elliott	Drunk Texan
Arthur Q. Bryan	Drunk Texan
Beal Wong	Wing Ling - Chinese Singer
Harry Seymour	Piano Player
Friedrich Hollaender	Accompanist
Bobby Robb	Boy Playing Baseball
Drew Roddy	Boy Playing Baseball
Peter Caldwell	Boy Playing Baseball
Harry Harvey Jr.	Boy Playing Baseball
Muriel Barr	Model
Gayle Mellott	Model
Lynn Baggett	Bit Part
Diana Barrymore	Bit Part

Released August 9, 1941
Warner Bros
Running time: 104 minutes
Black and White

Movie ad for Manpower

Because Humphrey Bogart is one of the major icons of classic cinema, one has to stop and realize that when he made his movies with George Raft, he was just a supporting actor who only got leads in B movies. He had a good chemistry with Raft, as indicated in their two films together, and Raft liked him. However, when plans were made for him to appear in *Manpower*, it was after he had scored big in *High Sierra* playing a role that Raft had turned down.

After *They Drive By Night*, the studio wanted a project to re-team George Raft and Ida Lupino, so they chose *High Sierra*, based on a story by W.R. Burnett. But the leading character, Roy Earle, was a gangster who dies at the end. He has redeeming qualities, coming to the aid of a disabled girl, and the director was once again going to be Raoul Walsh, but that was not enough for Raft to accept another hood role. He turned it down, was put on suspension, and the part went to Humphrey Bogart. Ida Lupino liked working with Raft, but wasn't terribly fond of Bogart, and he didn't endear himself to her on this project. Bogart was sarcastic, standoffish, and difficult throughout, so much so that when he was set to co-star with Lupino again in *Out of the Fog*, she arranged for him to be replaced with John Garfield.

Because of her amazing performance in *They Drive By Night*, Lupino was given top billing in *High Sierra*, while Raft would likely have had it if he'd taken the Roy Earle role, being a bigger star than Bogart. *High Sierra* changed that. Bogart's performance was so strong, and received so many raves, it catapulted him to stardom.

As a result, when it was planned for George Raft and Humphrey Bogart to appear together in *Manpower*, Raft no longer wanted to work with Bogart. Raft realized that *High Sierra* meant that Bogart would now be a co-star, and not a supporting actor. In fact, Bogart was confronted at the studio by Mack Gray, Raft's noted "man Friday" who had been with him since the 1920s. The press misconstrued it as Raft confronting Bogart, resulting in a fight, so that had to be rectified. An article in *The Los Angeles Times* stated:

> The statement, "We don't want you" resulted in reports that George Raft and Humphrey Bogart, two of the screen's recognized he-men, had gotten into a fist fight. The place was supposed to have been a screen-test on one

of the large sound stages at the Warner Bros. Studio. Raft was supposed to have hit Bogart and further eventualities were supposed to have been prevented by the interference of others. All the supposition simmered down to the fact that Mack Gray, man Friday for Raft, did have a verbal encounter with Bogart. Bogart had gone to the studio to make a test for a role in Raft's coming vehicle with Marlene Dietrich called *Manpower* when Gray is said to have made his utterance. Raft wasn't present at the time, say those who should know. No blows were struck.[56]

Bogart was then placed in the A-level programmer *The Wagons Roll at Night*, while George Raft came out of suspension.

George Raft was then offered the role of Sam Spade for what would become the quintessential film noir, *The Maltese Falcon*, which they planned to film after *Manpower*. However Raft did not want to work with John Huston, who was a first-time director, so he opted to exercise a part of his contract which gave him the right to turn down any remakes. *The Maltese Falcon*, based on the Dashiell Hammett book, had been filmed twice before. So Raft was once again suspended, and Humphrey Bogart was given the role, causing his star power to escalate further. Raft started work on *Manpower*.

There was some discussion of casting either Broderick Crawford or Victor McLaglen in the role that had once been considered for Bogart. Both of these were character actors, so their role would be a supporting part. But when Edward G. Robinson, a top star, agreed to take the role, it relegated George Raft down to third billing after both Robinson and female lead Marlene Dietrich, despite Raft having the film's lead role.

George Raft plays Johnny Marshall, a power lineman who works on high tension wires. During an emergency in a raging thunderstorm, his pal Hank McHenry (Edward G. Robinson) is seriously injured and almost killed. Hank can't climb the poles anymore, so he is elevated to foreman. An old veteran lineman, Pop Duval (Egon Brecher), whose estranged daughter Fay (Marlene Dietrich) recently moved to town, is killed during an ice storm. Fay reacts

---

56 George Raft-Humphrey Bogart Screen Test Denied. *The Los Angeles Times*. March 8, 1941.

George Raft and Marlene Dietrich in Manpower

without emotion to the news, which angers Johnny, but Hank becomes attracted to her. Fay works as a hostess and Hank, who notably strikes out with women, despite a bravado he puts on for the other guys, frequently visits her, even giving her money. When he proposes, she accepts, even though she admits she doesn't love him. Hank believes she will learn to love him. When Johnny is injured, he recuperates at Hank and Fay's home, when Fay reveals her attraction to him. Johnny rebuffs her, despite the palpable sexual tension, so she decides to leave Hank. When she goes to say goodbye to the girls at the club, she gets caught up in a raid and sent to jail. Johnny bails her out and insists she not leave Hank and break his heart. However, Fay goes to Hank and says she is leaving him because she is attracted to Johnny. Hank believes Johnny has betrayed him as a friend. He climbs the pylon with his bad leg where Johnny is working on high tension wires during another storm. The two fight, and, despite attempts by Johnny to hold on to

George Raft, Edward G. Robinson, Marlene Dietrich, Joyce Compton in
Manpower

him, Hank falls to his death. Johnny must then decide if he should act on his suppressed feelings for Fay.

George Raft's Johnny is presented as a leader, a somewhat heroic character even alongside the other men. Edward G. Robinson's Hank is someone Johnny admits he loves; a dear friend despite his faults, and his false sense of self-awareness.

When *Manpower* opens, it is established that Hank tries to loftily convince himself that he is just as handsome, just as virile, and just as desirable as any of the better-looking men, including Johnny. Robinson, an exceptionally versatile actor, is typically convincing in the role. Dancing happily with a woman who is not impressed with him at all, he believes himself to be quite graceful, while she complains he's stepping all over her feet. He convinces himself she is interested in seeing him the very next night. When he is injured, he mentions how he feels sorry for her that he won't be able to make that second date. In the hospital he is physically flirtatious with the pretty nurses, so much so that when his next bath is ready, two large male orderlies come in to do the job.

Johnny realizes that Hank is not a success with women, and isn't the "catch" he convinces himself to be, but never confronts him. The other guys sometimes dismiss him for not being able to "get a dame" and Hank responds violently. But because these men depend on each other in dangerous situations, they quickly cool down and apologize. It is an interesting dynamic. George Raft maintains a consistent cool, the sexy charismatic Ying to Robinson's misguided subordinate Yang. It is a fairly complex buddy-movie concept within the parameters of a fairly typical Warner Brothers programmer. The humor in *Manpower* is provided by Warner stalwarts Alan Hale and Frank McHugh, whose aggressive, boisterous hijinks include chasing pretty nurses when visiting Hank in the hospital, and pleasantly drunk at his wedding.

Manpower starts out as very much a "guy's movie" and Raoul Walsh had already been pegged as a man's director. In fact, Walsh was pleased that an actress at the level of Marlene Dietrich had been cast in the film, because he knew her presence would more than distract from the maleness of the movie. And it does. Suddenly Hank is smitten, and even when Fay honestly admits not loving him, his ego is such that he believes she'll eventually come around. When Johnny is staying with them, he never seems to pick up on any sexual tension. Even Johnny won't admit to his feelings when Fay admits hers, stating, "I never gave you a second thought."

The occasional misogyny softens in a lot of the scenes with Dietrich, especially the ones between her and Robinson where Hank is forced to confront his vulnerabilities. He is very soft and honest with her, and it's a testament to Robinson's acting ability that he is able to so seamlessly transition from acting tough to acting sweet.

George Raft and Edward G. Robinson didn't get along at first, because their approaches were so different, while their egos were quite massive. Robinson would instruct Raft how to approach a scene, sometimes even defying the director. He would also claim he needed some dialog in scenes where he had none, throwing the attention away from Raft who'd been at the center. In response, Raft was snarling and aggressive in their physical scenes. At one point he allegedly turned Robinson around too quickly, resulting in an argument that ended up in a physical altercation. Robinson went to his dressing room and wanted to be removed from the movie, but Walsh interceded and the two later made up. However, their fight made the newspapers, including on-set photos, concerning the top brass. Fortunately, that only added further interest in the movie. Robinson would later ask Raft for an autographed picture of himself, which he'd hang in his den with photos of his other co-stars. In their later years, each man recalled the other with respect and no rancor. They would appear in one more movie, many years after this one.

Despite what may have been a contentious off-screen relationship at the time, Robinson and Raft are really good together. The more tense scenes toward the end are convincing, but so are the ones where they are just palling around. The movie's love triangle may revolve primarily between them and Dietrich, but it's evident that Raft and Robinson's characters really love each other too.

Marlene Dietrich liked working with both actors, and would play phonograph records and dance the rhumba with George Raft between scenes. However, there was one scene that Raft was very concerned about doing, and it ended up causing Dietrich injury. According to Fredrick Othmann's Hollywood column:

At this writing Miss Marlene Dietrich is home nursing a sprained ankle and a swollen cheek. Mack Gray, the Man Friday of George Raft, is suffering the same kind of swelling, and Raft, the man who did all the damage, is suffering worst of all. He had to smack Miss Dietrich on both cheeks, whack-whack, in the manufacture of a movie called *Manpower*. So, he practiced all day on Gray, trying to make his slaps hard enough to look real, and soft enough not to hurt. He never succeeded on Mack. He either slapped too hard, or too gently. "It's a mighty tough job," Raft said. "I never hit a lady before and I'm scared of it." Whack-whack. He tried again on the cheeks-of Gray. Came time finally for Raft to go to work on Miss Dietrich and: Whack-whack. The guy must have been nervous. His first whack sent Miss Dietrich oft balance and she sprained her ankle. His second whack missed her other cheek and landed on her nose. The Dietrich blood dribbled onto a Warner Brothers carpet. She went home for repairs. Raft went home to kick himself. He came back to work next morning but Miss D. didn't. She reported by phone that the damage wasn't serious, but that her left cheek was puffed so that no amount of makeup could disguise it. So they're shooting around Miss Dietrich, and if Raft seems glum, everybody understands and without wise-cracks, either.[57]

Fortunately, there were no hard feelings from Marlene Dietrich, and the cast and crew understood it was an accident, but Raft felt terrible about it.

Manpower was a major box office hit, and despite his troublesome refusal of roles, the top brass at Warner Brothers were pleased with moviegoers' response to Raft. However, yet another conflict arose upon completion of the film. Universal was preparing a movie called *Broadway* in which they wanted George Raft to play himself in a fictionalized musical/crime drama that recalled his years on stage. Because he had been refusing so many roles for the past eight months, and he owed his home studio three more features, Warners would not loan him out. They wanted him to play an ex-gangster in a comedy-drama entitled *All Through The Night*. However, a deal was finally reached. Warners would loan Raft if Universal would loan them Robert Cummings for the film *King's Row*. They would pay $27,500, which would be taken from Raft's salary. As a result, *Broadway* became George Raft's next movie. The role in *All Through The Night* went to, of course, Humphrey Bogart.

---

57 Othmann, Fredrick. Hollywood column. *The Hanford Sentinel*. April 28, 1941

BROADWAY

Directed by William Seiter
Screenplay by Felix Jackson and John Bright, adapted by Bruce Manning, from a play by Phillip Dunning and George Abbott
Produced by Bruce Manning
Cinematography by George Barnes
Film Editing by Ted Kent

Songs:
The Darktown Strutters' Ball
Written by Shelton Brooks

Some of These Days
Written by Shelton Brooks

The Sidewalks of New York
Music by Charles Lawlor
Lyrics by James W. Blake

M-I-S-S-I-S-S-I-P-P-I
Music by Harry Tierney
Lyrics by Bert Hanlon and Ben Ryan

Where the Red, Red Roses Grow
Music by Jean Schwartz
Lyrics by William Jerome

La Cumparsita
Music by Gerardo Matos Rodríguez

Dinah
Music by Harry Akst
Lyrics by Sam Lewis and Joe Young

Sweet Georgia Brown
 Music by Maceo Pinkard and Ben Bernie
Lyrics by Kenneth Casey

Alabamy Bound
 Music by Ray Henderson
Lyrics by Buddy G. DeSylva and Bud Green

I'm Just Wild About Harry
Music by Eubie Blake
Lyrics by Noble Sissle

Yes Sir! That's My Baby
 Music by Walter Donaldson
Lyrics by Gus Kahn

When Irish Eyes Are Smiling
 Music by Ernest Ball
Lyrics by Chauncey Olcott and George Graff

Chicago (That Toddlin' Town)
Written by Fred Fisher

Three O'Clock in the Morning
Music by Julián Robledo
Lyrics by Dolly Morse

Cast:
George Raft	George Raft
Pat O'Brien	Dan McCorn
Janet Blair	Billie Moore
Broderick Crawford	Steve Crandall
Marjorie Rambeau	Lillian (Lil) Rice
Anne Gwynne	Pearl
S.Z. Sakall	Nick
Edward Brophy	Porky
Marie Wilson	Grace

Gus Schilling	Joe
Ralf Harolde	Dolph
Arthur Shields	Pete Dailey
Iris Adrian	Maisie
Janet Warren	Ruby
Dorothy Moore	Ann
Nestor Paiva	Rinalti
Abner Biberman	Trado
Damian O'Flynn	Scar Edwards
Mack Gray	Mack Gray
John Daheim	Andy
John Harmon	Harry
Tom Kennedy	Kerry
Sammy Stein	Slug
Charles Lane	Hungry Harry
Grace Lenard	Grace
Eve March	Mary
John Maxwell	Ed
Billy Nelson	Tommy
Jay Novello	Eddie
Henry Roquemore	Will
Fern Emmett	Will's Wife
John Sheehan	Oscar
Kenny Stevens	Ken Stevens
Harry Tyler	Wingy
Benny Rubin	Counsellor
Jimmy Conlin	Newsman
Eddie Bruce	Photographer
Frank Ferguson	Reporter
Pat Gleason	Reporter
Walter Tetley	Western Union Messenger
James Flavin	Doorman
George Ford	Club Patron
Jennifer Holt	TWA Stewardess
Linda Brent	Hat Check Girl
Kernan Cripps	Morgue Attendant
Harry Seymour	Piano-Tuner

Byron Shores	Manager
Joe Gray	Bootlegger
Joe Cunningham	Detective
Arthur Loft	Detective
Lee Phelps	Detective
Charles Jordan	Gangster
Larry McGrath	Gangster
Jimmy O'Gatty	Gangster
Tony Paton	Gangster
Charles Sullivan	Gangster
Anthony Warde	Gangster

Released May 8, 1942
Universal Pictures
Running Time: 91 minutes
Black and White

Broadway was originally a stage musical that was produced in 1926. It starred Lee Tracy as a dancer named Roy Lane, Thomas Jackson as a detective, and Paul Porcasi as a nightclub owner. Both Jackson and Porcasi repeated their roles in a 1929 movie version where Glenn Tryon played the dancer. When Universal planned to make a new version of the movie, producer Bruce Manning contacted George Raft and discussed how the dancer's life and exploits were similar to Raft's. Manning wanted to have Raft play the dancer as himself, not as a character named Roy Lane, and include a prologue where he tells the story, shown in flashback, and an epilogue in which he is a famous movie star. Raft liked the idea and turned down all of the projects Warner Brothers offered until they agreed to loan him to Universal for this movie. Universal paid $200,000 for the film rights to Philip Dunning and George Abbott's play.

   This was not the first time Universal had planned to borrow George Raft from Warner Brothers. In early 1941 there were plans to star him in the musical *Tango* and Raft planned to exercise the freelance provision in his Warner contract. But that film was never

Movie Ad for Broadway

made. Then later that same year, Universal and producer Bruce Manning wanted Raft to co-star with Rosalind Russell in a film called *Marriage of Inconvenience*, with William Seiter directing. This production was also cancelled due to the studio's inability to work around Ms. Russell's busy schedule.

Broadway features George Raft flying into New York from Hollywood, along with Mack Gray. He takes a walk on the streets of Broadway, and is surprised to discover a nightclub that was prominent in his past is now a bowling alley. Chatting with the night watchman, George reminisces about when he was a dancer during the prohibition era, his partner, Billie (Janet Blair) a gangster's girlfriend whose job is protected even when she arrives late. Her gangster boyfriend Steve (Broderick Crawford) murders a rival, arousing the suspicion of Detective Dan McCorn (Pat O'Brien). During a party, Steve and gangster Rinalti (Nestor Paiva) get into a fight over Billie. She later tells George Raft to keep away from Steve, but he ignores her advice. George confronts Steve who gets ready to shoot him, but Detective McCorn shows up. Steve tosses the gun to George and claims Raft was attempting to rob him. McCorn lets George escape to get more information about Steve, and he returns to the club so he and Billie can perform their tango specialty number. George confronts Steve in his office, and the two begin to fight. Then Pearl, a dancer who had been the girl of the rival gangster Steve killed, comes in and murders Steve. When McCorn arrives, George tells him what happened, and the detective protects Pearl by stating that Steve killed himself. The film then switches back to Raft and the night watchman. It is explained that Pearl confessed the next day, served her time in prison and is still living in New York. Raft also tells the watchman that Dan became a New York police commissioner. When asked about him and Billie, George admits they never married: "I never got the chance." The last shot is of George Raft walking away from the old club and down the streets of Broadway.

When word got around that the play was being redone as a period piece, columnists who were around for the play in the 1920s became nostalgic. Sidney Skolsky recalled that he considered the play "his story" and knew other columnists who felt the same. He also recalled that James Cagney had originally been attached to the original theatrical production:

> Cagney was supposed to play Roy Lane, but Jed Harris, the producer, decided otherwise "Cagney," said Jed Harris, "has too much menace for the part. He looks like he could take care of himself and the gangsters." Jed Harris was right. 'Cagney went into the movies and took care of himself and the gangsters. However, in the movie version, producer Manning has the same problem with Raft. Audiences would expect him to take care of the gangsters. However, George Raft means money at the box office and, therefore, producer Manning had to change the character of Roy Lane, hoofer, to fit the character of George Raft, hoofer and movie star.[58]

William Seiter was an interesting choice for a director. Seiter was very versatile, directing many films in various genres from the silent

---

58 Skolsky's Hollywood. Syndicated. March 19, 1942

era into the 1950s. Over time he appears to be best known for his work with comedians, including Wheeler and Woolsey in *Diplomaniacs*, Laurel and Hardy in *Sons of the Desert*, The Ritz Brothers in *Life Begins in College* (1937), The Marx Brothers in *Room Service* (1938), and Abbott and Costello in *Little Giant* (1946). His direction of *Broadway* is effective in handling the musical numbers and the dramatic sequences.

Broadway is the total package, offering great old songs, fun dance numbers, and, as the narrative, a tough action drama with gangsters and violence. Of course, it isn't George Raft's actual story despite some similarities, but moviegoers didn't care about that. They loved the hint of intrigue that surrounded George Raft and his real life gangster connections. Thus, when Universal advertised *Broadway* as based on Raft's story, theaters were filled to capacity. Raft even repeated his coin-flipping trick from *Scarface*. *Broadway* turned out to be a major hit, its box office tripling its production costs.

The one thing that hampers the film is the ending. Raft's final narration about what happened to everyone involved feels very abrupt. Also, there really isn't any resolution to his relationship with Billie, even though it was clear in the flashbacks that they had feelings for each other and the way Raft talks about her it sounds like he still does. But the film is effectively bracketed by the lone drifter persona Raft takes on in these scenes that frame the narrative, drifting back in to his old life and leaving just as suddenly and mysteriously as he entered.

Raft had some personal appearance obligations upon completing *Broadway*. One stop was Fort Dix where he attended his own Caravan of Sports, a government-approved boxing and wrestling show that Raft financed for the servicemen to enjoy.

By the time George Raft returned to his home studio of Warner Brothers, Humphrey Bogart had become a star in his own right, and at the same level as Raft. While George Raft was still able to ensure good box office with his name, the fact that the studio had another rugged leading man under contract made the troublesome actor less attractive. However, since James Cagney had recently left the studio and was doing independent productions, some of the Warner top brass felt they should hang on to Raft.

George Raft's contract with Warner Brothers was about to run out. The studio worked to find the right vehicle for him; one that would please the moviegoers and satisfy Raft. The result was *Background To Danger*. It turned out to be Raft's final film for Warner Brothers.

BACKGROUND TO DANGER

Directed by Raoul Walsh
Screenplay by W.R. Burnett based on a novel by Eric Ambler
Produced by Jerry Wald
Cinematography by Tony Gaudio
Film Editing by Jack Kilifer

Cast:
George Raft	Joe Barton
Brenda Marshall	Tamara Zaleshoff
Sydney Greenstreet	Colonel Robinson
Peter Lorre	Nikolai Zaleshoff
Osa Massen	Ana Remzi
Turhan Bey	Hassan
Willard Robertson	McNamara
Kurt Katch	Mailler
Curt Furberg	Franz Von Papen
Steven Geray	Ludwig Rader
Charles Irwin	Hotchkins
Manart Kippen	Ivan
Charles La Torre	Moustaffa
Georges Metaxa	L.V. Bastaki
Daniel Ocko	Igor Rashenko
Nestor Paiva	Koylan
Frank Reicher	Rudick
Fred Wolff	Reiger
William Yetter Sr.	Schneider
Pedro de Cordoba	Baba
Paul Porcasi	Customs Official with Joe
Georges Renavent	Customs Official with Ana
John Bleifer	Secretary
Dick Botiller	Plane Announcer

Jack Chefe	Elevator Operator
Jack Deery	Man at Train Station
William Edmunds	Waiter with Information
Carl Harbaugh	Butler
Dave Kashner	Newspaper Worker
James Khan	Train Caller
Liparit Liparit	Wagon Driver
Lou Marcelle	Commentator
Sylvia Opert	Nautch Dancer
Otto Reichow	Mailler's Henchman
Jean De Briac	Levantine Porter
Charles De Ravenne	Bellboy
Cap Somers	Chef
Nick Thompson	Butler
Tom Steele	Thug at Newspaper Office
John Van Eyck	Official
Antonio Samaniego	Policeman
Juan Varro	Policeman
Eumenio Blanco	Syrian Vendor
Frank Puglia	Syrian Vendor
Michael Mark	Hotel Night Clerk
Cosmo Sardo	Clerk
Ernst Hauessermann	Clerk
Jean Del Val	Clerk
Walter Bonn	German Officer
Robert Stephenson	German Officer
Irene Seidner	German Mother
Lisa Golm	German Daughter
Leo White	Whispering Agent
Alfred Zeisler	Attaché
Frederick Giermann	Attaché
Ray Miller	Chauffeur
Kurt Kreuger	Chauffeur
Mary Chan	Club Patron
Rudy Germane	Club Patron
Moy Ming	Club Patron
Yeghishe Harout	Turkish Policeman

Rafael Alcayde	Turkish Husband on Train
Fernanda Eliscu	Turkish Wife on Train
John Piffle	Fat Turk on Train
Nino Bellini	Turkish Secretary
Demetris Emanuel	Turkish Official
Hassan Ezzat	Turkish Conductor
Jerry Mandy	Italian on Train

Released July 3, 1943
Warner Bros
Running Time: 82 minutes
Black and White

Background to Danger began shooting in September of 1942 and by that November, George Raft had bought out his contract with Warner Brothers. It was an unusual situation according to Jack Warner:

> In one way my association with Raft was unique. When we had serious performance problems with other actors and actresses, I actually wound up paying of their contracts to get them off the lot. Raft says, "I had nothing but trouble with Jack Warner." After five pictures he wanted out. "Tell you what George, "I said, "Why don't we settle the argument for, say, ten thousand." "Fine," he said. And what do you know? He gave me a check for $10,000 and I practically ran to the bank with it before he could change his mind.[59]

Warner Brothers was no longer interested in keeping Raft active at the studio. He refused projects, wanted his films rewritten for his approval, and was repeatedly suspended. In the meantime, Humphrey Bogart emerged as a new star for the studio, based mostly on projects Raft turned down. By the time Raft was doing *Background to Danger*, Bogart had scored again with *Casablanca*, an enormous hit that won a Best Picture Oscar and became one of the iconic classics of Hollywood movies. So, George Raft was no longer worth the problems he created.

---

59 Yablonsky, Lewis. *George Raft*. NY: McGraw-Hill, 1974

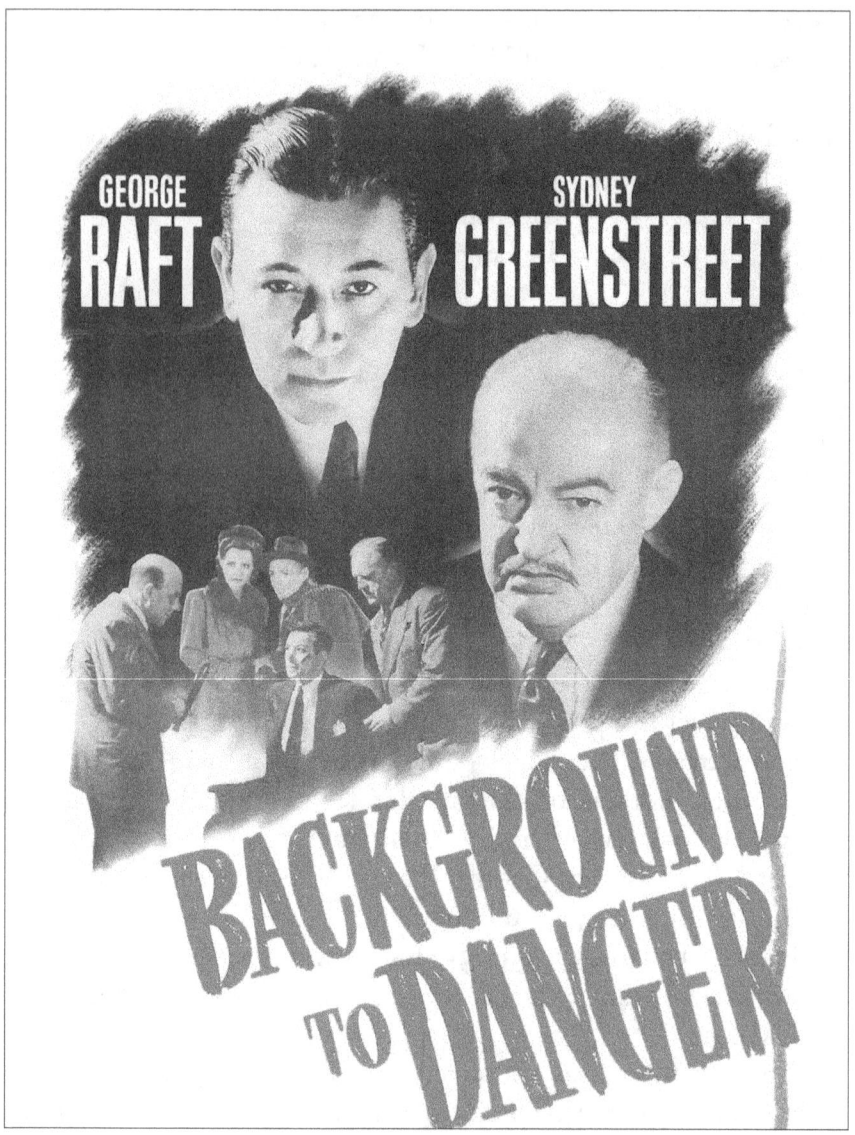

Movie Ad for Background to Danger

For his part, George Raft didn't want to be beholden to a studio, and have them foist projects on him that he didn't want to do. He instead preferred to freelance, and felt he had enough box office clout to do so. Raft was settled comfortably into a lifestyle of personal appearances as well as movies, and was enjoying a romantic relationship with actress Betty Grable that was noted in the press. Louella Parsons stated in her column:

> George Raft returned from New York without ever having visited a single night spot, not even his favorite, the Stork Club. That's because he is so true to Betty Grable, and much as he loves dancing he didn't go stepping with any other girl. He'll be back at Warners in six weeks and this time there won't be any squawk out of him, for he'll star in *Background to Danger*," by Eric Ambler, who is now serving with the British Commandos. It is just a year since George and Edward G. Robinson staged their front page battle in *Manpower* at Warners and he hasn't made a picture there since that time. Supporting-him in *Background to Danger* will be Sydney Greenstreet of *Maltese Falcon* fame. Jerry Wald, who will produce the picture, has handed it to Philip McDonald to write the adaptation.

After Parsons column had gone to press, W.R. Burnett, who had penned Raft's breakthrough film *Scarface* was hired for the adaption, and Peter Lorre, another *Maltese Falcon* actor was added to the cast.

Raft's demands continued on this project. Eric Ambler's novel was about an ordinary man who gets caught up in intrigue beyond his control, and having to find his way out of the situation. Raft insisted W.R. Burnett's screenplay be changed so that he was an undercover agent who heroically stops Nazis from creating conflict in the neutral country of Turkey, coming off as a veritable Superman. Burnett was blamed in the press for the change in the screenplay. Wood Soans stated in the *Oakland Tribune:*

> Ostensibly *Background to Danger* stems from a novel by Eric Ambler, but in translating the spy story to the screen, W. R. Burnett obviously decided that it wasn't worthwhile reading the book when all that was needed was a series of exciting sequences and a good cast. So. Warners put Raft in the role of Superman, the American spy chaser who is determined not to let Germany hornswoggle Turkey into abandoning its neutrality.[60]

---

60 Soans, Wood. George Raft in Spy Film. *Oakland Tribune* September 1, 1943

Peter Lorre, Brenda Marshall, George Raft in Background to Danger

However, W.R. Burnett stated in an interview with Patrick McGilligan in *Film Comment* magazine:

> I was always afraid that I'd have to face Eric Ambler after what we did to that. The point of *Background to Danger* was that this man was a salesman and suddenly things begin to happen to him that he can't understand. And he gets involved in all this espionage. But Raft wouldn't do it unless he was an FBI man. The whole story went out the window....[61]

The story has George Raft playing Joe Barton, who is undercover as a machinery salesman. He boards a Baghdad-Istanbul Express train at Aleppo and meets a pretty woman (Osa Massen) who asks him to hold an envelope for her as they reach the Turkish border. She believes she'll likely be searched, and he, as an American, will not. Joe agrees but when he later goes to her hotel to return her envelope, he finds she has been killed. He hides when the room is searched by Russian spy Nikolai Zaleshoff (Peter Lorre) and then sneaks out a window. As he leaves, he is seen by Nikolai's sister, and partner in espionage, Tamara (Brenda Marshall). Nazi Germany is attempting to force neutral Turkey into entering the war on the

---

61 McGilligan, Pat *Film Comment. 19* Jan/Feb 1983

side of the Axis. This is being led by Colonel Robinson (Sydney Greenstreet). Joe is picked up by Turkish police who turn out to be Nazi agents working for Robinson. Joe refuses to cooperate even while being beaten, and is rescued by Nikolai. Joe returns to his hotel and discovers it has been ransacked and the envelope is missing. It is revealed that Joe is an American spy when he reports to his superior (Willard Robinson) and is given an assistant (Turhan Bey). In Istanbul, Robinson arranges through bribery that the documents contained in the envelope are plans for the Russians to invade Turkey. Joe, Nikolai, and Tamara are captured. Joe punches one of the guards and Nikolai attempts to do the same, but fails and his shot to death. Joe and Tamara escape. After kidnapping an embassy official, Joe is informed as to where Robinson has gone, and stops the them from printing the story. Then he forces Robinson to burn the maps and turns him over to the Turkish police, where he is deported to East Germany to face execution. Joe and Tamara decided to work together, along with a romantic connection, and go off to Cairo for their next assignment.

Despite some typical Hollywood flag-waving of the period and Raft's insistence on being a heroic figure in defiance of the story and screenplay, *Background to Danger* was a box office hit. Raft might have been a problem for studio heads, but he was still very well-liked by the public. Sydney Greenstreet had been such a hit in *The Maltese Falcon*, he received billing above the title with George Raft. That film was such a massive hit, the addition of Peter Lorre also attracted moviegoers. Plus, a wartime audience welcomed a movie with a top star playing a heroic American who thwarted any Nazi advancement.

There are times when *Background to Danger* feels like an attempt to capitalize not just on *The Maltese Falcon* with its casting, but *Casablanca* as well. Raft's character feels not unlike Rick, and of course they share Greenstreet and Lorre. Perhaps the film would have worked better had Raft not insisted on not playing an Everyman character, although the revelation that his character is actually involved with all of this, and not just an ordinary guy caught up in espionage, was a surprise.

George Raft and Sydney Greenstreet in Background to Danger

According to Derek Sculthorpe's book *The Life and Times of Sydney Greenstreet,* novelist William Faulkner was employed at Warner Brothers to "work on troublesome scripts," stating:

> On viewing the first version of *Background to Danger* (Faulkner) diagnosed the problem as being "too much running around." He spent two weeks revising the script and creating new scenes. The film made more sense, but Faulkner's ability with dialog was somewhat less successful. At one stage, Greenstreet phoned producer Jerry Wald from the set to tell him that he simply could not deliver a particularly long and complicated speech as Faulkner had written it. The lines were duly modified. Faulkner's dialog was often altered on the set that way.[62]

While he appears to have gotten along well with Sydney Greenstreet, George Raft did have a problem with Peter Lorre. Recalling Lorre in later interviews as "a mean little guy," he recounted for

---

62 Schulthorpe, Derek. *The Life and Times of Sydney Greenstreet.* BearManor Media, 2018

Lewis Yablonsky that there was a scene where Lorre kept blowing smoke in Raft's face despite repeated warnings to stop. Eventually, Raft punched him, and Lorre fled to his dressing room. Raft did apologize but, "he never blew smoke in my face again."[63]

After completing this project, George Raft decided to get away from movies and join a troop going to England to entertain the USO. The soldiers enjoyed seeing the various stars in these shows, that predominantly featured favorites like Bob Hope and Joe E. Brown who offered much needed comedy. Raft would do one of his dance routines, much to the delight of the servicemen.

For his next movie, George Raft accepted a job over at Universal studios, where he had recently scored with *Broadway*, a film he enjoyed doing. The result was an all-star film with appearances by W.C. Fields, The Andrews Sisters, Jeanette MacDonald, and Donald O'Connor.

Raft liked the script because it allowed him to once again play an entertainer.

---

63 Yablonsky, Lewis. *George Raft*. NY: McGraw-Hill, 1974

FOLLOW THE BOYS

Directed by Eddie Sutherland
Screenplay by Lou Breslow and Gertrude Purcell
Produced by Charles Feldman
Cinematography by David Abel
Film Editing by Fred R. Feitshans Jr.

Songs:
I'll Walk Alone
(1944)
Music Jule Styne
Lyrics by Sammy Cahn
Sung by Dinah Shore

A Better Day Is Coming
(1944)
Music by Jule Styne
Lyrics by Sammy Cahn
Danced by Vera Zorina and Sung by a Chorus

Tonight
(1944)
Music by Walter Donaldson
Lyrics by Kermit Goell
Danced by Vera Zorina and George Raft and Sung by Chorus

The House I Live In
(1942)
Music by Earl Robinson
Lyrics by Lewis Allan
Sung by Delta Rhythm Boys

Beyond the Blue Horizon
(1930)
Music by Richard A. Whiting and W. Franke Harling
Lyric by Leo Robin
Sung by Jeanette MacDonald and joined by the soldiers

Sweet Georgia Brown
(1925)
Music by Maceo Pinkard, Ben Bernie and Kenneth Casey
Performed by Louis Jordan and his Orchestra
Danced by George Raft

Is You Is or Is You Ain't Ma Baby
(1944)
Written by Louis Jordan and Billy Austin
Performed by Louis Jordan and his Orchestra; vocal by Louis Jordan

Merriment
 Music by Agustín Castellón Sabicas
Performed by Carmen Amaya; Flamenco Dance by Carmen Amaya

Kittens With Their Mittens Laced
 Music and Lyrics by Inez James and Sidney Miller
Sung and Danced by Donald O'Connor and Peggy Ryan, accompanied by Charlie Spivak and His Orchestra

Shoo-Shoo Baby
(1943)
Music and Lyrics by Phil Moore
Sung by The Andrews Sisters accompanied by Freddie Slack and His Orchestra

I'll Get By
(1928)
Music by Fred E. Ahlert

Lyrics by Roy Turk
Sung by Dinah Shore

I Feel a Song Coming On
(1935)
Music by Jimmy McHugh
Lyrics by Dorothy Fields and George Oppenheimer
Danced by Vera Zorina and male chorus, including George Raft

The Bigger the Army and the Navy
Music and Lyrics by Jack Yellen, Ted Shapiro and Dan Dougherty
Sung by Sophie Tucker

Swing Low, Sweet Chariot
Written by Wallis Willis
Arranged by Henry Thacker Burleigh
Performed by Charlie Spivak and His Orchestra

I'll See You in My Dreams
(1924)
Music by Isham Jones
Lyrics by Gus Kahn
Sung by Jeanette MacDonald

Liebestraum No. 3 (A Dream of Love)
(1850)
Music by Franz Liszt
Performed on the piano by Artur Rubinstein

Bei Mir Bist Du Schön
(1932)
Music by Sholom Secunda
English Lyrics by Sammy Cahn and Saul Chaplin
Sung by The Andrews Sisters in a medley of their hits

Hold Tight, Hold Tight (Want Some Seafood, Mama)
(1938)

Written by Jerry Brandow, Buddy G. DeSylva, Edward Robinson,
Willie Spottswood and Leonard Ware
Sung by The Andrews Sisters in a medley of their hits

The Beer Barrel Polka
(1939)
Music by Jaromir Vejvoda (1927)
Czech lyrics by Vasek Zeman (1934)
English Lyrics by Lew Brown, Wladimir A. Timm (1939)
Sung by The Andrews Sisters in a medley of their hits

The Boogie Woogie Bugle Boy of Company B
(1941)
Written by Don Raye and Hugh Prince
Sung by The Andrews Sisters in a medley of their hits

I'll Be With You in Apple Blossom Time
(1920)
Music by Albert von Tilzer
Lyrics by Neville Fleeson
Sung by The Andrews Sisters in a medley of their hits

Pennsylvania Polka
(1942)
Written by Zeke Manners and Lester Lee
Sung by The Andrews Sisters in a medley of their hits

Victory Polka
(1943)
Music by Jule Styne
Lyrics by Sammy Cahn
Sung by The Andrews Sisters in a medley of their hits

Good Night
(1923)
Music and Lyrics by Leo Wood, Con Conrad and Irving Bibo
Performed by Ted Lewis and his Band; vocal by Ted Lewis

Besame Mucho
(1940)
Music by Consuelo Velázquez
Played by Charlie Spivak and His Orchestra

Mad About Him, Sad Without Him, How Can I Be Glad Without Him Blues
Music and Lyrics by Larry Markes and Dick Charles
Performed by Dinah Shore

Some of These Days
(1910)
Music and Lyrics by Shelton Brooks
Sung by Sophie Tucker

Cast:
George Raft	Tony West
Vera Zorina	Gloria Vance
Grace McDonald	Kitty West
Charley Grapewin	Nick West
Ramsay Ames	Laura
Frank Wilcox	Capt. Williams
Charles Butterworth	Louie Fairweather
Elizabeth Patterson	Annie
Regis Toomey	Dr. Henderson
George Macready	Walter Bruce
Mack Gray	Lt. Reynolds
Billy Benedict	Joe
Charles D. Brown	Col. Starret
Roy Darmour	Eddie
Ralph Dunn	Loomis
Grandon Rhodes	George Grayson
Addison Richards	MacDermott
George Riley	Jimmy
Janet Shaw	Phone Operator
Lennie Smith	Jitterbug Dancer

Carl Vernell	Terry Dennis
Emmett Vogan	Harkness
Theodore von Eltz	William Barrett
Anthony Warde	Captain
Billy Wayne	Fife
Edwin Stanley	Taylor
Nick Stewart	Lt. Reynolds
William Forrest	Edward Dobbs
Howard Hickman	Dr. Wood
Molly Lamont	Ms. Hartford
Frank Jenks	Chick Doyle
Jack Wegman	Mayor
Jack Whitley	Man
Jan Wiley	Phone Operator
Bill Wolfe	Zoot Suit Man
Duke York	Military Policeman
Thurston Hall	Man
Tom Hanlon	Announcer
Kay Harding	Woman in Montage
Carey Harrison	Colonel
Bill Healy	Ship Officer
Samuel S. Hinds	Officer
Leyland Hodgson	Australian Reporter
Stanley Andrews	Australian Officer
Martin Ashe	Man in Office
Robert Ashley	Jitterbug Dancer
Genevieve Bell	Mother in Montage
Lee Bennett	Acrobat
Nancy Brinckman	Phone Operator
Steve Brodie	Australian Pilot
Lane Chandler	Ship Officer
George Chirello	Welles' Assistant
Wallis Clark	HVC Committee Man
Clyde Cook	Stooge
Richard Crane	Marine Officer
Leslie Denison	Reporter
Bill Dyer	Messenger Boy

George Eldredge	Submarine Officer
John Estes	Hospital Patient
Clair Freeman	Dancer
Ralph Gardner	Patient in Leg Cast
Leonard Gautier	Performer
Doris Lloyd	Nurse
Anthony Marsh	Military Officer
Philo McCullough	Officer
Don McGill	Man
Michael Kirk	Man
Frank LaRue	Postman
Perc Launders	Studio Cop
Odessa Lauren	Phone Operator
Nelson Leigh	Bull Fiddler
John Meredith	Blind Soldier in MacDonald Act
Dennis Moore	HVC Officer
Edmund Mortimer	Theatregoer
Clarence Muse	Singer
Dick Nelson	Sergeant
Marie Osborne	Nurse
Franklin Parker	Man in Office
Cyril Ring	Laughtonpher
Alex Romero	Dancer
Bobby Barber	Soldier in W.C. Fields Routine
Steve Wayne	Soldier
John Whitney	Soldier
Walter Tetley	Soldier
Bernard Thomas	Soldier
Luis Torres	Soldier
Joel Allen	Soldier
Carlyle Blackwell Jr.	Soldier
Ed Brown	Soldier
Jimmy Carpenter	Soldier
Alan Cook	Soldier
John Duane	Soldier
Charles King	Soldier
Eddie Kover	Soldier

Don Kramer	Soldier
William Meader	Soldier
Mel Shubert	Soldier
John Cason	Soldier Listening to Radio
Hal Bell	Sailor
Doris Bren	Magic Maid
Linda Brent	Magic Maid
Rosemary Battle	Magic Maid
Eleanor Counts	Magic Maid
Majorie Fectean	Magic Maid
Janice Gay	Magic Maid
Lolita Leighter	Magic Maid
Mary Rowland	Magic Maid
Jane Smith	Magic Maid

Jeanette MacDonald, Orson Welles, Marlene Dietrich, Dinah Shore, Donald O'Connor, Peggy Ryan, W. C. Fields, Andrews Sisters, Ted Lewis, Artur Rubinstein, Carmen Amaya, Sophie Tucker, Walter Abel, Louise Allbritton, Evelyn Ankers, Louise Beavers, Randolph Scott, Noah Beery Jr., Turhan Bey, Nigel Bruce, Agustin Castellón Sabicas, Lon Chaney Jr, Peter Coe, Lois Collier, Alan Curtis, Andy Devine, Susanna Foster, Thomas Gomez, Gloria Jean, Elyse Knox, Maria Montez, Martha O'Driscoll, Robert Paige, Maxie Rosenbloom, Gale Sondergaard, Ted Lewis Orchestra, The Delta Rhythm Boys, Freddie Slack and His Orchestra, Charlie Spivak and His Orchestra, Louis Jordan and his Orchestra, Leonard Gautier's Bricklayers.

Released May 5, 1944
Universal Studios
Running Time: 122 minutes
Black and White

For his first movie after leaving Warner Brothers and striking out as an independent actor, George Raft took the lead in an all-star musical comedy that paid tribute to the Hollywood Victory Caravan. Raft had enjoyed entertaining troops with his dance act, and liked the script where he played an entertainer in a family act who

Vera Zorina and George Raft in Follow The Boys

needed work after vaudeville petered out, and discovered that these shows for the troops were essentially the same thing. This allows the film to present a series of specialty acts featuring everyone from The Andrew Sisters and Jeanette MacDonald to W.C. Fields.

George Raft plays Tony West who does a vaudeville act with his father Nick (Charley Grapewine) and sister Kitty (Grace MacDonald). After vaudeville fizzles out and they get fewer and fewer bookings, Tony heads to Hollywood and gets a job dancing in movies. Working for Universal, he connects with Gloria Vance ((Vera Zorina) first as a dancing partner on screen and then as her husband. World War Two breaks out and Tony tries to enlist but is told he has a bad knee and can't be accepted. He instead organizes a Hollywood Victory Committee, gathering stage, radio, and movie performers to do shows for the troops. His shows include a musical medley by The Andrews Sisters, Orson Welles doing his old magic act from Burlesque (at one point he saws Marlene Dietrich in half!), and W.C. Fields performing a billiard routine. Gloria discovers she is pregnant and wants to tell Tony, but he rebuffs her because he's too focused on his showbiz work. When Tony goes overseas to put on shows for the men in combat, he is killed during a submarine attack. Gloria then takes his place putting on shows for the military.

It is curious that an otherwise uplifting and patriotic movie has such an ending that is a bit of a downer. Tony and Gloria never really get to reconcile; he only finds out he is about to become a father right before he is killed because his sister breaks Gloria's confidence and tells him.

While it is not great cinema by any means, *Follow The Boys* holds up as a cultural artifact that entertains on several levels. It is an interesting collection of top entertainers from the war years. It features a lot of fun period music, comedy, and specialty acts. While the underlying narrative featuring George Raft and Vera Zorina is just a way to string together the various acts, there is an especially uplifting scene where Tony quickly puts together a makeshift show for an African American military unit, so they won't be overlooked, enlisting Louis Jordan and his band. Tony does his dance number to the tune of Jordan's band playing "Sweet Georgia Brown" as a rainstorm rages. "I can take it if you can," he yells triumphantly, and goes on with the show. The American patriotism presented in a movie like *Follow The Boys* is a fascinating look at an era, and a cultural attitude, that has long since passed us by. While nearly every studio did a movie like this (Raft has a cameo in *Stage Door Canteen*), *Follow The Boys* addresses segregated troops and makes sure to include them.

The film's premiere was quite a spectacle itself. Sophie Tucker sang, and George Raft danced to "Sweet Georgia Brown," just like he had in the movie. The film was enjoyed by exhibitors and the press syndicate representatives, resulting in books and publicity stories that ensured the movie would be a hit. Of course, moviegoers responded favorably to the many stars featured in the film.

A review in the trade magazine *Motion Picture Daily* responded favorably to the method and structure of *Follow The Boys*:

> There is an abundance of entertainment and stellar names galor in Charles K. Feldman's production *Follow The Boys*. In fact, it is overweighted with individual acts and star

appearances to such an extent that its story, an unpretentious one at best, eventually is lost in the maze of camp show entertainment which is poured so generously onto the screen, but is recovered to supply a tragic ending.

As expected, *Follow The Boys* was a major box office hit, and George Raft enjoyed not only having a fairly easy role to play, but also come off as someone who was selfless and heroic in context. Unfortunately, he and Vera Zorina did not get along. It was mostly due to her becoming difficult because she felt George Raft was too old to play her husband (she is sixteen years younger than he is). The studio let her know, quite bluntly, that it would be his name, not hers, that would draw an audience.

Because George Raft was in control of his destiny as an actor, and was also a successful star who ensured strong box office results, it was not difficult for him to find projects that he felt suited him. And, at first, this seemed like a good thing for his career. However, while going through several offers before taking the job for *Follow The Boys*, one of the films George Raft turned down was Billy Wilder's *Double Indemnity*, a true classic that is considered one of the finest noir films. While George having some control over his projects was generally a good thing, his penchant for passing on roles that would have benefited greatly still continued.

NOB HILL

Directed by Henry Hathaway
Screenplay by Wanda Tuchock and Norman Reilly Raine from a story by Eleanor Griffin
Produced by André Daven
Cinematography by Edward Cronjager
Film Editing by Harmon Jones

Songs
I Don't Care Who Knows It
Lyrics by Harold Adamson
Music by Jimmy McHugh

I Walked Right in With My Eyes Wide Open
Lyrics by Harold Adamson
Music by Jimmy McHugh

On San Francisco Bay
Music by Gertrude Hoffman
Lyrics by Vincent Bryan

What Do You Want to Make Those Eyes at Me For?
Music by James V. Monaco
Lyrics by Howard Johnson and Joseph McCarthy

San Francisco, the Paris of the USA
Written by Hirshel Hendler

Touring San Francisco
Music by Jimmy McHugh
Lyrics by Harold Adamson

Holy God, We Praise Thy Name
Written by Peter Ritter

San Francisco
Music by Bronislau Kaper and Walter Jurmann
Lyrics by Gus Kahn

Hello, Frisco!
 Music by Louis A. Hirsch
Lyrics by Gene Buck

When You Wore a Tulip and I Wore a Big Red Rose
 Music by Percy Wenrich
Lyrics by Jack Mahoney
Hello! Ma Baby
 Music by Joseph E. Howard
Lyrics by Ida Emerson

Cast
George Raft	Tony Angelo
Joan Bennett	Harriet Carruthers
Vivian Blaine	Sally Templeton
Peggy Ann Garner	Katie Flanagan
Alan Reed	Dapper Jack Harrigan
B.S. Pully	Joe the Bartender
Emil Coleman	Pianist
Edgar Barrier	Lash Carruthers
Joe Smith	Waiter
Charles Dale	Waiter
George Anderson	Rafferty
Olive Blakeney	Carruthers' Housekeeper
Doria Caron	Madeleine
Don Costello	Steve
Harrison Greene	Mr. Van Buren
Virginia Walker	Mrs. Van Buren
Rory Calhoun	Jose
Charles Cane	Chips Conlon

Robert Greig	Patton, Curruthers' Butler
William Haade	Big Tim, El Dorado Owner
Jane Jones	Ruby
Arthur Loft	Turner
Nestor Paiva	Luigi
Grandon Rhodes	Devereaux
Barbara Sears	Mrs. Devereaux
Joseph E. Bernard	Printer
Tom Dillon	Cop Chasing Katie
J. Farrell MacDonald	Cabby with Katie
Dorothy Ford	Tall Showgirl in Sally's Act
Bud Jamison	Singer
Joseph J. Greene	Headwaiter
Paul Hurst	El Dorado Doorman
Edna Mae Jones	Dance Hall Girl
William Murphy	Lucky Sailor at Tony's
Forbes Murray	Mayor
Helen O'Hara	Showgirl
Chief Thundercloud	Indian Chief
Lawrence Williams	Candidate
Jack Gordon	Bartender
Syd Saylor	Sailor Tourist at Wax Museum
Chick Chandler	Wax Museum Guide
Will Stanton	Tourist at Wax Museum
Lillian Salvaneschi	Dancer
Mario Salvaneschi	Dancer
Ralph Sanford	Politician
Eddie Hart	Politician
Sam Flint	Politician
George Lloyd	Politician
Harry Shannon	Policeman in China Town
Harry Strang	Policeman
Arthur Thalasso	Politician
Ralph Peters	Policeman
Brooks Hunt	Policeman
Fred Graham	Bouncer
Louis Bacigalupi	Bouncer

Robert Filmer	Bouncer
John Kelly	Bouncer
William Hunter	Bouncer
Susan Scott	Slummer
Carol Andrews	Slummer
Otto Reichow	Swedish Sailor
Sven Hugo Borg	Swedish Sailor
George Blagoi	Swedish Sailor
Jack Kenny	Club Patron
Phil Bloom	Club Patron
Edward Biby	Club Patron
Rube Dalroy	Club Patron
Fred Aldrich	Club Patron
Anton Northpole	Club Patron
Mathew McCue	Club Patron
George T. Lee	Lo, Tony's Chinese Servant
Beal Wong	High, Tony's Chinese Servant
Bruce Wong	Chinese Man
Jean Wong	Chinese Showgirl
Benson Fong	Chinese Servant
Eddie Lee	Chinese Man
Teri Toy	Chinese Showgirl
Freeman High	Specialty Singer
Sam Ash	Specialty Singer
Claire Emery	Acrobatic Dancer
Evelyn Dewey	Acrobatic Dancer
Mabel Boehlke	Acrobatic Dancer
Charlotte Dewey	Acrobatic Dancer
Darleen Garner	Acrobatic Dancer
Marie King	Acrobatic Dancer
Vicki Lang	Acrobatic Dancer
Virginia Lyndon	Acrobatic Dancer
Darlene Ottum	Acrobatic Dancer
Ben Jade	Acrobatic Dancer
Bonnadene Wolfe	Acrobatic Dancer
Priscilla White	Aerial Acrobatic Specialty
Gerald Mackey	Newsboy

Hugh Maguire	Newsboy
Eddie Nichols	Newsboy
Paul Graeff	Newsboy
Vincent Graeff	Newsboy
Robert Ferrero	Newsboy
Freddie Chapman	Newsboy
Irving Gump	Newsboy
Danny Hood	Newsboy
Mickey Mascari	Boy
David Polonsky	Boy
Marvin Davis	Boy
Ray Dolciame	Boy
Ronnie Pattison	Boy
Rudy Wissler	Boy
Jacqueline Huber	Girl
The Three Swifts	
The Troupers	

Released July 13, 1945
20th Century Fox
Running Time: 95 minutes
Technicolor

George Raft's first movie in color was almost cast with Fred MacMurray in the lead. Harry "Pop" Sherman originally bought the screen rights to Eleanore Griffin's story, which focused on a 10-year-old Irish girl coming to American to live with her uncle, finding out he is dead, and being adopted by a gambler. These rights were purchased from him by 20th Century Fox because they were currently enjoying success with Technicolor musicals set in the 19th century. Peggy Ann Garner was considered for the role of the child right away, based on her impressive performance in *Jane Eyre*. The adult leads were to be MacMurray, Lynn Bari, and Merle Oberon, with direction by Gregory Ratoff. Ratoff left the project in the Spring of 1944 and the studio assigned it to Henry Hathaway, who was reticent about making a musical; unfamiliar territory for him. The studio threatened him with suspension so he agreed to make the movie. When Fred MacMurray was not available to take the role, he was replaced by George Raft, with whom Hathaway had worked successfully in the past. The female leads were Joan Bennett, who worked well with Raft, and Vivian Blaine, a studio newcomer who had scored with Laurel and Hardy in *Jitterbugs* (1943). Louella Parsons announced in a June 1944 column:

> Just as we go to press, we hear that George Raft, who has done so nobly by himself, and Charles Feldman, in *Follow the Boys*, moves to the Fox Studios. George plays one of the leads in *Nob Hill*. Joan Bennett has the other top spot. Raft also is contracted for other pictures at Fox, although my understanding is this is not an exclusive contract.[64]

This indicates that Parsons, and assumably others, were noticing that George Raft was enjoying continued success as a freelancer, and was enjoying continued success and stardom without having an exclusive contract with a studio. Filming for *Nob Hill* began in the late summer of 1944.

Other columnists made mention that only a year earlier Vivian Blaine had a one-line bit part in a movie featuring Joan Bennett, and now in this film she not only co-stars with her, she ends up with the leading man at the end.

George Raft plays Tony Angelo, a nightclub owner in San Francisco at the turn of the century. His big draw is singer Sally Templeton (Vivian Blaine), who is in love with Tony. One night, Katie, a little girl (Peggy Ann Garner), arrives from Ireland looking for her Uncle, Pete Flannigan. The child had been living with her grandmother in Dublin, but when her grandma dies, she was sent to live with Uncle Pete. Sadly, she arrives to discover Pete has also died. Tony and Sally are very gentle, patient, and kind toward her, realizing she must be unsettled by these circumstances, and she becomes comfortable with them. Tony offers to pay her fare back to Ireland, but realizing the child has no place to go, is persuaded by Sally to let her stay. Tony gets connected with Harriet Carruthers (Joan Bennett) who wants him to support her brother (Edgar Barrier) in his campaign for district attorney. Upset with his attraction to Harriet,

---

64 Louella Parsons Column. Syndicated. June 3, 1944. International News Service

George Raft, Joan Bennett in Nob Hill

Sally takes a job at a rival club, which saddens Katie. When Lash wins the election, Tony realizes he has no future with Harriet, and after a bout with alcoholism, returns to a forgiving Sally. During all this tumult, Katie runs away, but is eventually found.

George Raft was enjoying picking his own projects and not having films foisted upon him that he didn't want to do, resulting in refusals and suspensions. The fact that his success and stardom remained unchanged was especially gratifying. Raft liked playing Joe Angelo, even though there are scenes where his character makes decisions that are negative. He is overall a good guy who runs an honest establishment, and his comforting parental affection for a frightened child is especially positive.

Raft and Peggy Ann Garner play off of each other very well. Katie respects Tony as a father figure, and he affectionately calls

George Raft, Peggy Ann Garner, Alan Reed in Nob Hill

her Shamrock and promises that he will someday marry Harriet and they'll all live in a house on a hill among the wealthy. When Tony realizes he was merely used by Harriet, and also lost Sally, he is honest with Katie that they will never live in that dream house on the hill.

Katie: What about Sally? Isn't she coming back here? Ever?

Tony: After the way I treated her, I wouldn't blame her if she never set foot in this place again the rest of her life

Katie: But a man's entitled to a bit of a slip.

Tony: Not the kind that I made. I was the prize heel of all time. I threw all that love and loyalty right back in her face.

Katie: Sally loves you Tony. If it'd help, she'd crawl up Nob Hill and back on her hands and knees.

Tony: Yeah. With me kicking her every foot of the way.

Peggy Ann Garner is very soulful in her role, and holds her own with these fine actors. Later this same year she would score big with a triumphant performance in *A Tree Grows in Brooklyn*.

Miss Garner's connection to George Raft extended beyond the movie. Responding to Raft's offscreen kindness, Peggy Ann heard that his birthday was September 26th and arranged for a surprise birthday party, complete with a cake. Raft was very moved by this gesture, and never forgot it. And, for the rest of her life, Peggy Ann Garner would recall George Raft among the kindest and most supportive actors she worked with as a child; a period that was not always happy for her.

Also while filming *Nob Hill*, Raft used his clout to help out a bit actor named Sven Hugo Borg. Raft remembered when he was filming *Spawn of the North* at Paramount, Borg, an uncredited extra, jumped into icy waters to rescue a stuntman. George arranged for Borg to appear in *Nob Hill*.

Nob Hill had everything movie audiences wanted, as World War Two continued to rage (it would finally end, months after this film's release). This movie offered all of the elements of escape – bright colors, an interesting story, well-developed characters, and period music. It was a big hit at the box office, earning millions for the studio, and became one of the top grossing films of 1945. It also continued George Raft's success as a freelancer.

George Raft would not be in another color film until *Black Widow* in 1954. And, coincidentally, Peggy Ann Garner would be in that movie also.

JOHNNY ANGEL

Directed by Edwin L. Marin
Screenplay by Steve Fisher, based on the story "Mr Angel Comes
    Aboard," by Charles Booth and adapted by Frank Gruber
Produced by William L. Pereira
Cinematography by Harry J. Wild
Film Editing by Les Millbrook

Song:
Memphis In June
Music by Hoagy Carmichael
Lyrics by Paul Francis Webster

Cast:
George Raft	Johnny Angel
Claire Trevor	Lily
Signe Hasso	Paulette Girard
Lowell Gilmore	Sam Jewell
Hoagy Carmichael	O'Brien
Marvin Miller	Gusty
Margaret Wycherly	Miss Drumm
J. Farrell MacDonald	Capt. Angel
Ernie Adams	Leslie
Edgar Dearing	Jim
Sam Flint	Barnes
Leyland Hodgson	Paul Jewell
Burt Holm	Isherwood
Jack Overman	Biggsy
John Indrisano	Joe
William J. O'Brien	Bartender
Mack Gray	Bartender
Jack Low	Bar Patron

Pat McKee	Barfly
Joey Ray	3rd Mate
Al Rhein	Checker
James Flavin	Matey
Al Murphy	Ship's Lookout
Jimmy O'Gatty	Sailor
Eddie Hart	Sailor
Alf Haugan	Sailor
Bill Williams	Sailor
Charles Sullivan	Sailor
Sailor Vincent	Crewman
John Hamilton	Harbor Master
Don Brodie	Harbor Master's Aide on the 'Putnam'
James Conaty	Harbor Board Member
Virginia Belmont	Cigarette Girl
Terry Morel	Cigarette girl
Rosemary LaPlanche	Hatcheck Girl
Ann Codee	Charwoman
Aina Constant	Secretary
Wade Crosby	Dock Watchman
Marcel De la Brosse	French Civilian
Louis Mercier	Cigar Maker
Philip Morris	Cop
Jack Perrin	Waiter
Theodore Rand	Headwaiter
O.M. Steiger	Frenchman
Jason Robards Sr.	Officer
Marc Cramer	Officer
Kernan Cripps	Official
Perc Launders	Official
Robert Andersen	Reporter
Bryant Washburn	Reporter
Chili Russell Hopton	Reporter
Carl Kent	Reporter
Rusty Farrell	Blonde
Chili Williams	Redhead
Eddie Lewis	Bit part
George Magrill	Bit Part

Released October 25, 1945
RKO Radio Pictures
Running Time: 79 minutes
Black and White

George Raft's first movie released during what would become the post-war era is, very appropriately, also his first official film noir. And the screen persona he had adapted and developed over his years in movies fit perfectly in this new genre of stylish crime dramas that are now referred to as "film noir" (French for "dark film"). This term was first used by French critic Nino Frank in 1946, but really didn't enter the American lexicon until many years later. In retrospect, films in the noir genre offer a stylish presentation within the parameters of crime on several levels, and usually featuring mysterious characters, low key lighting, and sudden bursts of violence. *Johnny Angel* offers all of those elements.

George Raft plays the title character, a sea captain. The film opens with him discovering a ship that he recognizes as a craft his father operates. It is sitting adrift in the fog, so Johnny goes aboard and finds that it has been abandoned. Realizing his father would never leave his ship this way, he believes it likely he has been killed. Johnny then sets out to investigate what happened. Johnny goes to see his employer George "Gusty" Gustafson (Marvin Miller). Gusty has a pretty wife named Lily (Claire Trevor) whom he adores, but who cares little for him, and an elderly woman, Miss Drumm, who had been his nursemaid as a child and to whom he feels beholden. Miss Drumm works as his secretary. He gets no information, so he returns to his father's vessel and finds a woman's shoe. A dockhand tells him that a woman was hiding on the ship when he had originally boarded to first investigate, so he seeks her out. Johnny meets cabbie Celestial O'Brien (Hoagy Carmichael) who takes him to the French Quarter. There he meets Paulette (Signe Hasso) and forcefully tries on the shoe he found. It first her perfectly. She avoids his relentless questioning, until a bouncer appears and fights with Johnny. This allows Paulette to escape. He later discovers Celestial has taken Paulette to a boarding house, and follows her there. She then finally gives him the details he is

George Raft in Johnny Angel

after, which are shown in flashback. She went to Johnny's father (J. Farrell McDonald) after her own father was murdered and framed for a gold bullion theft. Crew members mutinied and murdered Johnny's father, but the actual killer is a stowaway that Johnny now needs to identify. Meanwhile, Lily is in love with Johnny and plans to stab and kill Gusty so she will be free to have him, even though Johnny shows no interest. When they eventually go back to where Johnny expects to find answers, they find Gusty, still alive despite

Lily having stabbed him. He has a gun pointed at Johnny and confesses to being the killer of his father. Despite the gun, Johnny approaches him, but before Gusty can kill him, a shot is fired killing Gusty. It is Miss Drumm.

Along with being his first identified film noir, *Johnny Angel* is also George Raft's first experience working with director Edwin L. Marin. Marin was not a stylist, but was quite adept at handling a variety of genres. In a career that spanned low budget B movies and top drawer A pictures, Marin directed notable westerns (*Tall in the Saddle* with John Wayne), series movies (a few of the *Maisie* comedies with Ann Sothern), the Judy Garland musicals *Everybody Sing* and *Listen, Darling*, and MGM's screen version of Charles Dickens' *A Christmas Carol*. Marin would eventually direct George Raft in five different movies, including *Johnny Angel*, and each of them contain noir elements.

Raft's screen persona with its minimalist expression and penchant for subtle nuance, works well within the context of this dark murder mystery. Johnny has an emotional investment in his situation, being that it is his father whose ship is abandoned. And while he realizes the idea that his father might be alive is pretty much impossible, his offers a quietly jarring reaction when Paulette reveals that is, indeed, the case. Because Johnny is a ship captain as his father had been, there is an element of filial anguish as the father is something of a towering figure, even in death, that further shadows his son's intention to seek answers, and vengeance.

There isn't a great deal of suspense to the narrative mystery. Its outcome seems fairly obvious pretty early in the proceedings. But the steps Johnny takes, the complicated avenues he must venture across, and the obligatory bursts of violence that have come to define classic film noir, are all part of the neatly constructed package.

The supporting cast is carefully defined and placed. Claire Trevor's fine acting skills are exhibited strongly as her character suppresses her passions until finally succumbing to them with violence – and fails. As the femme fatale, Signe Hasso plays a character that starts out with defiance and ends up being helpful. Paulette is the quintessential noir character with answers she refuses to give, and an accent that adds that extra touch of intrigue. Her settling into a more cooperative connection blends nicely with Johnny's clearer understanding of events.

Hoagy Carmichael scored big this same year at Warner Brothers in *To Have and Have Not*, but his curious presence as a cab driver that offers ominous foreshadowing is another dark presence that further defines this film as quintessential noir.

Finally, *Johnny Angel* has great atmosphere—some of the opening scenes set around the boats are quiet and haunting.

While it now stands as one of George Raft's best movies and finest performances, *Johnny Angel* received a fairly unimpressed reaction from most critics. *Variety* stated:

> *Johnny Angel* is another in the seemingly never-ending series of maritime intrigues involving murder and lust. It is slow and plodding, with poor story development [from a story by Charles Gordon Booth, adaptation by Frank Gruber]. Raft is his invariably glowering self as a guy who really handles his mitts – and the dames – while Claire Trevor and Signe Hasso are the romantic interests. Rest of the cast is weighted down too much by the story, though of the feature performers, Hoagy Carmichael, the composer, as in the Bogart-Bacall *To Have and Have Not* for Warners, plays the character of whimsy with tongue in cheek.[65]

Despite having a star of George Raft's magnitude heading a good supporting cast, RKO didn't think *Johnny Angel* would be much more than double-feature fodder and let it go for a fairly inexpensive rental at theaters. This resulted in more engagements, and, surprising the studio, a very good response from moviegoers. *Johnny Angel* was one of the studio's biggest hits of the year. As a result, RKO asked George Raft to agree to a non-exclusive pact to make more films for the studio. During the post-war period, RKO became noted for its noir thrillers. Pleased with the film, and the experience, Raft agreed.

While RKO was finding the right property for George Raft to do next, the actor explored opportunities working in productions for independent producers. And his first, *Whistle Stop*, was yet another box office hit.

---

65 Johnny Angel review. *Variety*. 1945

WHISTLE STOP

Directed by Léonide Moguy
Screenplay by Phillip Yordan based on the novel by Maritta M. Wolff
Produced by Seymour Nebenzal
Cinematography by Russell Metty
Film Editing by Gregg Tallas

Cast:
George Raft	Kenny Veech
Ava Gardner	Mary
Victor McLaglen	Gitlo
Tom Conway	Lew Lentz
Jorja Curtright	Fran
Jane Nigh	Josie Veech
Florence Bates	Molly Veech
Charles Drake	Ernie
Charles Judels	Sam Veech
Carmel Myers	Estelle
Jimmy Conlin	Al - the Barber
Jimmy Ames	Mr. Barker
Jack George	Joe
Mack Gray	Bartender
Broderick O'Farrell	Barfly
Robert Homans	Sheriff
Charles Wagenheim	Deputy
Ewing Miles Brown	Townsman

Released January 25, 1946
Nero Films for United Artists release
Running time: 86 minutes
Black and White

Movie ad for Whistle Stop

Maritta Wolff's 1941 novel *Whistle Stop* won the Avery Hopwood Prize. Wolff's sordid story of a poor Midwestern family in the aftermath of the Depression was filled with edgy intrigue and sordid characters. It was really good movie fodder, but settled rather firmly on the "forbidden" list during these years of Production Code enforcement. When producer Seymour Nebenzal, screenwriter Phillip Yordan, and a lawyer, Herbert Silverberg, formed their own production company, it was to produce a film version of the Wolff novel. Reallzing he had to sanitize it in order to get any kind of release, Yordan worked hard to maintain some essence of the original book.

George Raft's availability as a freelancer who liked the screenplay was a real shot in the arm to the production. Raft was a star, a box office name, his movies were making money, and he wasn't beholden to any studio. Making a deal with him was not difficult. Ava Gardner had been doing only bit parts in movies for the past few years, getting somewhat better roles in B movies such as *Ghosts on the Loose* with The East Side Kids. Mickey Rooney told the author in a 2001 interview:

> When I was married to Ava Gardner and we found her a role in one of their (East Side Kids) pictures, I called Leo Gorcey and asked him to watch out for her. He helped her through the picture. Gorcey was nothing like his tough guy movie character. He was intelligent, friendly, and funny.[66]

Ava Gardner would always cite *Whistle Stop*, where she got a co-starring role opposite a star like George Raft, to be her breakthrough. By this time, however, she was married to bandleader Artie Shaw.

Columnist Sidney Skolsky took some credit for George Raft and Ava Gardner having met, stating in his column:

> It was at Romanoffs in a booth with Ava, and Raft came over to say hello to me. But, he wasn't fooling me or anyone in the booth. He really wanted to say hello to Ava and get an introduction. During the conversation Raft said to Ava, "I'd like to make picture a with you someday. You've got everything. You'd be great." It was a good approach. After all he couldn't give her the usual "How would you

---

[66] Neibaur, James L. *The Essential Mickey Rooney*. Rowman and Littlefield, 2016

like to be in pictures? I believe I can do something about it." She was in pictures.

Whistle Stop was announced as the next George Raft movie by Louella Parsons in a May, 1945 column. Jane Greer was, at that time, being considered for a role. The following month, actors Victor McLaglen and Tom Conway were announced. Conway was borrowed from RKO studios where he was appearing in the Falcon detective series, which he had inherited from his brother George Sanders. The final Falcon movie in the series would be released at the end of 1946. Ava Gardner was loaned to the production from MGM in July.

George Raft plays Kenny Veech, a small town man who lives with his parents and sister and has no job or any real ambition. The only money he makes is through small time gambling, and he spends it in the local taverns. His ex-girlfriend Mary (Ava Gardner) returns to the small town after several years. She had left because it was evident that she had no future with a loafer like Kenny. Her family owned the home in which the Veeches are living, so as that sole heir it now belongs to her and she arranges to have a room there for the time being. She is welcomed by Mrs. Veech (Florence Bates), Kenny, and his sister Josie (Jane Nigh). Mary is disappointed when she discovers that Kenny hasn't really changed his lifestyle at all. Mary attracts the attention of bar owner Lew (Tom Conway), much to Kenny's chagrin. One of Lew's bartenders, Gitlo (Victor McLaglen) hates him. He asks Kenny to join him in murdering Lew and stealing the funds from a fair he runs annually. Kenny is reticent at first, but reluctantly agrees in order to win Mary back. Mary discovers the scheme and detains Kenny until Lew is safely away. Angry, she leaves the Veech home and goes to a hotel, but eventually admits she never stopped loving Kenny, despite his flaws. Kenny says that he will change for her, and gets a job working for the railroad company. Jealous, Lew frames Kenny and Gitlo for murder, and they are pursued by police. Kenny is shot and injured but he and Gitlo escape by train to Detroit. Gitlo then returns to confront Lew, is shot by him, but strangles him before he dies. The police realize the frameup, and Mary goes to Detroit to get Kenny.

Critics were not pleased with *Whistle Stop*, many believing this low budget indie production was a real misfire. Bosley Crowther in *The New York Times* stated:

> This plainly remote and artificial concoction lacks flavor, consistency, reason and even dramatic suspense. And it is also abominably acted—which covers about everything. Apparently, Seymour Nebenzal, who produced it, had a vague idea that his film was to be a searching mirror reflecting one of life's small ironies. It isn't. It is just another cheaply manufactured melodrama in which a girl of rather dubious reputation wavers between two men. Ava Gardner, who plays the female, brings nothing but appearance to the role, and George Raft, miscast completely, plays the bum in a bored gangster style. Tom Conway is curiously urbane for a tavern keeper in a small town and Victor McLaglen goes solemnly heavy as a vagabond bartender.[67]

Meanwhile, the critic for *The Chicago Tribune* appeared to only be impressed with Victor McLaglen and was especially harsh toward Ava Gardner:

> Victor McLaglen, as Gitlo, does the best work of the entire cast. The role is perfectly suited to him, and he turns in an able performance. George Raft, as Kenny, is fairly inexpressive, and Ava Gardner's Mary is pretty bad. Her acting is overdone to the point of amateurishness. Florence Bates and Jorja Curtright are far better as two other women who love the worthless Kenny.[68]

Moviegoers however disagreed. *Whistle Stop* was another hit for George Raft, and it helped to advance Ava Gardner's career. Ava recalled years later:

> I enjoyed *Whistle Stop* mainly because George Raft was so much fun. We went dancing on a couple of occasions and George danced like a dream. *Whistle Stop* was my first leading role and as such I finally did get noticed.[69]

---

[67] Whistle Stop Review. *New York Times*. March 18, 1946

[68] Whistle Stop Review. *Chicago Tribune* January 2, 1946

[69] Aaker, Everett. *George Raft: The Films*. McFarland, 2013

Despite its low budget, *Whistle Stop* remains compelling and exciting, using all of the basic elements of film noir. Despite his seemingly one-dimensional laziness, Kenny is a multi-faceted character. He is streetwise and capable, he is attractive to women (his interest in Mary upsets his girl Fran, played by newcomer Jorja Cutright), and he has the ability to sustain employment if he chooses to do so. Mary acts as a veritable conscience. His lack of ambition and drinking is why she left town, and her leaving is the reason he continues to drink and slack. Mary's return changes him. He considers actual murder, but ends up working. The film ends with that satisfaction.

Yordan did not support the casting of Raft in this film at all, but he did a good job, and believably sells Kenny's change of heart when the events of the film prompt him to straighten out. Ava Gardner was lovely in this, and in the scene where Mary and Kenny reunite when she first comes back to town—you can sense the history that exists between the two characters. The addition of the train whistles being heard in the background through most of the movie was a nice touch also.

George Raft's career continued to flourish as a freelancer and he was enjoying the freedom to choose his own scripts, and liked the fact that indie productions allowed him greater creative input. He agreed to star in another independent production when approached by indie producer Benedict Bogeaus to star in a film about a tough political manipulator. Raft was impressed that the script was written by Fred Finklehoffe, who had just won an Oscar for *Meet Me in St Louis*. The director would be Edwin L. Marin, who had directed Raft in the successful RKO feature *Johnny Angel*. The cinematographer would be Karl Struss, whose work included Murnau's *Sunrise* and Chaplin's *The Great Dictator*. Finally, Raft would be reteamed with one of his favorite co-stars of the past, Sylvia Sidney. It looked like the perfect project for his next movie, so Raft agreed to star in *Mr. Ace*. It turned out to be a very bad decision.

MR. ACE

Directed by Edwin L. Marin
Screenplay by Fred F. Finklehoffe
Produced by Benedict Bogeaus
Cinematography by Karl Struss
Film Editing by James Smith

Cast:
George Raft	Eddie Ace
Sylvia Sidney	Margaret Wyndham Chase
Stanley Ridges	Toomey
Sid Silvers	Pencil
Jerome Cowan	Peter Craig
Sara Haden	Alma Rhodes
Alan Edwards	Pembroke Chase III
Roman Bohnen	Prof. Joshua L. Adams
Joyce Bryant	Nightclub Singer
Gordon B. Clarke	Nightclub Pianist
Joe Gray	Gentleman Gene Delmont
Stanley Andrews	Tomahawk Club Boss
Mack Gray	Mack
Al Hill	Mack's Henchman
Charles Sullivan	Mack's Henchman
Ben Hall	Tommy
Walter Baldwin	Bookie
Dewey Robinson	Tom
Lester Dorr	Reporter at Party
Ben Erway	Tomahawk Club Politico
Harold Miller	Margaret's Party Guest
William H. O'Brien	Party Guest
Bess Flowers	Party Guest
James Conaty	Party Guest

Sam Harris	Nightclub Patron
Eric Wilton	Nightclub Patron
Larry Steers	Man on Stage at Radio Forum
Mary Field	Lady with Question on Radio Forum
Truman Bradley	Radio Forum Moderator
Bert Moorhouse	Election Vote Tallier on Telephone
Brooks Benedict	Man Entering Elevator

Released August 2, 1946
Benedict Bogeaus Productions for United Artists release
Running Time: 84 minutes
Black and White

When George Raft and Sylvia Sidney last co-starred in a movie, it was Fritz Lang's *You and Me* several years earlier. At that time, Sidney had top billing. This time, Raft does. Despite both being noted as often being difficult, they got along well on the two earlier films they had done together, and were happy to be reunited for this project. Sidney only made a couple more movies after *You and Me* after which she left movies and retired to her farm in New Jersey for five years. She returned to co-star with James Cagney in *Blood on the Sun*, and then went into this film. Sidney would continue acting in films and later television until her death in 1999, appearing in such later films as *Beetlejuice* and *Mars Attacks*.

Edwin L. Marin was back to direct at Raft's insistence, and Sylvia Sidney approved of this choice. Producer Benedict Bogeaus hired one of the best cinematographers in American films in Karl Struss, and, as indicated previously, the story and screenplay is by Fred Finklehoffe, his first since winning an Oscar for *Meet Me in St Louis*. Both Sylvia Sidney and George Raft were coming off of projects that were box office hits, Sidney garnering more attention in that she had just returned to movies after a years-long hiatus. And the story deals with the new post-war American culture, specifically women entering positions that had predominantly been male oriented, in this case politics. This is a project that seemed to have everything going for it. And it was a resounding box office flop, George Raft's first failure in many years.

Movie ad for Mr. Ace

George Raft plays the title role, Eddie Ace, a political boss who is asked to help congresswoman Margaret Wyndham Chase (Sylvia Sidney) run for governor. With Eddie's assistance she could conceivably attain the position. Margaret's husband, Pembroke Chase III (Alan Edwards) wants a divorce, but she won't agree, because it would disrupt her political plans. After meeting her powerful friends, Eddie still isn't sure he believes women should be in politics. Margaret remains strong, attempting to convince the men that she'd make a good governor, but even as Eddie begins to fall for her, he still can't shake his belief that women don't belong in politics. Margaret is strategic. She talks to one of Eddie's cronies, Mr. Toomey (Stanley Ridges), and with his help she gets nominated. She is confronted by her husband, who threatens to reveal an affair with Eddie Ace, which Ace will back up, if she doesn't pull out of the race. She agrees to do so. Joshua Adams, a political professor (Roman Bohnen), initially had misgivings about her being governor, but believed she actually could succeed if she had more heart. Adams convinces Margaret to run independently as a reform candidate who opposes the current political climate, and she wins the election. She then discovers Eddie Ace was behind her, helping Adams. They meet and Ace tells her that he just wants her to be the best governor she can be.

Production on *Mr Ace* was shut down when George Raft became ill during shooting and had to take time off. According to the press:

> George Raft, screen heavy, yesterday was confined in Cedars of Lebanon Hospital with an attack of pleurisy, which Dr. Myron Prinzmetal said would keep him hospitalized for several days. Production of a picture in which he is starring at General Service Studios will continue with shooting of scenes in which he does not appear.[70]

However, when Raft's illness kept him hospitalized for weeks, there was some discussion of shutting down the project completely. He was released from the hospital after three weeks, and told to rest at home for one more week before he could return to work. Producer Bogeaus chose to keep the project active.

Columnist Sheila Graham visited the set as production was wrapping up and spoke to George Raft:

> "I can't act; I'm a personality," says George Raft. It is the last day and the last scene in his picture, *Mr. Ace*. This was originally titled *Congresswoman*, then *Mr. Ace and the*

---

70 George Raft Confined by Attack of Pleurisy. *Los Angeles Times*. February 12, 1946

Queen, and now it's whittled down to Mr. Ace, all Raft. "What makes you think you can't act?" this reporter asks Georgie. It seems that some of the reviewers of Whistle Stop made this disparaging statement. True or false, the picture is making a fortune at the box office. And whatever it is that Raft has, it has kept him in the starring ranks tor 15 years, Director Ed Marin has saved the rain scene for the end. Raft was seriously ill with pleurisy and was in the hospital for three and a half weeks, and the picture was delayed. "So now you don't care whether George gets a cold?" this columnist kids Mr. Marin. He swears he does and that he loves our George. I do, too. I can't say the same for Sylvia Sidney, co-starring with Raft in *Mr. Ace*. As usual, she is in a hurry, even when the picture is finished and she has absolutely nothing to do, except reply on the run "I don't know," when I ask about her future plans. She doesn't know, but I collected on a bet that she would make this reply when I asked the question.[71]

Mr Ace should have been a much better movie, given its subject matter and the talent of the screenwriter, director and cast. Women had entered the workforce out of necessity during the war due to the shortage of men. They also entered sports and the political world. And, when the war was over, they were expected to return to the kitchen and allow the men to take their rightful place as the breadwinners. Well, women enjoyed the independence of working and making their own money, and this film deals with one aspect of that. There is even one scene where a character chastises Margaret because she isn't "cooking, cleaning, or even having a baby!"

Unfortunately, despite this rather daring material for the times, and its cultural significance now, as history, *Mr. Ace* just isn't a very good movie. It plods along slowly, with only marginal interest, and never becomes compelling enough to offer any real suspense or excitement. Moviegoers of the period responded unfavorably according to these reports from exhibitors:

> Ruined George Raft as a drawing card for us. They want action from him and this one failed from every angle.

---

71 In Hollywood Today. *Sheila Graham*. Syndicated. April 2, 1946

> What a relief it would be if George Raft got his clothes mussed up once in a while.
> This was a dismal box office flop. Scarcely grossed film rental for the feature. There was no interest in the picture and no drawing power in the stars.[72]

Other studies have indicated that George Raft's career started a veritable toboggan slide downhill after this movie's lack of success, but this isn't accurate. While a flop does indeed disrupt momentum, especially a star who is free-lancing projects, George Raft's career was hardly over. RKO, still buoyed by the success of *Johnny Angel*, had a screenplay ready and Raft approved with the provision that he be allowed to rewrite portions to make his character more sympathetic, and that Edwin L. Marin direct him. Since Marin had directed *Johnny Angel*, the studio agreed. The movie would be produced by Joan Harrison, a screenwriter who was, at the time, one of only three female producers in Hollywood. Ironic that Raft would go from a semi-feminist movie to a film produced by a woman. And, fortunately, *Nocturne* was a box office hit.

---

72 Mr Ace. What The Picture Did For Me. *Motion Picture Herald*. Various, 1947

NOCTURNE

Directed by Edwin L. Marin
Screenplay by Jonathan Latimer from a story by Frank Fenton and Rowland Brown
Produced by Joan Harrison
Cinematography by Harry J. Wild
Film Editing by Elmo Williams

Cast:
George Raft	Police Lt. Joe Warne
Lynn Bari	Frances Ransom
Virginia Huston	Carol Page
Joseph Pevney	Ned 'Fingers' Ford
Myrna Dell	Susan Flanders
Edward Ashley	Keith Vincent
Walter Sande	Detective Halberson
Mabel Paige	Mrs. Warne
Bern Hoffman	Eric Torp
Queenie Smith	Queenie
Mack Gray	Gratz
Robert Andersen	Pat
Janet Shaw	Grace Andrews
John Banner	Charles
Greta Granstedt	Clara
Virginia Keiley	Lotus Evans
Rudy Robles	Eujemio
Lucille Casey	Bessie
William Challee	Olsen
Virginia Edwards	Mrs. O'Rourke
Antonio Filauri	Nick Pappas
Pat Flaherty	Flannigan
Sam Flint	Mr. Barnes

Jack Norton	Charlie
Gladys Blake	Pantages Theatre Cashier
George Goodman	Keyboard Club Manager
Benny Burt	Keyboard Club Bartender
Al Rhein	Keyboard Club Waiter
Lillian Bronson	Gotham Cashier
Phil Baribault	Dark Room Assistant
James Carlisle	Elderly Man
Carol Forman	Receptionist
Dorothy Adams	Angry Apartment House Tenant
Edward Clark	Apartment House Clerk
Matt McHugh	Coffee Attendant
Lee Frederick	Attendant
Ted O'Shea	Dancer
John Rice	Doorman
Paul Stader	Practical Life Guard
Bert Moorhouse	Movie Director
Joey Ray	Assistant Director
Donald Kerr	Gaffer
Dick Rush	Studio Policeman
Harry Harvey	Police Doctor
Lorin Raker	Police Coroner
Al Hill	Policeman Flynn
Edgar Dearing	Policeman with Injured Susan
Willie Bloom	Policeman
James Pierce	Policeman
Roger Creed	Policeman
Robert Malcolm	Chief of Detectives
Lloyd Dawson	Man
Tex Swain	Man
Robert Terry	Man
Arthur Tovey	Man
Mel Wixon	Man
Carol Donell	Woman
Connie Evans	Woman
Betty Farrington	Woman
Monya Andre	Woman

Eleanor Counts   Woman
Norma Brown   Woman
Betty Hill   Woman

Released by October 29, 1946
RKO Radio Pictures
Running time: 87 minutes
Black and White

George Raft and director Edwin L. Marin teamed again with a film noir for RKO with *Nocturne*. Produced by Joan Harrison, a longtime creative associate of Alfred Hitchcock, the film that resulted was appropriately dark, mysterious, compelling, and quite an improvement over *Mr. Ace*. And where *Mr. Ace* was Raft's first box office flop in years, *Nocturne* was a moneymaker.

Joan Harrison was a much better producer than Benedict Bogeaus. Her tenure with Hitchcock helped her to better understand the filmmaking process, while her penchant for realism was also evident. According to the press:

> For his starring role in RKO's *Nocturne*, George Raft will have the benefit of advice from one of Broadway's most famous detectives, Barny Ruditsky. Producer Joan Harrison, a stickler for realism, wants Raft to be an authentic replica of a real detective, not one of those unbelievable creatures we often see on the screen. Ruditsky worked on cases involving famous gangsters for 20 years.[73]

George Raft plays police lieutenant Joe Warne who goes to investigate the death of Keith Vincent, a composer. The crime scene reveals that Vincent was working on a new song, "Nocturne," at the time of his death. All signs point to suicide, but Joe believes there is more to it and continues his investigation, against the wishes of the department. Susan Flanders (Myrna Dell), a woman who introduces herself as a house maid, enters the scene and claims she slept through everything because she had earplugs in. But Joe is aware of her criminal past and she is taken in for questioning. Vincent

---

[73] Virginia Vale column. Western Syndicate Press. June 6, 1946

George Raft in Nocturne

has written the name Dolores on his sheet music. Joe thinks it is a clue, but discovers that Vincent called all of his girls by that name. He gets this from Eujemio (Rudy Robles), a house boy, who enters the scene with items Vincent had sent him to buy. Joe's determination and aggressive manner gets him into fights and in trouble with the department, who ask for his badge. Undaunted, he continues investigating. It appears that Frances Ransom (Lynn Bari) might be the murderer, but as Joe gets closer to her, he does not believe she committed the crime. He discovers that fellow musician Ned "Fingers" Ford found out that Vincent had an affair with his wife, and it is he who committed the murder.

It is interestingly offbeat that the film involves Joe trying to determine whether or not Vincent's death was murder or suicide, but the opening scene informs the viewer that it was the former. Possessing that knowledge and knowing that Joe's hunch is right makes for an experience that's not quite the same as trying to merely unravel the mystery; we are rooting for him to prove he's right to everyone who is trying to stop him.

George Raft continues to exhibit the sort of low key demeanor that works well in post war film noir. As he investigates with dogged determination, he maintains his cool even in situations where he

George Raft in Nocturne

has to resort to violence. One such situation involves the massively imposing Eric Torp (Bern Hoffman) a very large man who does not intimidate Joe. A powerful man, Torp essentially moves the piano around the club floor for Fingers to play. His connection to Fingers is revealed to be much deeper when Susan Flanders is beaten by him, but refuses to reveal any information. Raft's steely eyed approach to the character is not much different than most of the roles he has played, but it works very effectively in this context.

Because Edwin L. Marin never landed on a specific style, directing perhaps even more westerns than crime dramas, his penchant for noir was more a skill for visuals than a stylistic approach to the genre. The opening scene, with a woman sitting quietly, her face never revealed, while Vincent composes "Nocturne" at the piano offers several different shots, from different angles, and the sudden shot that kills Vincent is jarring and effective. The camera moves in this opening scene are remarkable—the camera travels from outside and through the window before landing on Vincent sitting at the piano.

The supporting cast is strong. Lynn Bari had appeared in a bit part then years earlier in George Raft's movie *It Had to Happen*, but by the time of this film, her status had risen to where she was now his co-star. Joe Pevney had been a Broadway actor and would later direct such films as *Three Ring Circus*, *Female on the Beach*, *Man of a Thousand Faces*, and *The Plunderers*. He also directed many TV shows including episodes of *The Munsters*, *Bonanza*, and *Star Trek*. In this film, he is a wicked presence who successfully conveys a prototypical noir villain.

George Raft was pleased with once again playing a good guy on the side of the law and liked the fact that he had an amusing mother figure (Mabel Paige) to better humanize his character in a positive manner. The mother is an enjoyable addition, especially during a sequence where she and her friend playfully try to solve the murder. That sort of comedic scene sounds like it would be out of place in a movie such as this, but it worked – it was the same type of humor Alfred Hitchcock would occasionally insert in his movies. Also, this movie contained many great shots of Hollywood and LA, particularly the RKO lot itself, which is fun for the viewer.

One of the chief reasons Raft liked working with Edwin L. Marin as a director is because Marin was open to his suggestions. This sort of creative input pleased Raft, and he had rewrites done on the script for *Nocturne* to make his character more positive.

After the debacle of *Mr. Ace*, George Raft needed a hit. And with a better producer and studio backing, *Nocturne* was a financial success for the studio and helped put Raft's career back on track. Exhibitors who had written off Raft as "washed up" after *Mr. Ace* admitted to being "pleasantly surprised" at how good this movie was and how well it did in their theaters. The half-a-million-dollar profit the movie garnered for RKO doesn't seem like a lot in the 21st century, but in 1947 it was formidable for a middle-budget movie of this sort.

RKO wasn't sure of this film's likely success, despite how well *Johnny Angel* had done. The sent it out as a double feature in most markets with their B-level comedy *Genius at Work*, starring Wally Brown and Alan Carney. Brown and Carney were a low rent Abbott and Costello who made a handful of 60 minute low budget features that were used as the bottom half of double feature programs. In the era of double features, it was usual for theaters to run a silly comedy with a serious drama to balance the program. To ensure box office for their studio, RKO paired *Nocturne* with one of their own releases as a second feature. It appears that *Nocturne* could have stood alone, and is unlikely that having *Genius at Work* on the program added anything to the box office. But theater owners reported in the trades that audiences enjoyed both movies.

By now George Raft had established himself as a movie tough guy who usually played detectives. He was no longer typecast as a gangster like he had been at Paramount during the 1930s. Although he is well known for having turned down top movies over the years, many of which helped develop Humphrey Bogart's stardom, during this period Raft was making choices that were usually beneficial to his career.

About a month before *Nocturne* was released, George Raft was responding to the criticism and poor box office of *Mr. Ace*, not yet realizing that this next film would be a hit. He decided that he might be more successful financing his own films. So, Raft met with a producer friend, Sam Bischoff, and formed his own production company, Star Films. Bischoff arranged a four picture deal with release through United Artists, who specialized in indie film productions. After approving a script, Raft asked Marin to direct him, feeling very comfortable with the director's methods and approach. So, George Raft's next movie, *Intrigue*, started filming in April of 1947.

INTRIGUE

Directed by Edwin L. Marin
Screenplay by George Slavin and Barry Trivers
Produced by Samuel Bischoff
Cinematography by Lucien Andriiot
Film Editing by George Arthur

Cast:
George Raft	Brad Dunham
June Havoc	Mme. Tamara Baranoff
Helena Carter	Linda Parker
Tom Tully	Marc Andrews
Marvin Miller	Ramon Perez
Michael Ansara	Ramon's Radio Man
Dan Seymour	Karidian
Hassan Ezzat	Karidian's Henchman
Bob Gilbert	Karidian's Henchman
Hassan Khayyam	Karidian's Henchman
Alex Montoya	Karidian's Henchman
Al Rhein	Karidian's Henchman
Edna Holland	Miss Carr
Marc Krah	Nicco
Nancy Hsueh	Mia
Philip Ahn	Louie Chin
Marya Marco	Ling
Philson Ahn	Chinese Official
Phil Taylor	Eddie Lane
Jay C. Flippen	Mike, the bartender
Reginald Billado	Air Force Pilot at Bar
Ralph E. Winters	Air Force Pilot at Bar
Bess Flowers	Table Extra in Bar
Charles Lane	Hotel Desk Clerk

Joe Gray	Hotel Guest
David Leonard	Headwaiter
Nan Wynn	Dinner Club Singer
Peter Chong	Editor
Rodd Redwing	Spy in Editor's Office
Wei Fan Hsueh	Doctor
Jean Wong	Hospital Nurse
Leon Lontoc	Mechanic
Michael Visaroff	Ship's Captain
Victor Sen Yung	Western Union Clerk
Gordon B. Clarke	Hotel Cigar Stand Clerk
Paul Fierro	Lead Thug
Stan Ross	Warehouse Thug
Ronald Louie	Orphan
Kenneth Chuck	Orphan
Richard Wang	Orphan
Hayward Soo Hoo	Orphan

Released October 15, 1947
Star Films, Inc. for United Artists
Running Time: 89 minutes
Black and White

A great deal of publicity was made when George Raft decided to start his own production company with producer Sam Bischoff. Of the four picture deal, Raft was to star in three of the films, while the other, a film noir entitled *Pitfall*, would feature Dick Powell.

Powell had been a successful juvenile in 1930s musicals, but was having trouble maintaining the same success in the 1940s. After success in Preston Sturges' *Christmas in July* (1940), Powell was relegated to acting as support for Abbott and Costello in one of their comedy features, *In the Navy* (1941). Powell redefined his career with the noir classic *Murder My Sweet* (1944), so George Raft and Sam Bischoff securing him for *Pitfall* (1948) was good for their film that would not happen to star Raft.

Bischoff had $5 million to spend on his four productions, and, being a veteran producer, knew how to wisely distribute the money.

George Raft in Intrigue

It looked like a great situation for him and for George Raft. Filming on the first movie for their company, *Intrigue*, was announced in the press at the end of 1946 with the intention to begin filming in the Spring of 1947. Edwin L. Marin was already secure as director, and the film was cast with reliable supporting players like Dan Seymour, Charles Lane and Tom Tully. Raft requested Marvin Miller as his chief nemesis, having worked well with him in *Johnny Angel* at RKO, also directed by Marin.

Producer Bischoff wanted Gloria Swanson to play a key role as the main villain of the narrative. Swanson had not appeared in a film since 1941's *Father Takes a Wife*, save for a recently discovered curio from 1946; a one-reel short where she offers advice to the lovelorn as Miss Gloria. According to Hedda Hopper's column:

> After seeing a test of Gloria Swanson, Sam Bischoff wants her for *Intrigue* opposite George Raft. She'd have the very meaty role of the head of the black market in China. Gloria wants a lot of do-re-mi, but Bischoff's willing to pay.[74]

Unfortunately, the deal never materialized and Miss Swanson would instead wait until *Sunset Boulevard* (1950) for her return to feature films.

June Havoc was then cast in the villainous role of Madame Baranoff, making her first film appearance in two years. Ms. Havoc left films to concentrate on stage work after appearing in *Brewster's Millions* (1944). After completing *Intrigue*, Ms. Havoc appeared in *Gentleman's Agreement* which won the Oscar for Best Picture. Once the screenplay by veteran Barry Trivers and newcomer George Slavin was approved, and with the director and cast set, filming commenced on George Raft's first movie for his own company.

George Raft plays Brad Dunham, a pilot who has been court-martialed and is now living in post-war China involved with smuggling goods into the country. When he doesn't get an increase in pay, he steals back his latest smuggled goods and holds them until being allowed to see the boss, Tamara Baranoff (June Havoc). She agrees to give him a cut of the profits. Brad is then reunited with an old reporter friend, Marc Andrews (Tom Tully) who is in Shanghai investigating crimes within the black market. Tamara is upset about Marc's stories and wants Brad to do something about it, but she is especially upset by Brad's attentions to a pretty social worker, Linda Arnold (Helena Carter). A rival black market operator, Caridian (Dan Seymour), visits Marc and reveals Brad's involvement with the smuggling ring he is investigating. Thugs steal Marc's latest story revealing everything and everyone, and when he plans to deliver the carbon, he is knifed by a man in a passing car. He hands the carbon to Brad, who delivers it to the paper. It reveals that

---

74 Hedda Hopper in Hollywood. Syndicated. April 9, 1947

June Havoc, George Raft, Helena Carter in Intrigue

Tamara's testimony resulted in Brad's court-martial. Brad opens up the warehouse of black market goods and allows citizens to take everything. Brad goes to Tamara and forces her to write a confession exonerating him. Her henchman Ramon (Marvin Miller) enters with a gun, but a fight ensues, and when the gun goes off, the stray bullet kills Tamara. Ramon is arrested, and Brad connects with Linda.

For his first film with his own company, George Raft found a good screenplay, had a good cast, and a good director, resulting in a hit movie. The freedom that Raft had been enjoying since breaking from Warner Brothers continued as a freelancer, even without a big studio behind him. Compare that to when James Cagney broke with the same company to make indie films. Cagney's subsequent releases, *Blood on the Sun, Johnny Come Lately,* and *The Time of Your Life* allowed the actor to stretch a bit, as was his intention, but he did not enjoy the same success as he had at Warner Brothers where he starred in top movies that received awards and award nominations. *The Time of Your Life,* based on the William Saroyan play, was something of an artistic achievement for Cagney, but alienated his fans, who wanted action dramas. By the end of the 1940s, Cagney returned to Warners and once again played a gangster, in *White Heat,* who dies violently at the end of the movie.

George Raft's approach was different. He didn't want to play hoods or heavies, wanted to be the good guy, the hero, and also desired the creative freedom to have some input beyond just acting. He was not a filmmaker, nor a writer, but did have ideas that better adhered to his vision as per his screen persona. Raft realized he was not an actor with the same skill set as, say, Spencer Tracy, but he believed he could at least match the popular John Wayne at using his skills in a manner that best suited his style and approach. He had been consistently doing so since becoming a freelance actor.

Now, with *Intrigue*, George Raft takes this one step further. As being co-owner of his own company with the producer of his films, he had even greater control. Comfortably surrounding himself with talent that understood his approach, especially director Edwin L. Marin, the results were successful.

However, there were still aspects beyond Raft's control. *Intrigue*, for instance, was originally supposed to be about smuggling blood plasma, not canned goods. It was discovered that Chinese-American relations could be hampered if the film was made with that element of the narrative, and Raft agreed to change it. Motion pictures had an enormous impact on the culture during this shaky post-war period, and Raft realized this. He always felt, however, that changing this element and making the smuggling of goods more commonplace, made the narrative less – well – intriguing, despite the film's title.

Still, the performances here are strong, and Raft continues to successfully anchor the narrative with a really grounded performance. He is not a detective, but is still investigating to clear his name. He

Helena Carter, George Raft in Intrigue

is no stranger to crime and the underworld, being tangentially connected. He has a buddy who takes chances and it results in tragedy. He has a good girl he loves, and a bad girl who loves him. All of these have become a sort of formula for a successful George Raft movie, and *Intrigue* is just that. Edwin Schallert in *The Los Angeles Times* called it, "an intense melodrama which offers George Raft one of his best roles."[75]

There are some amusing, sentimental moments in *Intrigue* by way of a tangential scene that takes place at an orphanage where social worker Linda is employed. When Brad goes to visit her, he enjoys connecting with the children and engages them in a baseball game by acting as umpire. The scene is used to point out that the kids aren't getting enough food, causing one young boy to collapse while running bases, thus ending the game. It is the black market that is limiting their supplies. So while the scene is wisely connected to the narrative, it is a fun respite from the noir aspect.

Intrigue was filmed from April thru June of 1947 and was released on October 15, 1947. About a month before the film's release, reporter Armand Archer caught up with George Raft and asked him about his running his own production company. Raft joked

75 Intrigue review. *The Los Angeles Times*. March 3, 1948

that he was now in the throes of middle age and had to find something to fall back on:

> In spite of George's modesty, he has been a moneymaker in Hollywood for 15 years, an enviable record. In the next couple of years will be making films for his own company. He will, however, appear in these films because he knows the Raft name still brings money to the box office. After he establishes his name as a producer, he hopes to get a production berth at a major studio. "At that time," Raft said, "I can go to them and be able to say, "See what I've done. I know a little about this end of the business." After all, when you've been around as long as I have, you should learn something."[76]

Shortly after the release of *Intrigue*, a movie George Raft had already appeared in for producer Benedict Bogeaus was released. Bogeaus' production company had previously produced the Raft feature *Mr Ace*, which had been a box office flop. Raft had a two-picture deal with the producer, and spent two weeks in late 1945 filming his part in an ensemble drama, *Christmas Eve*, which didn't come out until 1947, after the release of *Intrigue*. Unfortunately, it was another box office flop.

---

76 Hollywood Chatter. *New York Democrat and Chronicle*. September 13, 1947

CHRISTMAS EVE

Directed by Edwin L. Marin
Screenplay by Lawrence Stallings from a story by Arch Oboler
Producer Benedict Bogeaus
Cinematography by Gordon Avil
Film Editing by James Smith

Cast:
George Raft	Mario Torio
George Brent	Michael Brooks
Randolph Scott	Jonathan
Joan Blondell	Ann Nelson
Virginia Field	Claire
Dolores Moran	Jean Bradford
Ann Harding	Aunt Matilda
Reginald Denny	Phillip Hastings
Douglass Dumbrille	Dr. Bunyan
Claire Whitney	Mrs. Bunyan
Carl Harbord	Dr. Doremus
Dennis Hoey	Williams
Clarence Kolb	Judge Alston
Molly Lamont	Harriet Rhodes
John Litel	Joe Bland
Walter Sande	Mario's Hood
Joe Sawyer	Private Detective Gimlet
Konstantin Shayne	Gustav Reichman
Andrew Tombes	Auctioneer
Robert Dudley	Robert
John Indrisano	Gateman
Eddie Parks	Beer Drinker
Mike Ragan	Page Boy Bringing Package
Charles Sherlock	Chauffeur

Bert Stevens	Commuter at Terminal
Marie Blake	Reporter
James Conaty	Reporter
Edgar Dearing	Police Sergeant
Paul Kruger	Policeman
J. Farrell MacDonald	Policeman
Brick Sullivan	Policeman
Al Hill	Bartender
Ernest Hilliard	Assistant Bartender

Released October 31, 1947
Benedict Bogeaus productions for United Artists
Running time: 88 minutes
Black and White

Alternate title: *Sinner's Holiday*
Some studies, including his own autobiography, claim Robert Altman contributed to the script without credit

George Raft was pleased with being offered this film as his second Benedict Bogeaus production because it was an ensemble piece that required little time and effort, and he would be sharing the screen with some top level performers. His request for Edwin L. Marin to direct was once again accepted, making this a very comfortable experience for Raft. Unfortunately, as with his previous Bogeaus film, *Christmas Eve* flopped at the box office, once again affecting George Raft's momentum.

While it is not one of Raft's best films, *Christmas Eve* is somewhat better than its reputation. An interesting story that allows vignettes featuring such top talent as George Brent, Randolph Scott, and Raft, *Christmas Eve* is an uneven but sometimes compelling melodrama that ties together well at the end.

George Raft plays Mario Torio who had once been taken in as an orphan, along with two other boys, by a wealthy woman, Matilda Reid (Ann Harding). Mario finds out that Matilda's crooked nephew Phillip Hastings (Reginald Denny) is trying to have her judged as incompetent so he can be given charge of her millions.

Movie ad for Christmas Eve

He wants to go to her, but has a possible 20 year prison sentence for criminal activities in America. He has since settled comfortably as a wealthy club owner in South America. The other two orphans are shown in separate vignettes. George Brent is Michael, a playboy with no money who is trying to find a way to acquire some money. Johnny is a hard drinking rodeo performer who gets involved with a female detective investigating a baby racket at an orphanage. Each of these three men's stories are separate, but they come together at the end when they arrive at Matilda's house for Christmas Eve, convincing the judge (Clarence Kolb) that the eccentricities of Matilda are harmless and even rather amusing.

George Raft's vignette as Mario is the most interesting of the three, as he exhibits a typically solid demeanor as a successful club owner complete with white dinner jacket. However the woman with whom Mario is connected (Virginia Field) has secretly stashed millions for an escaped Nazi liason (Konstantin Shayne) who ties Mario up and slaps him around despite the woman's protests. Of course Mario escapes and defies the warnings of an FBI man (John Litel) about returning to America.

George Brent had been a handsome leading man at Warner Brothers during the 1930s, but left movies to help teach flying during the war effort. When he returned it was determined that as he got older, he had lost his looks and was relegated to B movies and indies. Brent was a good actor, and accepted a role against type in *The Spiral Staircase* (1946), which was a big hit. When he made *Christmas Eve* he was teamed in his segment with Joan Blondell, another popular Warner performer during the 30s.

Randolph Scott was best known for westerns, and the affable, pleasantly sloshed rodeo rider was a good role for him. But it was also his last role in a non-western movie. For the remainder of his career, until his 1962 retirement, Randolph Scott appeared exclusively in westerns.

Even though the overall tone was a bit all over the place it is somehow gratifying that all three actors played roles that adhered to their strengths; Brent being a playboy, Scott being someone connected to cowboys/the West, and Raft being someone with a criminal background.

Ann Harding plays the elderly Matilda even though the actress was actually a full year younger than George Raft. She is made up to look older and plays her character well, being both tough and comical. Her eccentricities include having her cream and sugar for her coffee via delivery by electric train, because it reminded her of her boys.

There is a plot twist involving Raft's character. It appears the trouble he is in was because he was covering up for the nephew to spare Matilda's feelings. This is all straightened out in the end when all three men do indeed show up on Christmas Eve.

There are times when the film drags a bit, and the separate vignettes each have a somewhat different rhythm, making the movie uneven and loosely episodic rather than having a tighter more organic structure. But it is still a reasonably entertaining movie, an average film, and not as weak as its reputation, and poor box office, would have one believe. It probably didn't help that the film has such a holiday specific title for a movie that doesn't have a lot to do with Christmas outside of the characters gathering for Christmas dinner at the very end.

Christmas Eve was financed by a company called Walter E. Heller & Co, who sued the production when its poor box office resulted in their being owed $223,000 on their investment. They initiated foreclosure hearings on the film. The story was remade for television in 1986 with Loretta Young in the Ann Harding role.

For his next film, Raft continued his pact with RKO, who had enjoyed good box office returns on his previous films for the studio. *Race Street* was another film noir and would be the last time Edwin L. Marin directed a George Raft film. It also turned out to be the best Raft movie that Marin directed.

RACE STREET

Directed by Edwin L. Marin
Screenplay by Martin Rackin, suggested by a Maurice Davis story serialized in Turf and Sports Digest from December, 1945 to March, 1946
Produced by Nat Holt
Cinematography by J. Roy Hunt
Film Editing by Samuel E. Beetley

Cast:
George Raft	Gannin
William Bendix	Runson
Marilyn Maxwell	Robbie
Frank Faylen	Dickson
Harry Morgan	Hal Towers
Gale Robbins	Elaine Gannin
Cully Richards	Mike Hadley
Mack Gray	Stringy
Russell Hicks	Easy Mason
Tom Keene	Al
William Forrest	Nick
James Nolan	Herbie
George Turner	Dixie
Richard Benedict	Sam
Dean White	Big Jack
Freddie Steele	Monty
Wong Artarne	Lee
Edna Ryan	Lucille
Charles Lane	Switchboard Operator-Clerk
Jason Robards Sr.	Apartment Desk Clerk
Reginald Billado	Clerk
Barry Brooks	Intern

James Bush	Male Nurse on Ward
Mary Kent	Central Receiving Nurse-Receptionist
George Chandler	Waiter
George Goodman	Turf Club Waiter
Oliver Cross	Turf Club Headwaiter
Charmienne Harker	Cigarette Girl at Turf Club
Jane Worland	Hat Check Girl
Joan Myles	Cigarette Girl
Hercules Mendez	Chef
Michael Wallace	Headwaiter at Billy'
Robert Dudley	Watchman
Cy Kendall	Shoeshine Customer
Mickey Martin	Elevator Boy
Sam McDaniel	Garage Attendant
Carl Saxe	Detective
Michael St. Angel	Clerk
Al Murphy	Drunk
Joe Gilbert	Nightclub Patron
Larry Steers	Nightclub Patron
Paul Power	Nightclub Patron
Bert Stevens	Nightclub Patron
Al Rhein	Man in Joe's Bar
Frank J. Scannell	Bar Patron
Eric Wilton	Bar Patron
Frank McLure	Racetrack Spectator
James Conaty	Racetrack Spectator
William H. O'Brien	Racetrack Spectator
Franklyn Farnum	Bit
Eddie Arden	Bit
Mike Lally	Bit
June Pickerell	Bit
George Murray	Bit

Released June 22, 1948
RKO Radio Pictures
Running Time: 79 minutes
Black and White

Plans for George Raft to star in *Race Street* were announced in the press in early 1947 and William Bendix was indicated as co-star at the same time. However, early newspaper accounts offered much different stories than what the film turned out to be. An item in the *New York Daily News* stated:

> George Raft and William Bendix will be teamed by RKO Radio as rivals in *Race Street*, a melodrama of racketeering and the fourth estate. Raft will portray a former war correspondent reduced to handicapping horses for New York daily as a result of a slip made overseas. Bendix will play a bookie king who tries to buy him off when Raft's selecting talent proves uncanny.[77]

Some elements of this idea do appear in the finished film, and it is far more accurate than what Edwin Schallert's column stated a couple of weeks later:

> The return of Anne Jeffreys from her big *Street Scene* engagement in New York is being counted on tentatively for July. At that time, if she is free, even temporarily, of her run of the play contract, RKO will bring her back to pictures for *Race Street*, which will star George Raft and William Bendix. And there's no doubt that stardom is in sight for Anne, after her success in the stage musical, as well as, prior to that, in a grand opera. The only odd thing is that the film slated for her is not a musical, but a race track tale, as its title implies, with Bendix scheduled to portray her father and Raft a newspaperman who falls in love with Miss Jeffreys in the story.[78]

Anne Jeffreys ended up being placed by RKO in the Randolph Scott western *Return of the Badmen*, after which she returned to the stage for a few years. When she returned to the screen in the early 1950s, it was for television, including a starring role on the series *Topper*. She didn't appear in another theatrical feature until 1962.

Marilyn Maxwell was hired for the leading female role in *Race Street*, and William Bendix did not play her father, nor did George

---

[77] Raft and Bendix To Appear. *New York Daily News*. January 12, 1947

[78] Lead in Race Street awaits Anne Jeffreys. *Los Angeles Times*. January 29, 1947

Raft play a newspaperman. Maxwell had been playing small roles in comedies and musicals at MGM, including *Lost in a Harem* with Abbott and Costello, and *The Show Off* with Red Skelton. She would later connect with Bob Hope for several films (and, allegedly offscreen as well) and would include strong dramatic turns in movies like *Champion*, a boxing drama with Kirk Douglas.

Edwin L. Marin was set to direct, which was announced by the press rather triumphantly making mention of his previous hit films with George Raft:

> Edwin L. Marin has been signed by RKO to direct *Race Street*, a melodrama of racketeering and the Fourth Estate, in which George Raft will star. Marin directed Raft in two previous RKO pictures, *Johnny Angel* and *Nocturne*, both of which rate high in this star's list of box-office successes.[79]

Marin was pleased to discover he would be able to take advantage of the San Francisco location sites -- the city in which the film was set. RKO announced that they wanted to be more authentic with their contemporary dramas, and shoot on location:

> RKO announced that *Race Street*, George Raft's third starring vehicle for this studio, will be shot almost entirely in and around San Francisco. This is in line with its policy of shooting major productions in authentic locales and backgrounds. *Race Street* is scheduled to start on Aug. 18. Dozens of well-known newspaper, night clubs, racing, sport and historic spots will be used In filming this melodrama of race track rackets and the Fourth Estate.[80]

The filming of *Race Street* began in August of 1947, just a couple of months after George Raft completed work on *Intrigue*, and continued through to late September. While some of it was indeed shot on location, there were also plenty of scenes that took place on the convenient studio sound stages.

George Raft plays racketeer Dan Gannin, who is informed by his trusted bookie Hal Towers (Harry Morgan) that a group of rival gangsters are insisting he pay protection money. Dan wants to

---

79 Raft Gets Vehicle in Race Street. *Rochester Democrat and Chronicle*. February 28, 1947

80 Arthur Pollock's Theater column. *Brooklyn Daily Eagle*. August 15, 1947

Movie ad for Race Street

get out of the gambling rackets and has started a new legit nightclub which is set to open that night. Dan tells Hal that he wants him to buy into the club and also leave the rackets. Hal is tenacious and wants to fight the syndicate that is threatening him. Dan is at the club opening with his girl, Robbie (Marilyn Maxwell). When Hal does not show up to Dan's club opening as promised, he goes over to Hal's apartment along with police detective Barney Runson (William Bendix), a longtime friend of both men. They find Hal lying dead at the bottom of a flight of stairs. Barney warns Dan not to retaliate, to let the law take care of things. Dan does not listen. When Dan is offered protection money, he goes along with it in order to find out who killed Hal. Circumstances continue with Dan being kidnapped, roughed up, and even discovering that Robbie is connected with the syndicate. But he is determined to find out who killed his friend. Robbie claims she was forced to go along with the racketeers and begs Dan's forgiveness. He believes her until he leaves her apartment and hears the desk clerk connecting a phone call from her to Dickson, the head racketeer (Frank Faylen). Realizing for sure that he has been double-crossed, Dan returns home and is put in protective custody by Barney. As they are leaving the apartment, they are met by Al (Tom Keene) who had been one of Dan's bookies, but is now working for Dickson. Dickson then enters and Dan lunges at him and starts a fight, as Barney joins. When Dickson prepares to shoot Barney, Dan dives between them and takes the bullet, then knocks out Dickson. Dan dies in Barney's arms.

Race Street is really a celebration of a cinematic formula, not only of film noir, but of what has become a typical George Raft movie. Its noir elements include a voiceover narration by William Bendix as the Barney character, the film's moral compass. He's just as tough as the others but chose a career path on the side of the law, rather than the rackets. George Raft's character of Dan is somewhere in the middle. He made his mark in the rackets, generated enough money, and now wants to settle into the clean life of a nightclub owner. Unlike Barney, Dan was not willing to start at the bottom and engage in a struggle. He made money a quicker, easier way, albeit illegal. Thus, when Hal is murdered by thugs, both Dan and Barney are aware of the type, but have different ways of confronting it. And, of course, Dan has no intention of heeding Barney's warnings to back off and allow the law to take care of things.

In one of the film's strongest scenes, the men have just discovered Hal's dead body, and Barney is sternly warning Dan not to retaliate. Barney is repeating himself, but Dan angrily stares straight ahead, doesn't even budge, throughout. And we realize what he is thinking. George Raft is one of the few actors who could convey so much by just staring without moving his face, body, even his eyes. Just that stern, straight-ahead look informs the viewer of just what the character is thinking.

Raft turns in one of his best performances. He does a great job walking that line between good guy and shady guy as he normally does, but the emotional stakes felt higher thanks to the close involvement of his character's friends.

Along with the dark imagery and the narration, the script also throws in a few catchphrases. Dan (and Hal) use the phrase "Stay with it," as a declaration of encouragement and triumph. Barney uses "What a coincidence" in a sarcastic, all-knowing manner. It's a bit cheeky, but with the best of intentions. And it is certainly calculated, but it is what audiences wanted to see. Finally, there is a dollop of sentiment underlying the narrative, and especially at the conclusion. Barney and Dan have a conflict as to their perspective. They are not adversaries, in fact they are friends, but Dan's approach is from the perspective of a racketeer, while Barney's is from a detective's standpoint. So when Dan dies and the picture fades to a night time shot of San Francisco, and we hear Barney's narrative voiceover conclude with, "I'm still here, because I had a good friend," it sentimentally ties up their relationship effectively, despite its being a cliché.

Race Street was something of a transition for RKO and for George Raft. It began production while Dore Schary was still in charge of the studio, and concluded just as Howard Hughes took over. And, it was the last film in which Raft was directed by Edwin L. Marin. Marin switched to directing exclusively westerns, leaving this film for work at 20th Century Fox, and also at Warner Brothers. When his Warner film *Colt 45* became one of the top box office hits among the studio's western films, they signed Marin to a contract. Sadly, Marin died in 1951, only three years after completing *Race Street*. Because he was not a stylist in the manner of John Ford, Marin is not known as a top western film director. And although he has the same cleverness as any film noir director, he has not been given enough attention for his work in this sub-genre either. Marin did some of his best work with George Raft.

Race Street was another moneymaker, and the studio was pleased with the results. However, George Raft was eager to produce another film for his own production company. Raft was presented with a script by producer Joseph Ermolieff, who had a deal to produce it for RKO in 1939, but the production was cancelled (resulting in Ermolieff suing the studio). He wanted Raft and Sam Bischoff to consider producing *Outpost in Morocco* through their Star Productions. Raft liked the script, and even though this story about the French Foreign Legion was very atypical for him, he decided to film it with himself in the lead. He and Bischoff even arranged to shoot some location footage in Morocco.

OUTPOST IN MOROCCO

Directed by Robert Florey
Screenplay by Charles Grayson and Paul de Sainte Colombe from
 a story by Joseph Ermolieff
Produced by Joseph Emrolieff and Samuel Bischoff
Cinematography by Lucien Andriot
Film Editing by George M. Arthur

Cast:
George Raft	Capt. Paul Gerard
Marie Windsor	Cara
Akim Tamiroff	Lt. Glysko
John Litel	Col. Pascal
Ernö Verebes	Bamboule
Eduard Franz	Emir of Bel-Rashad
Crane Whitley	Caid Osman
Damian O'Flynn	Commandant Louis Fronval
Michael Ansara	Rifle Dispenser
John Doucette	Card-Playing Soldier
Ivan Triesault	Leader
James Nolan	Legionnaire Colonel's Aide
Gordon Armitage	Legionnaire
George Bruggeman	Legionnaire
Jackie Searl	Legionnaire
Paul Bradley	Nightclub Patron
Ralph Brooks	Nightclub Patron
Shep Houghton	Nightclub Patron
Perk Lazelle	Nightclub Patron
Sol Murgi	Nightclub Patron
George Nardelli	Nightclub Patron
Barry Norton	Nightclub Patron
Suzanne Ridgway	Nightclub Patron

Cosmo Sardo	Bartender
William Wilkerson	Arab

Released May 2, 1949
Moroccan Pictures for United Artists
Running time: 92 minutes
Black and White

George Raft was pleased to be acting in a film that was quite unlike his usual work, and to be bringing his established screen persona into another setting. An adventure about the Foreign Legion with some location shooting was quite a stretch from *Scarface* or even *Johnny Angel*. Location shooting in Morocco was completed far ahead of time, a full month before director Robert Florey was hired.

Raft wanted Ava Gardner to play his leading lady, but she was not available, so Marie Windsor was cast. Windsor had been in films for the entire decade of the 1940s but usually in brief, uncredited parts until scoring opposite John Garfield in *Force of Evil*. This is what led her to *Outpost in Morocco*, at four times her previous salary.

Joseph Ermolieff had originally brought the story to RKO in 1939 who planned to film it, but cancelled the production once World War Two broke out. Ermolieff responded by suing the studio. It was nearly ten years later when Ermolieff struck deal with George Raft and Sam Bischoff to make the movie with their Star Films production company. They merged with Ermolieff and created Moroccan Films and received financial support from Pathe in France.

After Raft got permission to film in Morocco with actual members of the Foreign Legion as extras, he traveled there in December of 1947 with second unit director Richard Rosson and cinematographer Lucien Androit who spoke fluent French. They spent three months filming battle scenes and chases around the base at Bal Archard, returning in March of 1948 with over 80,000 feet of film. It was then up to the filmmakers to match this footage with resemblant locations in the US, and prepare a shooting script. Interiors were shot at the Samuel Goldwyn studios in Los Angeles.

Marie Windsor and George Raft in Outpost in Morocco

George Raft plays Captain Paul Gerard of the Foreign Legion who is leading a troop to a fort, but must stop in Bel-Rashad. He is assigned to escort Cara (Marie Windsor), daughter of the Emir, to Bel-Rashad, and investigate anti-French corruption. It takes tend days, during which Gerard and Cara fall in love. Gerard ten-day journey Gerard and Cara fall in love. Upon arriving, Gerard meets with Commandant Fronval (Damian O'Flynn) and Lieutenant Glysko (Akim Tamiroff). During his investigation, Gerard finds that the people are being armed with modern firearms, but is found out, so he hides out with Cara and then escapes. When he goes to report this to headquarters, he and his troop discover it has been destroyed and the Legionnaires, including Commandant Fronval are dead. Gerard then orders that the Emir in Bel-Rashad be captured. Lt. Glysko instead captures Cara as a hostage. After the Emir destroys the fort's water supply, a rainstorm is greeted with cheers from the troops but it destroys the makeshift mud wall they built to replace the concrete one that was felled by the Emir's men. Gerard then orders his men to plant land mines along the route that leads to the now missing wall. Cara rides through the minefield to warn her father, forcing Gerard to order the detonation of the mines and kill Cara, the Emir, and his men. The warriors then lay their rifles down in front of Gerard and his men, indicating peace has been restored.

Even though a foreign legion action drama seemed incongruous for George Raft, moviegoers didn't seem to mind. They liked the fact that the film had a lot of action, and that Raft was a crusading soldier who made decisions as well as sacrifices. It enjoyed a reasonable profit at the box office. And while Raft really did little more than utilize his same screen persona in another setting, his natural ability did shine through. Always effective when exhibiting his minimalist low-key nuance, Raft's reaction is especially powerful when he must sadly be forced to give the order that results in Cara's death.

Reviews were generally good with the critic for the trade magazine *Motion Picture Daily* stating:[81]

> All of the color, intrigue, and adventure popularly associated with Africa and the French Foreign Legion runs through this Moroccan Pictures production. An added element of authenticity is provided by the fact that much of the picture was filmed in Morocco with the aid of hundreds of Spahis, the famed native cavalry. There are moments of suspense and an abundance of drama and action. Under the directorial guidance of Robert Florey, *Outpost in Morocco* is well-knit. Florey has employed the native cast with vigor and imagination and has capture their wild dash across the plain with excellent treatment.

While his most recent films as a freelancer had mostly been successful at the box office, George Raft also realized he wasn't quite the star he had been and was seriously considering retirement. Even after he accepted his next role, *Johnny Allegro* at Columbia, with Nina Foch as his co-star, he was telling the press that his days in movies might be numbered:

> George Raft telling why he wants to retire sounds sad indeed. "What the heck! I'm not getting any better pictures. And 1 figure youth must supplant age." He'd like

---

81 Outpost in Morocco review. *Motion Picture Daily*. March 25, 1949

to keep on acting all right, with box office names like Rita Hayworth, Joan Crawford, Greer Garson, and Barbara Stanwyck for co-stars. Or Ava Gardner, a virtual unknown when she starred with Raft in *Whistle Stop.* "I tried to get her for *Outpost in Morocco,* George related, "Metro said they had her lined up for many things. I help everybody but myself. Everybody else gets a break but me. Maybe I'm not any good." George's recent co-stars have been Marie Windsor, Marilyn Maxwell, and June Havoc. His present assignment teams him with Nina Foch. All talented lovely gals but not the box office draw of Crawford or Stanwyck. After an RKO picture here in March, and a probable picture In Paris in the summer, George wants to retire to a villa on the French Riviera. Maybe he'd fly back occasionally to produce pictures if it could be arranged or as George says: "If anybody had faith in my ability." Retirement as an actor would end nearly 20 years on the screen in which he has made about 50 pictures. He has never looked at himself on the screen after one quick peek in his first picture: "I ran like the devil." [82]

While it is difficult to determine if George Raft was truly serious about leaving movies, financial obligations kept him working. And he was committed to a few upcoming projects, the first of which was *Johnny Allegro.*

---

82 George Hansacker "Hollywood" column. Syndicated. January, 1949

JOHNNY ALLEGRO

Directed by Ted Tetzlaff
Screenplay by Karen DeWolf and Guy Endore from a story by James Edward Grant
Produced by Irving Starr
Cinematography by Joseph Biroc
Film Editing by Jerome Thoms

Cast:
George Raft	Johnny Allegro
Nina Foch	Glenda Chapman
George Macready	Morgan Vallin
Will Geer	Schultzy
Gloria Henry	Addie
Ivan Triesault	Pelham Vetch
Harry Antrim	Pudgy
William Phillips	Roy
Eddie Acuff	Sam
Mary Bear	Nurse Baldwin
Paul E. Burns	Gray
Frank Dae	Dr. Jaynes
Sol Gorss	Jeffrey
Thomas Browne	Frank
Walter Rode	Grote
Frank O'Connor	Coroner
George Offerman Jr.	Elevator Boy
Joe Palma	Guard
Steve Pendleton	Police Detective
Fred F. Sears	Desk Clerk
Larry Thompson	Operator
Harlan Warde	Coast Guard Officer
Matilda Caldwell	Servant

Chuck Hamilton	Armored Car Guard
Brick Sullivan	Armored Car Guard
Sayre Dearing	Man in Basement
Franklyn Farnum	Man in Basement
William H. O'Brien	Nightclub Waiter
Cosmo Sardo	Waiter
Barry Norton B	Nightclub Patron

Released May 26, 1949
Columbia Pictures
Running time: 81 minutes
Black and White

When George Raft started appearing in crime dramas of the same basic style and manner, it was accepted, or dismissed, as a predictable formula that had become common for Raft during this period of his career, as the term film noir hadn't happened. Raft had been freelancing since the mid 1940s with reasonable success despite a couple of misfires. And it was film noir that seemed to be the best place for his low-key stoicism.

Johnny Allegro is just such a movie, and contains all of the basic elements of the sub-genre, some of which became cliches. But Raft's stoic manner, his quiet delivery, and his squinty nuanced stares fit the title role of this admittedly formulaic drama, that contains some interesting, offbeat elements.

George Raft plays the title role, a former racketeer who escaped from prison, joined the O.S.S. and risked his life to save others, becoming a hero. Now settled into a quiet, successful business as a florist, he is greeted by Glenda (Nina Foch), a pretty blonde in a hotel lobby who hugs him and whispers for him to pretend he knows her. He goes along with it, helping her to evade a police detective, and then, over a period of days, the two become romantically involved. Johnny is then met by a government agent named Schultzy (Will Geer), who knows of Johnny's past. Johnny agrees to go quietly with him, but Schultzy believes Johnny's war heroism is notable enough to allow him a second chance. He asks Johnny to get as much information about Glenda as possible. Johnny sets up a

Movie ad for Johnny Allegro

scene where he shoots and kills a policeman and insists that Glenda flee with him so he doesn't get caught. They go to a secluded island where they are met by Morgan Vallin (George Macready), who turns out to be Glenda's husband. Suspicious, he asks Johnny to turn over his gun. Johnny is especially unsettled about this because the gun remains filled with blanks from the fake cop killing. Vallin doesn't believe in guns, preferring a bow and arrow, and is an excellent marksman with that weapon. Johnny fakes illness and goes to a hospital where he secretly meets with Schultzy, who tells him Vallin's plans to flood the area with counterfeit money. Johnny is asked to find out where that counterfeit money is hidden. Glenda remains attracted to Johnny, and Vallin discovers this and threatens Johnny. When Vallin is preparing to leave the island, Johnny contacts Schultzy so he and his men move in. Glenda stops Vallin from shooting Johnny with his bow and arrow and when the men confront each other and fight, Vallin is killed.

Johnny Allegro was originally titled *The Big Jump* when George Raft signed on to play the lead in August of 1948. It was his first film at Columbia since *She's Gotta Have It* in 1935. Jane Greer was originally sought for the female lead, but it eventually went to Nina Foch, who was under contract at Columbia. Foch had scored on Broadway in *John Loves Mary* and was touring with the play when Columbia head Harry Cohn summoned her back to start making pictures or, he stated, Rodgers and Hammerstein would owe his studio $5000. Filming went so long on *Johnny Allegro* that George Raft missed an opportunity. RKO wanted him to star in Don Siegel's *The Big Steal*, but Raft was still active on this film when production started. Robert Mitchum replaced him and, ironically, that film's leading lady was Jane Greer.

Critics were becoming dismissive of George Raft's established approach to his screen roles. Bosley Crowther of *The New York Times* stated in his review of *Johnny Allegro:* "Nothing with any vague resemblance to vivid acting is contributed by Mr. Raft, who has become one of the most indifferent and comatose actors extant."[83] Raft's performance wasn't really any different than most of the roles he'd been playing since freelancing. It's just that his part in *Johnny Allegro* was a very low-key character. Johnny is experienced, weary, and settled. His eventual circumstances have him careful, cunning, a cynic who is no stranger to dangerous situations. Johnny has accomplished a prison escape and decorated war heroism in his time. The dangers of gangsters and threats hardly phase

---

83 Johnny Allegro review. *The New York Times*. May 31, 1949.

him. And George Raft handles this role effectively, always looking as though he is thinking, studying, and calculating as he moves through the proceedings. There is even a short dance sequence.

The 23 year age difference between Raft and leading lady Nina Foch wasn't really out of the ordinary during this era. In fact, Raft was, curiously, one of the few actors who claimed to be older. Raft was born in 1901 but claimed to have been born in 1895. Even in interviews from this period he would call himself past 50 rather than nearing 50. But despite this age difference, the actors connect well on screen.

George Macready's Morgan Vallen character is an offbeat villain with the odd quirk of preferring the bow and arrow as a weapon. He loftily explains how its scope and accuracy is superior to a gun, and demonstrates its effectiveness more than once in the movie. Johnny quips, "how would someone commit suicide with that?" Macready is the sort of post-war accented villain who represents the stereotypical invader. His living in seclusion on an island as he plans a massive counterfeiting exercise is as diabolical as any of the violence he exhibits. He and Johnny respect each other while also despising each other. It is an effective dynamic.

Vallen's character and the island setting turns this noir into something resembling *The Most Dangerous Game* in its final act which is a bit incongruous with the movie's first half, but t certainly made the film feel more memorable than it might have otherwise.

Ted Tetzlaff was an Oscar nominated cinematographer who became a director in 1941. This is the same Ted Tetzlaff whom Raft accused of favoring Carole Lombard when they did *Rumba* years earlier, and whom he believed was doing the same thing on the film *The Princess Comes Across*, promoting Raft to walk off the project. Apparently, George Raft had no such misgivings for Tetzlaff as a director, and his helming of this movie was most effective in maintaining its suspense and interest.

Johnny Allegro ended up being made for a reasonable budget because Columbia was a pretty strong studio by this time. George Raft's old co-star Humphrey Bogart was making films at the studio at the same time, and the two did get together while Raft was working on *Johnny Allegro*. According to actor Emil Sitka, who appeared regularly in Columbia short comedies:

> George Raft and Humphrey Bogart would come to our set together and watch The Three Stooges work. A lot of the bigger stars working at Columbia used to do that. Raft and Bogart would come on the set, greet (producer-director) Jules (White), talk to the Stooges briefly, and then watch us shoot a few scenes. They were nice guys and seemed really fascinated by the slapstick we were doing.[84]

Johnny Allegro ended up being the most commercially successful film noir George Raft did during the post-war era. Raft was comfortable and satisfied with the film's success and had several projects lined up, including another movie for RKO and a cameo that would take him on location in France. But first, Raft was summoned by director Roy Del Ruth, with whom he'd worked on three other films. Del Ruth had his own production company now, and wanted George Raft to star in an offbeat film noir that had a distinct religious theme. Raft accepted, and *Red Light* featured him in one of his best performances from this period.

---

84 Interview with the author - 1980

RED LIGHT

Directed and Produced by Roy Del Ruth
Screenplay by George Callahan from a story by Don "Red" Barry
Cinematography by Bert Glennon
Film Editing by Richard Heermance

Cast:
George Raft	John Torno
Virginia Mayo	Carla North
Gene Lockhart	Warni Hazard
Raymond Burr	Nick Cherney
Harry Morgan	Rocky
Barton MacLane	Strecker
Arthur Franz	Jess Torno
Ken Murray	Ken Murray
Stanley Clements	Bellboy
William Frawley	Hotel Clerk
Arthur Shields	Redmond
Frank Orth	Stoner
Phillip Pine	Pablo Cabrillo
William Phillips	Ryan
Robert Espinoza	Miguel
Movita	Trina
Brick Sullivan	Red, a Truck Driver
Bob Perry	Red's Helper
Victor Sen Yung	Vincent, Houseboy
Al Hill	Burt
Edwin Max	Max Appleby aka Bert Adams
Leonard Bremen	Bookie
Claire Carleton	Waitress
Bill Cartledge	Elevator Operator
Paul Frees	Bellhop

Mack Gray	Bookie
Chuck Hamilton	Detective Arresting Nick
Bob Jellison	Man in Hotel Room
Soledad Jiménez	Pablo's Mother
Phyllis Kennedy	Chambermaid
Joe Kirk	Reporter in Newsreel
David Leonard	Man Reading Bible
Sol Murgi	Convict
Jack Overman	Hotel Clerk
Charles Ferguson	Reporter at Airport
John Wald	Reporter at Airport

Released September 30, 1949
Running Time 83 minutes
Roy Del Ruth productions for United Artists
Black and White

George Raft was comfortable having worked with Roy Del Ruth in the past, and the script he was given appealed to his interests. Del Ruth's production company was formed in 1947 and produced three feature films of which *Red Light* was the third. Del Ruth was a director whose worked dated back to the Mack Sennett silent comedies, despite the man himself being describe as a very serious, unsmiling sort (garnering him the nickname "Laughing Boy" in some quarters). Del Ruth was one of the highest paid directors through the 1930s into the early 1940s, but his stature took a hit with the negative critical reaction to *The Babe Ruth Story* (1948), made for his own company. *Red Light* was the followup.

Raft liked the screenplay for *Red Light* because it was an offbeat approach to the usual crime thriller he had been making. There was a religious subtext, a sadistic and brutal villain, and Raft's character was allowed to expand beyond the stoicism for which he was (sometimes negatively) known and show real emotion in some scenes.

George Raft plays Johnny Torno, a businessman who owns and operates a trucking company. His brother Jess (Arthur Franz) is a priest who had just been released from a World War Two prisoner-

George Raft in Red Light

of-war camp, this event being captured in a newsreel. Nick Cherney (Raymond Burr) is serving time in prison for having embezzled from Johnny's company when he sees the newsreel footage. Nick is to be released from prison in another four years, so he concocts a scheme to get even with Johnny by hiring a former inmate acquaintance named Rocky (Harry Morgan) to murder Jess, and to have this happen before Nick's release from prison, giving him an air-tight alibi. Johnny finds Jess in his hotel room dying. Jess's parting words indicate the key to the murder can be found in the room's Gideon bible. However, the bible is missing. Unsettled by the lackluster methods of the police investigation, Johnny decides to investigate on his own. Questioning everyone who had stayed in the room, he meets Carla (Virginia Mayo) who agrees to help him. Rocky decides to blackmail Nick while the two are on a train, so Nick attacks Rocky and throws him off the moving train, ostensibly to his death. Nick fears Johnny has found the bible, so he goes to his office to search. While there, he sees company manager Warni Hazard (Gene Lockhart) whom he pursues. Hazard hides under a propped-up train car in the freight yard. Nick finds him and kicks out the jack, causing the car to crush Hazard. Johnny finally finds the bible in the possession of Pablo Cabrillo (Phillip Pine), a veteran blinded during the war, who keeps it for sentimental comfort. He agrees to let Johnny look inside. The message is Romans 12:19 which speaks against vengeance. Nick, nearby, believes he is no longer in danger and leaves. As he gets to the stairs, he is met by an enraged Rocky who survived the fall from the train. There is a shootout, alerting Johnny, who is injured, but Rocky is killed, and before he dies, he reveals Nick as the one who planned Jess's murder. Nick escapes and is pursued by Johnny and the police. Nick tries to shoot Johnny but his gun is empty. Johnny refuses to shoot Nick because of the message in the bible. Nick turns to run and steps on a live cable connected to the neon sign on Johnny's building, and is electrocuted.

Roy Del Ruth had set up his production company at the low budget Monogram Studios in 1947 to make *It Happened on 5th Avenue*. He was going to follow it up with this film, originally titled *Mr Gideon*, after purchasing the original story's rights from Don "Red" Barry, who had made his name as a cowboy star in B westerns. Monogram formed Allied Artists to make more prestigious movies, and that is where Del Ruth produced *The Babe Ruth Story*. It was decided that Monogram would arrange for United Artists to handle the distribution of *Red Light* along with another of their films, *Gun Crazy*.

Del Ruth shot some location footage in San Francisco in 1947 but production on the film was delayed. There were plans to cast Robert Ryan as Johnny, Edward G. Robinson as Nick, Charles Bickford as Rocky and William Bendix as the detective. George Raft signed to play Torno in February of 1949 after Raymond Burr, Harry Morgan, and Barton MacLaine were already cast. Virginia Mayo was borrowed from Warner Brothers around the same time. Filming began in March of 1949.

While George Raft has opportunities to show some real emotion in scenes, the focus on this film's villain and his sadistic brutality makes a nice contrast. Raymond Burr became so well-known for his later television work as crusading defense lawyer Perry Mason or wheelchair-bound lawman Ironside, it is something of a revelation to explore his earlier work and find that he established himself in bad guy roles, perhaps most notably in Alfred Hitchcock's *Rear*

George Raft and Virginia Mayo in Red Light

Window (1954), and in the Dean Martin - Jerry Lewis comedy *You're Never Too Young* (1955). Burr adds a great deal of creepy elements to the Nick character, his satisfied smirk and chuckle after crushing Hazard under a train car being especially notable.

The contrast this offers against the more grounded Johnny character is discernible. George Raft has become quite comfortable in this type of role, and when he is called upon to exhibit greater emotion, speaking more loudly with a yearning and pleading in his voice, it not only exhibits his character's desperation, but the ability of the actor to recall earlier films like *Souls at Sea* where similar reactions were utilized.

As a further contrast, the character of Rocky as played by Harry Morgan (then still billed as Henry Morgan), is a gruesomely snarling counterpart to the more low-key evil of Nick. While Nick is cool and passionless, Rocky is trembling and aggressive. Nick's evil is in his actions. Rocky's are displayed by his manner. Their own conflict seems inevitable even at the outset of the narrative.

Virginia Mayo was a working actress on her way for much of the 1940s, mostly working in comedies and musicals. She appeared opposite Bob Hope in *The Princess and the Pirate* and supported Danny Kaye in several of his hit movies, including *Up in Arms, Wonder Man, The Kid from Brooklyn, The Secret Life of Walter Mitty,* and *A Song is Born.* Mayo appeared in a remarkable six feature films in 1949, but it was an important year for her. Just prior to *Red Light,* Mayo turned in one of her finest performances in one of her best films, *White Heat.* Playing the smart-talking moll of a vicious gangster played by James Cagney, she holds her own effectively against one of the actor's most explosive, manic performances. There is a scene in *White Heat* where Cagney was to kick a chair out from under her, causing her to fall. Cagney was reticent about doing the scene, hurting a woman, despite his character being a cruel and violent psychopath. Cagney insisted Mayo fall comfortably onto a couch so it was not as harmful and aggressive. The is mentioned because in *Red Light,* George Raft had similar misgivings about his character brutalizing Mayo's, as reported in the press:

> George Raft may be a tough guy on and off the screen, but when it comes to women apparently he just goes soft. The *Red Light* script called for rugged Raft to slug Virginia Mayo. Raft refused. Producer Roy Del Ruth argued. Then pleaded. But it was no good. George said no. Finally Mr Del Ruth got an idea: Virginia was in front of the camera Raft was offstage At the proper moment Georgie slapped his hands hard and Virginia reacted as if she'd taken it on the chin. And that's how the scene was shot with George never laying a hand on his leading lady.[85]

The cast for *Red Light* is rounded out by several familiar names, including Barton MacLaine as a police detective who is annoyed by Johnny's intrusive investigation, as well as William Frawley, Victor Sen Yung, and Stanley Clements in smaller roles.

Critics were generally satisfied with *Red Light*, and some pointed out that Raft exhibited more emotion in some scenes. However, they continued to dismiss his nuanced minimalist style of acting as

---

85 Lloyd Sloan. And You Hear Such Interesting Stories. *Los Angeles Evening Citizen News.* April 9, 1949.

merely limited and often dull. Moviegoers continued to disagree and *Red Light* was successful at the box office. However, production costs were somewhat higher than the usual low budget thriller, so the profit this film made was not as strong.

Red Light is one of the better George Raft movies of the postwar era, but the religious theme seems a bit distracting and even forced. It doesn't organically fit into the context too comfortably. But that's really a trifling quibble based on the compelling drama and solid performances. It is a well-crafted movie, enhanced further by Dimitri Tiomkin's score

Some may argue that the religious themes are interesting, especially since it is something not often seen in noir. But it does often feel like the movie is at odds with itself. We have Jess and the Bible warning against violence, but then the rest of the movie has so many violent scenes, including the trailer dropping on Hazard and Nick's death—his electrocution, which isn't the fault of any other character, and almost feels like he's been struck down by God. But even though the moment at the end where we move to a close-up of Raft's face as he has his epiphany that he shouldn't kill Nick seems a bit forced, it is commendable how the film quickly establishes that Torno is not a religious man, even though he cares deeply for his brother. This makes it feel more like his character undergoes some sort of positive change over the course of the film.

Red Light is a great looking movie—the lighting we see in the church scene and that final shot of the neon sign as the end credits role are notably strong visuals.

For his next movie, George Raft was back at RKO for one last time. However, despite still having fans, and having been a leading man in successful projects for decades, Raft was beginning to lose his stature. His films were profitable, but less so than they once had been, and it had been some time since he had the backing and support of a major studio. While his freelancing had been comparatively successful, interest in his type of movie started to wan. And his upcoming RKO movie was yet another crime thriller.

A DANGEROUS PROFESSION

Directed by Ted Tetzlaff
Screenplay by Martin Rackin and Warren Duff
Produced by Robert Sparks
Cinematography by Robert de Grasse
Film Editing by Frederic Knudtson

Cast:
George Raft	Vince Kane
Ella Raines	Lucy Brackett
Pat O'Brien	Joe Farley
Bill Williams	Claude Brackett
Jim Backus	Police Lt. Nick Ferrone / Narrator
Roland Winters	Jerry McKay
Betty Underwood	Elaine Storm
Robert Gist	Roy Collins - aka Max Gibney
David Bauer	Matthew Dawson
Jonathan Hale	Roger Lennert - Lucy's Attorney
Paul Maxey	Judge Thompson
Frances Morris	Mrs. Frances Farley
Mack Gray	Fred - Taxi Driver
Yvonne Rob	Vi
Lynne Roberts	Miss Wilson
Dick Ryan	Gus, Policeman
Michael St. Angel	Roberts - Law Firm Receptionist
Burk Symon	Herman
Jim Drum	Wally
Gloria Gabriel	Kane's Secretary
Nancy Valentine	Dawson's Secretary
Charmienne Harker	Cigarette Girl
Kenner G. Kemp	Customer in McKay's Restaurant
Phyllis Kennedy	Maid in Kane's Apartment

Allen Wood	Bellhop
Harry Brown	Room Clerk
Dick Dickinson	Thin Man
Frank Shannon	Barman
Don Dillaway	Drunk
Buck Harrington	Prisoner
Mike Lally	Policeman
Barry Brooks	Detective
William J. O'Brien	Clerk
Allan Ray	Clerk
Ken Terrell	Man
Ralph Volkie	Man
Terry Wilson	Man

Released November 26, 1949
RKO Radio Pictures
Running time: 79 minutes
Black and White

A Dangerous Profession was originally called *The Bail Bond Racket,* and was written with Humphrey Bogart in mind. Bogart was interested, but a deal was never reached. Then Fred MacMurray used his own money to option the screenplay for himself to star. Nicholas Ray was the planned director. MacMurray never did end up making the film so it ended up in the hands of RKO.

Then RKO studio president Howard Hughes announced that there were plans for Lewis Milestone to direct the film and Jane Russell to play the female lead. The direction went to Ted Tetzlaff, and Jean Wallace was hired for the leading female role, along with Pat O'Brien and Jim Backus just as the film was ready to go into production. Filming began in May of 1949 but after a few days, Jean Wallace was believed to be wrong for the part and was replaced by Ella Raines.

George Raft plays bail bondsman Vince Kane an ex-cop who joins his detective friend Nick Ferrone (Jim Backus) to the home of Claude Brackett (Bill Williams) who has just been arrested for a bond securities theft that Ferrone had been pursuing for years.

Ella Raines and George Raft in A Dangerous Profession

Vince notices some familiar items belonging to Brackett's wife and leaves his business card. The wife, Lucy (Ella Raines), shows up at Vince's office the next day, and it is revealed they were once a couple and her leaving had affected him greatly. Lucy and her lawyer Lennert (Jonathan Hale) want Vince to bail out Claude, but they only have $4000 of the $25,000 necessary. Vince refuses. The next day a mysterious man named Dawson (David Bauer) shows up with $12,000, so, coupled with the $4000, Vince would only have to add $9000 to make Claude's bail. He agrees to do so, much to the chagrin of Joe Farley (Pat O'Brien). Nick is upset that Vince bailed out Claude, who killed a cop during his years-old crime. Vince questions a cigarette girl that Claude had once dated, and she helps him find the elusive Dawson's office and describes a man with a giant expensive ring who is involved. He doesn't get to see him, but believes he is not a lawyer but instead a gangster's patsy. He also realizes he is being followed. He then goes to see Lucy,

George Raft and Pat O'Brien in A Dangerous Profession

who is trying to hide the fact that Claude jumped bail. She proclaims her love for him, but skeptical Vince thinks she is using him to buy time for Claude. When an angry Nick informs Vince that Claude has been murdered trying to skip town, he confronts Dawson who tells him where the man that hired him is living. Vince begins to realize that racketeer Max Collins is the man with the ring who hired Dawson. Vince sets up a situation with his partner, who wants to buy him out, and Collins, where he gets a confession. Lucy contacts police, and she and Nick arrive just after a brawl in a car that stumbles into the street results in Collins being knocked out and Joe being shot.

This is the film George Raft got from RKO when production on *Johnny Allegro* ran too long and he lost out on playing in *The Big Steal*. Unfortunately, *The Big Steal* was the better film. *A Dangerous Profession* was only fair, a meandering story that was decidedly not as compelling as Raft's previous crime dramas. Ella Raines is effective as the female lead, and it is good to see Pat O'Brien in a tough talking character role. O'Brien was quite past his popular Warner

Brothers prime of the 1930s, but he had worked with George Raft in *Broadway* a few years earlier, and would do so again in *Some Like it Hot* several years later. O'Brien would later dismiss this movie as "a dog," but his performance is very steady and strong.

Jim Backus is the film's moral anchor, providing occasional narration and scoring highly as the honest, angered detective. During this period, Backus had settled into a successful career playing sturdy, supportive character parts that resonated effectively. A few years later he would stretch as an actor with the iconic role as James Dean's timid, emasculated father in *Rebel Without a Cause* and would define the latter part of his career in comedies on television, notably *I Married Joan* with Joan Davis, and *Gilligan's Island* as quirky millionaire Thurston Howell III.

A Dangerous Profession is an adequate film, not a bad one (the *New York Times* called it "exceedingly ordinary"), but its biggest problem was its failure at the box office. George Raft's previous three films for RKO were box office hits, but *A Dangerous Profession* lost $280,000 (equivalent to roughly $3 million in 21st Century money). Raft's movies had been steadily making money, but his most recent efforts made comparatively less than those produced only a year earlier. This harmed the actor's once-lofty standing as a freelance film actor.

George Raft decided that perhaps his status in American films was such that he would have better opportunities in Europe, so after appearing in a cameo as himself in *Nous Irons a Paris* (English title: *We Shall Go To Paris*), Raft accepted the lead role in a film to be produced in England, titled *I'll Get You For This* (released in America as *Lucky Nick Cain*). But while he could still secure lead roles, even he realized his time as a top movie star was over. He even began stating in interviews that he made some bad decisions regarding the roles he turned down, and that he perhaps should never have stopped playing hoods.

Despite these misgivings, George Raft's screen persona had now been established as a wise, calculating, pragmatic investigator of crime, either as a detective, or as a citizen who was dissatisfied with how the police were conducting an investigation and pursued one himself. And this is how he was presented in his final films as a leading man.

LUCKY NICK CAIN

Directed by Joseph M. Newman
Screenplay by George Callahan and William Rose, adapted from the novel by James Hadley Chase.
Produced by Joe Kaufmann
Cinematography by Otto Heller
Film Editing by Russell Lloyd

Cast:
George Raft	Nick Cain
Coleen Gray	Wonderly
Enzo Staiola	Toni
Charles Goldner	Massine
Walter Rilla	Mueller
Martin Benson	Sperazza
Peter Illing	Ceralde
Hugh French	Travers
Peter Bull	Hans
Elwyn Brook-Jones	The Fence
Constance Smith	Nina
Greta Gynt	Claudette
Donald Stewart	Kennedy
Norman Shelley	Mr. Langley
Margot Grahame	Mrs. Langley
Lilli Molnar	Prisoner
Hannah Watt	Prison Matron
Anthony Dawson	Agent
Valerie de Cadenet	Blonde
Martin Miller	Photographer
Paul Beradi	Man in Nightclub
Ernest Blyth	Man in Nightclub
Charles Hammond	Man in Nightclub

Released March 3, 1951
Romulus Films for 20th Century Fox release
Running time: 97 minutes
Black and White

While George Raft realized he wasn't the star he once had been, even though he continued to be cast in top billed lead roles, his status wasn't helped by the fact that he was off American screens for two years before *Lucky Nick Cain* hit US theaters. This movie was filmed and released as *I'll Get You For This* in England several months after production completed, and by the time it hit United States theaters, it was 1951, two years after the release of *A Dangerous Profession* which had been a box office disappointment.

George Raft in Lucky Nick Cain

George Raft stars as Nick Cain a gambler from America who is vacationing in San Paolo, Italy. Nick is surprised at the welcome he receives from Miles Travers (Hugh French), a hotel manager, Francisco Sperazza (Martin Benson), a casino owner, even police chief Armando Ceralde (Peter Illing), being told that his gambling prowess is notable and his presence significant. Nick goes to the casino that night and meets a fellow American, Kay Wonderly (Coleen Gray). When Kay suffers a losing streak and is indebted to the casino, Sperazza agrees to forget about the debt if she'll keep Nick in San Paolo. They go to Nick's room where he is knocked out by liquor that Travers has drugged. Ceralde tells Nick that a treasury agent from the US was found murdered in his room, and the murder weapon was in Nick's possession. Realizing he's being framed, Nick forces Ceralde, Sperazza, and Travers to drink the drugged liquor at gunpoint and escapes with Kay. When they attempt to flee with a florist's delivery truck, its owner, Massine (Charles Goldner), threatens them with a gun and takes them to his apartment. Once hearing their story, he agrees to hide them. Nick then investigates the agent's murder, uncovers a deal involving Sperazza and Ceralde with German businessman Eric Mueller, and that Kay is romantically involved with Sperazza. It all ends up being an international counterfeiting ring, which Nick and Massine uncover.

Lucky Nick Cain was a US-British co-production done independently on location with American actors, while British actors appeared in the supporting roles. One of the interesting dynamics in *Lucky Nick Cain* was Nick's relationship with Toni, a young boy played by Enzo Staiola, best known for Vittorio DeSica's classic *The Bicycle Thief*. A shoeshine boy who idolizes Nick, Toni benefits the gambler by agreeing to stay with Kay while he and Massine investigate further. Raft recalled for columnist Sheila Graham: "He couldn't understand a word of English. I gave the kid every cue with my hand. He doesn't know what he was saying, but he knew what it was about." Graham went on to call the film "One of George's best."[86]

Coleen Gray recalled this film as one of the best experiences in her career, and that George Raft was "a lovely gentleman" who

---

86 Sheila Graham column. Syndicated. February 28, 1951

"knew his lines and wanted to do his best at all times."[87] From all that has been written about the production, it appears to have been a comfortable experience for all involved. And, the resulting movie is good, certainly better than *A Dangerous Profession* had been.

Reviews were uniformly good with Variety calling the film "A well-done chase melodrama that will cut a fair swath at the box office. Raft is well cast as the big time Yank gambler. It is the type of role he's often done in the past and he plays it with a sure hand."[88]

While it was a good, typical of George Raft film, when *Lucky Nick Cain* was finally released in the US, it went out as the second feature as a part of a double-bill, an status usually held by a quicky B movie that served to support the top billed movie. Often *Lucky Nick Cain* was paired with another potboiler and sold as two B movies to play at neighborhood theaters. Quite a comedown for an actor whose films had usually garnered stand alone bookings at major movie houses.

George Raft then signed a three-picture deal with producer Bernard Luber, who did very little in movies and is perhaps best remembered for having co-produced the second season of television's *The Adventures of Superman*. The three films Raft made for Luber were released by poverty row studio Lippert Pictures. And they were the last films in which George Raft received top billing.

---

87 Aaker, Everett. *George Raft: The Films*. McFarland, 2013
88 Lucky Nick Cain review. *Variety*. February 28, 1951

LOAN SHARK

Directed by Seymour Friedman
Screenplay by Martin Rackin and Eugene Ling from a story by Rackin
Produced by Bernard Luber
Cinematography by Joseph F. Biroc
Film Editing by Al Joseph

Cast:
George Raft	Joe Gargen
Dorothy Hart	Ann Nelson
Paul Stewart	Lou Donelli
John Hoyt	Vince Phillips
Helen Westcott	Martha Haines
William Phipps	Ed Haines
Charles Meredith	F.L. Rennick
Henry Slate	Paul Nelson
Russell Johnson	Charlie Thompson
Margia Dean	Ivy
Benny Baker	Tubby
Lawrence Dobkin	Walter Karr
Robert Bice	Steve Casmer
Virginia Carroll	Netta Casmer
George Eldredge	Mr. Howell
Ross Elliott	Norm
William Tannen	Rourke
Harlan Warde	Lt. White
Robert B. Williams	Scully
Barbara Wooddell	Mrs. Hilton
Keith Richards	Buckley
Spring Mitchell	Nancy
William Phillips	Baski

Robert Karnes	Police Lieutenant
John Roy	Police Officer
Russell Custer	Officer
Mike Ragan	Garage Thug
Jack Daley	Borrower
Mike Donovan	Plant Guard
William H. O'Brien	Waiter
Frank O'Connor	Bartender
Brick Sullivan	Diner Patron
Rudy Germane	Club Patron
Joe Hinds	Club Patron
Jack Gordon	Worker
Herschel Graham	Worker
Claire Carleton	Nagging Wife

Released May 23, 1952
Encore Productions for Lipper Pictures release
Running Time: 77 minutes
Black and White

Martin Rackin originally wrote the story for *Loan Shark* for Warner Brothers in 1949, but the studio turned it down. He then revamped the screenplay with Eugene Ling and sold it to producer Bernard Luber for his Famous Artists production company, who planned to make it with George Raft in the lead. Famous Artists entered into a deal with the low budget poverty row studio Lippert Pictures.

Robert Lippert had been vice president of Screen Guild Productions (the president was Joseph Blumenfeld), a low budget studio begun in 1945, notable only for some B-level color films, such as *Scared To Death* which turned out to be Bela Lugosi's only movie in color. Lippert took over as President in 1949 and renamed the company Lippert Pictures. While their films were generally unremarkable B-level second-features, there were some notable highlights, including Samuel Fuller's *The Steel Helmet*, and the noted *Superman and the Mole Men* (1951) which featured George Reeves' first appearance as Superman, just prior to the TV series debut.

The deal Famous Studios made with Lippert was that Bernard Luber would make a film and Robert Lippert would distribute it. Lippert agreed to give away 75% of each film's profit in an effort to get better directors and actors on these projects. This was the ideal time to get an actor at the level of George Raft. While he was not the top star like he had been, his name still meant enough at the box office, so he was quite a coup for an independent producer releasing through a poverty row studio. Raft was given $25,000 up front and 25% of the profits.

George Raft had now passed 50, but still retained a screen presence that resonated if given the right part. His having signed onto the project impressed Lippert enough so that he gave the movie a budget of $250,000, much larger than his usual productions. Director Seymour Friedman had entered films with *Trapped By Boston Blackie* and had since developed as a specialist in B-level crime dramas, which was perfect for this project. Cinematographer Joseph Biroc had effectively filmed Raft in *Johnny Allegro*, so he was hired for the project. Biroc had filmed Frank Capra's *It's a Wonderful Life*, and would later be cinematographer on such diverse films as *Viva Las Vegas*, *Blazing Saddles*, and *The Towering Inferno*, for which he won an Oscar. At the time he filmed *Loan Shark*, he had successfully done other noir-based crime dramas such as *The Killer That Stalked New York* and *Cry Danger*.

As it turned out, despite being distributed by a low budget studio that resulted in fewer theaters than a large company, *Loan Shark* turned out to be a very strong, effective B-level crime drama that deserves some attention.

George Raft plays Joe Gargen, a former boxer who has just been released from prison after serving three years for assault with a deadly weapon. All he did was hit a guy, but because he boxed professionally, his hands were considered lethal weapons. He goes to the home of his sister Martha (Helen Westcott), where he plans to live until he can find a job and get his own place. Martha's husband Ed (William Phipps) works for a tire company where he and several workers have become victimized by loan sharks. It is an organized ring run by Lou Donelli (Paul Stewart) and the tire company's manager F.L. Rennick (Charles Meredith) asks Joe

Dorothy Hart and George Raft in Loan Shark

to work undercover and find out who these loan sharks are. Joe doesn't want anything more than an ordinary job so he turns the offer down. However, when his brother-in-law is killed for trying to organize against the loan sharks, Joe changes his mind. He makes it clear with Rennick that he is to be left alone to do things his way, and that nobody else should know what he is doing. So, Joe gets a job in the factory and starts his secret investigation. He gets to know Charles Thompson (Russell Johnson), who has a connection to the operation, and soon gets to meet Donelli as well as bookkeeper Walter Karr (Lawrence Dobkin) and the boss, Vince Phillips (John Hoyt). They give Joe a job making collections, which turns his family and friends against him, but he accepts their anger in order to remain undercover. Eventually Joe finds out everything necessary, and when he insists on more money, it arouses suspicion from Donelli, but not from Phillips who continues to trust him. Joe finally threatens to reveal their business operations to police unless he gets $50,000. However, when Walter Karr pulls a gun on Joe, he flees and is pursued by Phillips and Karr. Joe manages to shoot them both, and it is revealed what he had been doing to his family and friends.

George Raft's romantic interest in *Loan Shark* is played by Dorothy Hart. Gail Russell, another star whose status had dipped, was sought for the female lead, but her personal problems were such that she was unable to do the film. The romance that Raft's character of Joe encounters is Ann Nelson, a friend and neighbor of Martha's whose brother works at the plant. Theirs is a tumultuous relationship, because she believes Joe has betrayed everyone, especially when he beats up her brother at the request of the loan shark operation. Joe reluctantly does so in order to keep up the ruse.

The entire structure of *Loan Shark* is very effective. Even as the film opens, prior to the credits, a murder is committed on screen, shown from the perspective of the murder victim—we see a fist quickly coming toward the lens of his glasses, and then the glass shatters. It's brutal, and also creatively staged. The lead-up to that moment has the camera following the backs and feet of the victim and his pursuers, their feet loud on the sidewalk. It is a very jarring, brutal opening that sets the pace for the remainder of the movie. The film maintains this brisk pace, and the events that unfold in the narrative are consistently compelling. There is even a rather artful visual for the ending of the movie, when the camera pans up to a theater marquee that states The End.

Critical comments were good and the moviegoers who saw the film were pleased. Art Cullison, the noted media critic in Akron, Ohio, stated in his On With The Show column, "Raft, of course, takes easily to these tough melodramatics in a script that allows him to do what's best."[89] However, Lippert's distribution was limited compared to the other studios. *Loan Shark* played major cities, but not all of the small towns. And because this type of movie, and George Raft's box office significance, had been diminished in popularity, *Loan Shark* was the second feature on double bills, usually

---

89 Raft in Familiar Role Goes Outside Law to Catch Racketeers. *Akron Beacon Journal.* June 12, 1952

with little more than the title and a few names occupying marginal space in the ad.

George Raft continued with his deal to make two more movies under these circumstances for Bernard Luber. The next one had him traveling back to England for location shooting in London, and once again with a larger budget than the usual Lippert release. It was released as *Escape Route* in the UK, but by the time it was released in the US, it was entitled *I'll Get You.*

I'LL GET YOU

Directed by Seymour Friedman
Screenplay by John Baines and Nicholas Phipps
Produced by Bernard Luber
Cinematography by Eric Cross
Film Editing by Tom Simpson

Cast:
George Raft	Steve Rossi
Sally Gray	Joan Miller
Clifford Evans	Michael Grand
Reginald Tate	Col. Wilkes
Patricia Laffan	Irma
Frederick Piper	Inspector Reid
Cyril Chamberlain	Bailey
Arnold Diamond	Max
Arthur Lovegrove	Phillips
Anthony Pendrell	Rees
Norman Pierce	Inspector Hobbs
John Warwick	Security Chief Brice
Roddy Hughes	Porter
June Ashley	Blonde Contact In Flat
Grace Arnold	Neighbor
Ernest Blyth	Morgue Attendant
Howard Douglas	Taxi Driver
Harry Towb	Immigration Officer

Released January 6, 1953
Banner Films for Lippert
Running Time: 88 minutes
Black and White

Alternate title: Escape Route

I'll Get You is another Lippert release through producer Bernard Luber, once again directed by Seymour Friedman, only this time shot on location in England (*Loan Shark* was filmed in Hollywood). *I'll Get You* was filmed shortly after production concluded on *Loan Shark*. Once again George Raft was paid $25,000 along with 25% of the profits. Once again the film was given a larger budget than the usual *Lippert* release. And, once again, it received scant release, playing for short periods as the bottom half of double bills, and given little attention from moviegoers.

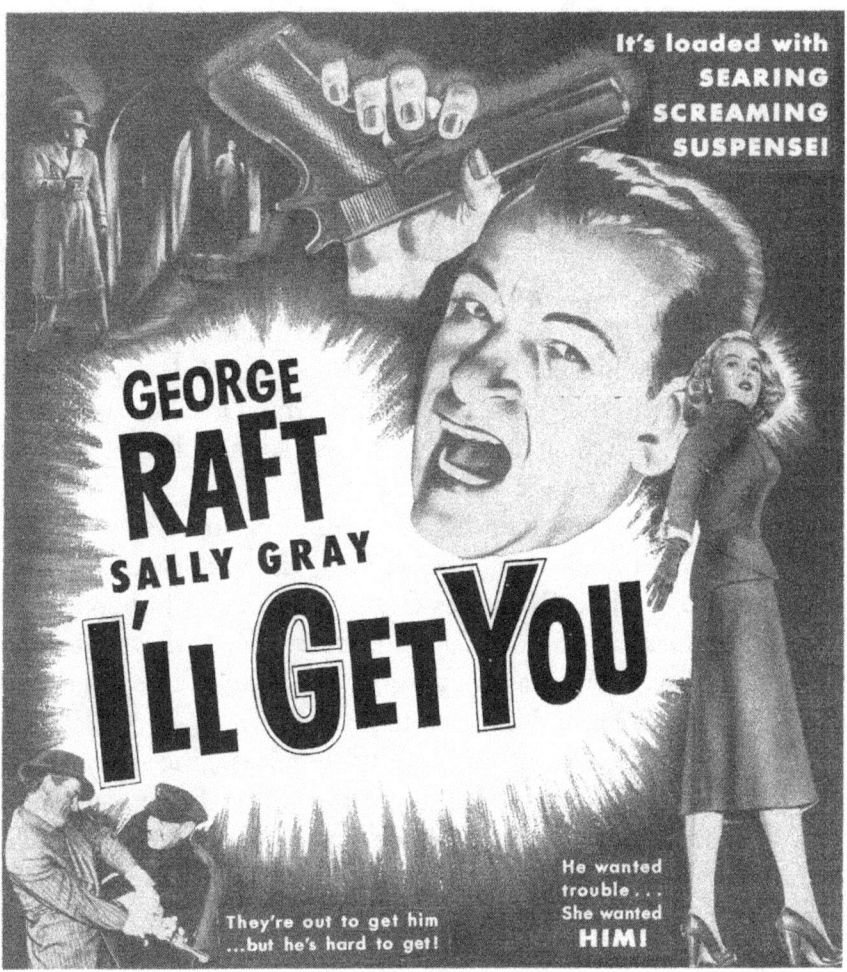

Movie Ad for I'll Get You

George Raft plays Steven Rossi, an American assistant to a jet designer who has been abducted along with several other scientists. Rossi flies to London to investigate, and through a series of contacts, finds his way to Michael Grand (Clifford Evans), a German manufacturer who had once offered Rossi a job. When he gets to Grand's hotel room, he instead finds Joan Miller (Sally Gray) who takes Rossi at gunpoint to Colonel Wilkes (Reginald Tate). Claiming to want a job from Grand, Wilkes has Rossi stay with Joan, who keeps a watch on him overnight. Rossi discovers that Wilkes is British Intelligence and incorporates Rossi in his attempt to capture Grand, who is behind the kidnappings. Rossi agrees, but wants to use his own methods. Joan, also an agent, helps Rossi. They reach Grand's secretary, Irma (Patricia Laffan), who tells of his whereabouts, then phones and warns him. They find Grand in an abandoned building, and he tries to shoot Rossi, but it is thwarted by Joan. Joan later follows Irma to a beauty shop where she communicates with Grand who is hidden in a curtained area. A burned-out car is found with two bodies inside. One is identified as Irma, but the other is not believed to be Grand. This arouses the suspicion Inspector Reid of Scotland Yard (Fredrick Piper). Wilkes and Reid find out that Rossi is an FBI agent. Rossi and Joan return to the beauty shop where Grand is sending a shortwave message. When he hears them, he burns some documents and leaves out the back way

When Rossi enters, he saves some of the documents but Grand gets away. Rossi goes to the docks in disguise and leaves a trail so Joan can follow him. Rossi sees Grand and follows him, but Joan loses track. Grand and Rossi fight and there is a gunshot that alerts Joan and police. Rossi attacks and subdues Grand in a freight elevator, the police arrive, and the scientists are freed.

It is unfortunate that at the time of its release, the moviegoing public had grown tired of George Raft's crime thrillers and dismissed them as too similar to each other to have much merit. While Raft had long ago established a screen persona, and his crime films were following a fairly distinct formula, he really wasn't walking through them with indifference as some studies have accused.

Now older, George Raft comes off as a seasoned old pro whose subdued demeanor still offers the same subtle nuance and pragmatic approach as he had in his best film noir performances. This was his style, it was effective, and it worked well in *I'll Get You* as it had in his other films. It can be argued that *Loan Shark* had been the better film, with tighter pacing, more artful direction, and situations that were more compelling. But *I'll Get You* is not a bad movie, and offers the murky darkness, bursts of violence, and mysterious figures that are staples of the formula in which Raft was now working.

One moment in the film generated some notice in the press. At one point, when Raft first meets Joan, she first subdues him with judo. A blurb in Erskine Johnson's column stated:

George Raft's fans can start cringing. In *I'll Get You*, his leading lady is a military intelligence operator, an expert at judo, who throws him to the floor the first time they meet.[90]

This is a bit of an exaggeration, but it apparently was jarring for some viewers that an older Raft plays a character who is overpowered by a woman.

I'll Get You was usually paired in double features with the Lippert-produced western *The Tall Texan* topping the bill, and another Lippert subject, the 3-D novelty short subject *A Day in the Country*. This program made the rounds in neighborhood theaters for short runs, with the 3-D subject getting the most attention, and *The Tall Texan* getting whatever was left. The short, narrated by comedian Joe Besser who was working with Abbott and Costello on their TV show, and would later join The 3 Stooges, took advantage of the popular-but-brief 3-D craze of the 50s. The western feature was competent-but-standard fare. *I'll Get You* has held up best among the films on the program, but at the time it generated the least interest.

George Raft was becoming more disillusioned with movies, and was considering looking into television and well as perhaps returning to dancing. But first he had one more Lippert movie to do for Bernard Luber, *The Man From Cairo*.

---

90 Closeups and Longshots. Erskine Johnson column. Syndicated. July 30, 1952

THE MAN FROM CAIRO

Directed by Ray Enright
Screenplay by Eugene Ling, Phillip Stevenson, Janet Stevenson
    from a story by Ladlisas Fordor adapted by Edoardo Anton
    and Ugo Velona
Produced by Bernard Luber and Livio Dall'Oglio
Cinematography by Maria Albertelli
Film Editing by Mario Serandrei

Cast:
George Raft	Mike Canelli
Gianna Maria Canale	Lorraine Beloyan
Massimo Serato	Basil Constantine
Guido Celano	Emile Touchard
Irene Papas	Yvonne Lebeau
Richard McNamara	Agent Charles Stark
Alfredo Varelli	Prof. H. M. Crespi
Leonardo Scavino	Police Capt. Akhim Bey
Mino Doro	Major C. Blanc
Anthony La Penna	Colonel Fournier
Franco Silva	Armeno
Angelo Dessy	Pock-marked Thug
Henri Vidon	Bit
Rossana Galli	Bit

Released November 27, 1953
Eros Films for Lippert Pictures
Running time: 81 minutes
Black and White

Gianna Maria Canale and George Raft in The Man From Cairo

The third and final film in George Raft's deal with independent producer Bernard Luber was also the weakest. It was shot on location in Italy, but its budget was $100,000 less than the previous Lippert releases produced by Luber. George Raft once again got the $25,000 salary and 25% of the profits, but due to limited release and perhaps some creative bookkeeping, none of the Lippert releases showed a profit. Thus, the $25,000 is all George Raft got for each film.

George Raft plays Mike Canelli, an American tourist in Algiers who is mistaken for American agent Charles Stark (Richard McNamara). Several investigators with French intelligence have been found dead while investigating one million francs in gold that went missing during World War Two. Stark was flown in by French intelligence with the belief that an American undercover might not be detected. Stark is a friend to Canelli, who happens to run into him and mentions he'll be looking for a man with four fingers on one hand. When Canelli is questioned by those believing he is the American agent, this clue comes up and arouses his suspicion.

From this point the film takes on the typical formula that had pretty much run dry for George Raft. Even though his solid presence anchors a narrative that has its mysterious characters, evil villains, and femme fatales, the formula moves more slowly in this film, because of a fairly convoluted narrative. Also, the innocent bystander who becomes a man wrongly accused isn't a character that works as well for Raft; there's an air about his character that makes him feel too worldly for such a role.

The Man for Cairo is not a bad film, but it isn't as striking or compelling as the two previous crime dramas Raft made for Lippert release. It moves along rather sluggishly and its only real interest is historical. It is an early film for actress Irene Papas, and the final film for director Ray Enright, whose career dated back to the silent era and later included a lot of programmers at Warner Brothers featuring such stars as Humphrey Bogart, James Cagney, and several Joe E. Brown comedies. And, *The Man From Cairo* was also the last film for which George Raft would receive top billing.

Shortly after the release of his previous Lippert film, *I'll Get You*, George Raft starred on television in *I Am The Law*, a syndicated TV series in which he starred as NYPD detective George Murphy. Raft was in his element, had some money invested in the project, which was produced by comedian Lou Costello and his brother Pat. It was a good show, arguably better than the movies Raft had been doing, but it generated little interest among TV distributors. Debuting in February of 1953 it was already off the air that July, a few months before the release of *The Man From Cairo*.

This was George Raft's final film release of 1953. As 1954 began, Raft was involved in a traffic accident that resulted in his hospitalization. According to the press:

> Actor George Raft entered St. John's Hospital in Santa Monica yesterday for what his physician termed observation and treatment of an arm injured in a traffic accident. Dr. Danny Leventhal said Raft was pitched forward when

another car struck him from behind on the Arroyo Soco Parkway last Saturday.[91]

The following October, other drivers in the three-car pileup attempted to sue Raft, accusing him of being negligent. This was likely an attempt to obtain some notoriety and money from one they perceived to be a wealthy movie star.

However, a couple of months later, Raft was moved by a testimonial dinner given in his honor. The press stated:

George Raft, one of the movies' toughest tough guys, is an old softie after all. The veteran movie gangster wept openly last night as the Friars Club tossed him a stag testimonial banquet marking his 25th year on the screen. Perhaps the saddest note of all came in Raft's speech of gratitude. The greying actor, a little paunchy now, looked around at studio heads Jack L. Warner, Darryl Zanuck and Dore Schary on the speaker's dais and then said: "This is a great honor for a fellow who hasn't done a thing in a year. The other day someone asked me to sing two choruses of Sweet Georgia Brown in a picture about the, life of Ben Bernie. That's the kind of offers I get nowadays." But the evening was mostly filled with laughs, 90 per cent of them bawdy. Although such high-priced comics as Martin and Lewis, George Burns and Parkyakarkus were on the program, it was a former light heavyweight champion of the world who got most of the laughs. Slapsie Maxie Rosenbloom introduced as "Marlon Brando's diction teacher," said it was Raft who first taught him how to fight "Dis bum Raft picked me up when I didn't have a quarter to my name, recalled Maxie. "Now I owe $20,000. Thanks, George!"[92]

With his movie career now at low ebb, and television not having worked out either, George Raft busied himself with a Las Vegas act where he could perform some of his dancing routines. He admitted to being quite nervous going back to the stage again after so many years, but the shows were popular and successful, giving the actor much needed confidence.

---

91 Actor George Raft Enters Hospital. *Los Angeles Times.* January 16, 1954
92 Raft Weeps at 25-year Testimonial. *Oakland Tribune.* March 23, 1954

Approaching his situation with introspection, Raft decided that he'd like to play a hood again after fighting that image for over a decade. He even told the press that it might have been a bad idea for "going straight." So, he accepted an acting offer from MGM to play a gangster in their film *Rogue Cop* which would star Robert Taylor. George Raft's movie career had come full circle – he was once again playing a gangster in a supporting role at a major Hollywood studo.

ROGUE COP

Directed by Roy Rowland
Screenplay by Sydney Boehm based on the novel by William P. McGiven
Produced by Nicholas Nayfack
Cinematography by John Seitz
Film Editing by James E. Newcom

Cast:
Robert Taylor	Det. Sgt. Christopher Kelvaney
Janet Leigh	Karen Stephanson
George Raft	Dan Beaumonte
Steve Forrest	Eddie Kelvaney
Anne Francis	Nancy Corlane
Robert Ellenstein	Det. Sidney Y. Myers
Robert F. Simon	Ackerman
Anthony Ross	Father Ahearn
Alan Hale Jr.	Johnny Stark
Peter Brocco	George 'Wrinkles' Fallon
Vince Edwards	Joey Langley
Olive Carey	Selma
Roy Barcroft	Lt. Vince D. Bardeman
Dale Van Sickel	Manny
Ray Teal	Patrolman Mullins
Nicky Blair	Marsh
Nesdon Booth	Det. Garrett
Dallas Boyd	Patrolman Higgins
Paul Bryar	Patrolman Marx
Richard Deacon	Stacey
Russell Johnson	Patrolman Carland
Robert Burton	Insp. Adrian Cassidy
Lillian Buyeff	Gertrude

Phil Chambers	Det. Dirksen
Guy Prescott	Det. Ferrari
George Taylor	Dr. Leonard - Coroner
Michael Fox	Rudy
Connie Marshall	Frances
Milton Parsons	Tucker
Dick Simmons	Det. Ralston
Joseph Waring	Rivers
Carleton Young	Dist. Atty. Powell
Jimmy Ames	News Dealer
Benny Burt	Pool Hall Proprietor
Jack Chefe	Waiter at Turf Club
Gene Coogan	Truck Driver
Jonathan Cott	Policeman
Herbert Ellis	Bartender
Mitchell Kowall	Guard
Harold Miller	Turf Club Patron
Gilda Oliva	Italian Mother
Dick Ryan	Elevator Man
Jeffrey Sayre	Policeman
Budd Buster	Parker
George Selk	Parker
Jack Victor	Morgue Orderly
Paul Brinegar	Clerk
Paul Hoffman	Clerk

Released September 17, 1954
Metro-Goldwyn-Mayer
Running time: 92 minutes
Black and White

George Raft's last few independent films received so little attention, by the time he was hired by MGM to play a supporting role in *Rogue Cop*, it was called a comeback in the press. Newspaper articles claimed that Raft hadn't made a movie in five years, when in fact he had been consistently active throughout that time. The press cited *A Dangerous Profession* as his last movie, because it was

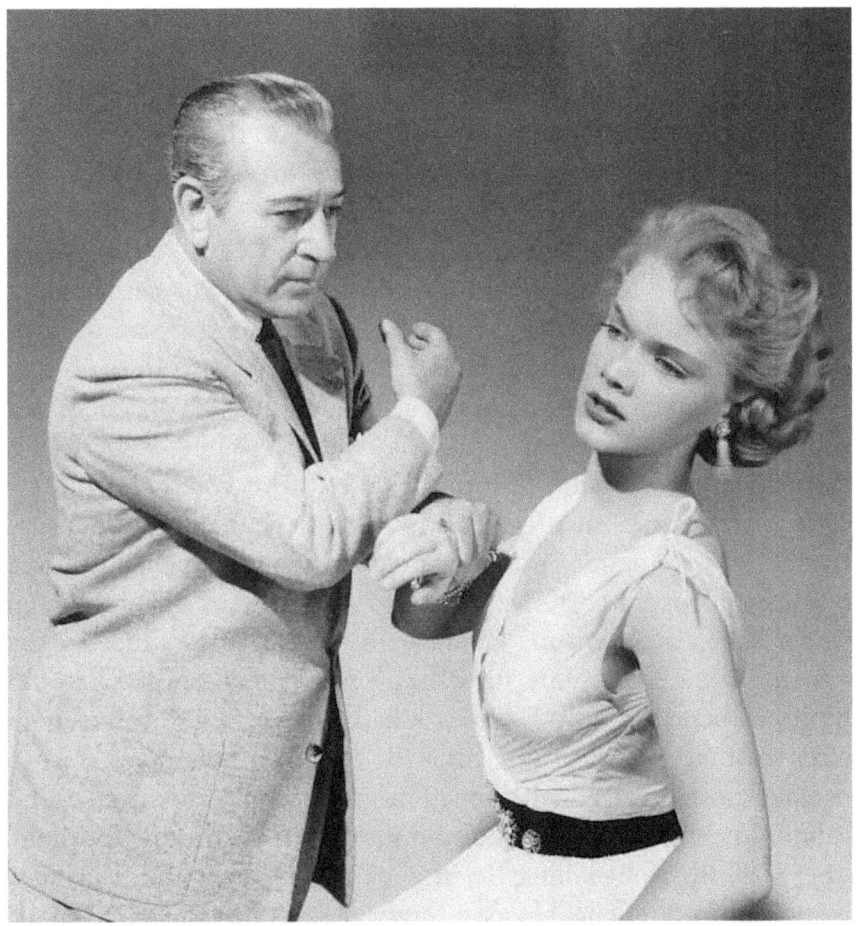

George Raft slaps Anne Francis in Rogue Cop

his last for a major studio, while only some accounts briefly mentioned that he appeared in a few low budget indie productions and some films overseas. Ironically, it can be argued that both *Lucky Nick Cain* and *Loan Shark* were superior to *A Dangerous Profession*.

Rogue Cop isn't George Raft's movie at all. It is really Robert Taylor's film, and he is very good as a crooked cop whose honest-cop brother is being threatened by gangsters. The head gangster is played by Raft, who had established himself as a pragmatic good guy investigating criminal activity in so many movies, perhaps his once again playing a hood is part of this "comeback." Raft being cast was a result of his plea at the recent Friar's dinner. Dore Schary, who was in attendance, offered him the part. He wasn't interested at first, but Robert Taylor realized it'd be good to have him in the role and went to see him with the script. It was Taylor's plea, and a reading of the script, that convinced Raft to do the film.

MGM had purchased the screen rights to William McGiven's novel in November of 1953, assigning the screenplay to Sidney Boehm, who had adapted *The Big Heat*. Robert Taylor signed on to do the movie in March of 1954, while the supporting cast of Janet Leigh, Steve Forrest, and George Raft were hired a month later. Filming began in May of 1954.

George Raft plays mob boss Dan Beaumonte, who has received cooperation from crooked cop Christopher Kelvaney (Robert Taylor). However, Kelvaney's brother Eddie (Steve Forest) is an honest cop who sees a suspect flee a murder scene. Beaumonte insists that Kelvaney stop his brother from identifying the man, but Eddie refuses to cooperate. Kelvaney tries to get Eddie's girl, nightclub singer Karen Stephenson (Janet Leigh) to persuade Eddie, but she also refuses. Beaumonte hires Langley (Vince Edwards) to kill both brothers, but only Eddie is killed. Thereafter Kelvaney goes after the mob himself, using his skills as a detective, in an effort to convict those involved with the murder of Eddie. He captures and subdues Eddie but Beaumonte and some men are waiting for them. There is a shootout killing Beaumonte and his gang, but Kelvaney is mortally wounded. He asks forgiveness as he is taken away by ambulance.

For his return to A-list movies, George Raft not only agreed to play a gangster again, he also agreed to a supporting role, although his third-billed name does appear above the title. Playing an evil gangster as an older man, he exhibits significant cruelty against his much younger girl, played by Anne Francis. This dynamic is interesting in that Raft always had misgivings when playing a character who was rough with women. However, unlike during his past stardom where he could refuse roles and insist his character be rewritten, Raft was now one whose last four films received only marginal interest, so his landing a role at MGM in a major film was now something of a coupe. Despite his past stardom, George Raft did not have the clout to insist on any changes.

It is interesting to compare he character Raft plays in *Rogue Cop* with his character in *Scarface*. Both are supporting roles as a gangster. In the first he is a young man who is up-and-coming in the mob world. And in this film, he is an older man who has reached the top and is settled there. He is slower in pace, but not due to a creeping menacing feeling, but because of an abject weariness that is sustained by his cunning and cruelty. If anything gets in the character's way, he has various levels of power to make it go away. His antagonist is perfect for the protagonist Kelvaney.

Robert Taylor was also aging into his roles. Once a young, handsome romantic leading man, Taylor was now past 40 and taking on parts that were more suited to a middle-aged man. As Kelvaney, he is a man who is ashamed of his past, but in too deep to refuse anything. His reluctance doesn't matter. He must try to convince his honest younger brother to play along with the demands of a mob boss. Taylor conveys his inner turmoil effectively, presenting himself as a defeated character with an edge who is trying to survive within the circumstances he's created for himself. Joining MGM in 1934, Robert Taylor would eventually remain with the studio for 25 years; the longest tenure there of any other actor, save for Lewis Stone, who had a lifetime contract that ended with his sudden death after 29 years.

For the women in the film, Janet Leigh was coming to the end of her eight years at MGM. *Rogue Cop* would be her last movie for that studio under this contract. The New York Times would report in their April 17, 1954 issue that the actress signed with Universal Studios.

Anne Francis would recall for Hedda Hopper: "This is the one part I've been waiting for." Director Roy Rowland said of Francis:

> The first time I read the story she popped into my mind, the association of Anne and the part of the girl drunk stems back to an evening when we were entertaining some friends, including Anne and her husband Bam Price, in our home. Anna went behind the bar and started mixing something fancy; then she did an imitation of a drunk which we all thought was clever. I was impressed by the

strange contrast of that little girl face and her imitation of a silly drunk.[93]

Critics were generally pleased with *Rogue Cop* and it was a big hit at the box office, earning nearly $2 million over its budget. George Raft turned in an excellent performance in a hit film for a major studio. He hoped that this might allow for some greater opportunities in character roles, and he was willing to play the bad guy. However, his next project was for writer-director-producer Nunnally Johnson, who was interested in casting Raft as a detective in his color-Cinemascope production *Black Widow*.

---

93 Hedda Hopper column. *The Los Angeles Times*. October 10, 1954

BLACK WIDOW

Directed, Produced, and Screenplay by Nunnally Johnson
Story by Patrick Quentin from the novel *Fatal Woman* by Hugh
    Wheeler and Richard W. Webb
Cinematography by Charles G. Clarke
Film Editing by Dorothy Spencer

Cast:
Ginger Rogers	Carlotta 'Lottie' Marin
Van Heflin	Peter Denver
Gene Tierney	Iris Denver
George Raft	Detective Lt. C.A. Bruce
Peggy Ann Garner	Nancy 'Nanny' Ordway
Reginald Gardiner	Brian Mullen
Virginia Leith	Claire Amberly
Otto Kruger	Gordon Ling
Cathleen Nesbitt	Lucia Colletti
Skip Homeier	John Amberly
Hilda Simms	Anne
Mabel Albertson	Sylvia
Bea Benaderet	Mrs. Franklin Walsh
Harry Carter	Police Sgt. Welch
Richard H. Cutting	Police Sgt. Owens
Anthony De Mario	Tony – Bartender
Aaron Spelling	Mr. Oliver
James Stone \	Fritz - Stage Door Attendant
Frank Wilcox	Zachary Paige
Geraldine Wall	Gwen Mills
Nesdon Booth	Police A.P.B. Man
Paul Kruger	Policeman
Oliver Cross	Bar Patron
Frances Curry	Maid

Virginia Maples	Model
Forbes Murray	Man in Hallway
Jeffrey Sayre	Photographer
Wilson Wood	Costume Designer
Michael Vallon	Coal Dealer
Pat White	Party Guest in Red Dress
Arthur Tovey	Party Guest
Bert Stevens	Party Guest
Monty O'Grady	Party Guest
Cosmo Sardo	Party Guest
Franklyn Farnum	Party Guest
Dick Gordon	Party Guest
Robert Haines	Party Guest
Kenner G. Kemp	Party Guest
Harold Miller	Party Guest
Paul Bradley	Party Guest
Steve Carruthers	Party Guest
Paul Cristo	Party Guest

Released October 29, 1954
20th Century Fox
Running Time: 95 minutes
Color

Black Widow is George Raft's first movie in color since *Nob Hill*, which was also made for 20th Century Fox and also featured Peggy Ann Garner in the cast. Garner was then only a child and shared many scenes with Raft. In this film, they share no scenes together. Her character is dead before his shows up.

After the ballyhoo of George Raft once again playing a hood in *Rogue Cop*, he is once again a seasoned, pragmatic, no-nonsense detective in *Black Widow*. Some newspaper accounts built this up by stating Raft was expanding his work as a detective on TV's *I Am The Law* into a feature film in color and Cinemascope. Others indicated that George Raft would be playing on the right side of the law for a change, ignoring that fact that other than the recent

Van Heflin, Ginger Rogers, George Raft, and Reginald Gardiner in Black Widow

Rogue Cop he had been doing so quite regularly for some years and in many films.

Raft once again has a supporting role in *Black Widow*, and again his fourth-billed name does appear above the title. Unlike *Rogue Cop*, which had a stand-alone star in Robert Taylor despite a strong supporting cast, *Black Widow* is an ensemble film which features pretty significant roles for such screen luminaries as Raft, Garner, Van Heflin, Ginger Rogers, Reginald Gardiner and Gene Tierney. So, Raft's supporting role is an important one, settled comfortably in the ensemble.

Despite Ginger Rogers and George Raft appearing for the first and only time together in a movie, two of the screen's greatest dancers have no scene where they dance together. Of course, it wouldn't fit comfortably in this narrative at all, but it is still rather ironic.

George Raft appears as Lt. Bruce, who is called upon to investigate the sudden suicide of a young woman named Nancy (Nanny) Ordway (Peggy Ann Garner), having apparently hanged herself in the apartment of Broadway producer Peter Denver (Van Heflin). His wife Iris (Gene Tierney) is out of town, but is aware that Nanny was staying with Peter. When she comes home, it is she that finds Nanny's dead body hanging from the shower rod. Peter had met Nanny a few months earlier at the home of actress Lottie Marin (Ginger Rogers) and her husband Brian Mullen (Reginald Gardiner). Nanny was an aspiring writer and had been using the Denvers' apartment to write during the day. When Lt. Bruce begins investigating, the suicide looks like murder and all signs point to Peter. Further information indicates that Nanny was living with a brother and sister (Skip Homeier and Virginia Leith) whom she met while working in a bar and grill. She revealed false info to the girl and agreed to marry the boy. Nanny was engaged in a secret affair with Brian Mullen and made it look like it was Peter Denver, all as part of a plot to advance her own career and social standing. When Mullen admits his affair with Nanny to Peter, the room is bugged and Lt Bruce overhears. During an interrogation of the suspects, Lt Bruce accuses Mullen of Nanny's murder. Lottie tries to implicate Dan, but it is shown he has an alibi for the time she provides. After intense questioning from Lt. Bruce, Lottie confesses to having killed Nanny and making it appear like a suicide. Peter is cleared as having no more than a platonic relationship with Nanny.

In an ensemble film like *Black Widow,* where all of the actors are noteworthy and a certain level of performance is expected, it is commendable that everyone does an impressive job in their roles. Ginger Rogers heads the cast in a part that had been first offered to Tallulah Bankhead and Joan Crawford, both of whom turned it down. Rogers is able to tap into both her comedic and dramatic skills by playing an affected actress whose self-importance and vindictive nature blend nicely. Van Heflin, in a role first offered to Gregory Peck, is especially good as the accused man who desperately works to clear his name. Van Heflin rocketed to stardom back in 1941 with his Oscar winning role for Best Supporting Actor as a drunken, paranoid gangster's buddy. For the remainder of his career he could play silly comedy (*Weekend With Father*) and guilt-ridden paranoia (*Airport*). He plays Peter as a successful man who is both bewildered and disturbed by his circumstances, but has a determination to clear himself as innocent.

Garner won a Juvenile award, special Oscar, for her work in films like *A Tree Grows in Brooklyn* and *Junior Miss*, later appearing as a teenager in *Bomba The Jungle Boy* and *The Loveable Cheat*. She hoped her performance in *Black Widow* would establish her in adult roles in movies, but it was not to be.

George Raft also hoped that his work in *Black Widow* would further advance his career, working off the success of *Rogue Cop*. Nunnally Johnson was quite pleased with his work, and indicated Raft was quite cooperative:

> Raft would show up on set word-perfect and looking no older at age fifty-three than he had at age thirty-nine. He learns his lines very well... he's not an actor in particular. He was a personality that was very well fitted for that period. He's a nice guy to be with.[94]

Raft is very good in the role, quite comfortable as the weathered, accomplished detective who had little trouble finding the necessary clues in his investigation, especially when assisted by his chief suspect who is desperate to clear his name.

There is some really beautiful colorful photography in this movie, but it is perhaps a bit too "pretty" for noir when it needs to feel gritty. Gene Tierney is not given a meaty enough role to match her talents.

Black Widow doubled its production costs at the box office, but that was considered to be only a moderate success, not a big hit. Reviews were mixed, many critics being dismissive of the formula plot and the ensemble cast merely a gathering of familiar names to

---

94 Johnson, Nunnally (1969). Recollections of Nunnally Johnson oral history transcript. University of California Oral History Program

get Americans out of the house, away from their televisions, and back in theaters.

For his next film, George Raft was re-teamed with Edward G. Robinson for the first time since 1941's *Manpower* during which they had a tumultuous, even violent relationship on the set. However, at this time Robinson was graylisted during the notorious Red Scare. This list was similar to the blacklist but because Robinson was cleared after naming names before the House UnAmerican Activities Committee, he was considered graylisted. Because he was called in to testify, the major studios would not hire him for top roles, despite being cleared. However, his being cleared meant that he could find work in supporting roles at the majors, and in smaller independent films. During this time, Robinson appeared in movies like *Big Leaguer, Vice Squad,* and *The Violent Men,* Raft was at the point in his career where his stardom had plummeted drastically and a recent comeback wasn't too successful. Thus, the two were re-teamed for an independent production with Raft's old business partner Sam Bischoff.

A BULLET FOR JOEY

Directed by Lewis Allen
Screenplay by Geoffrey Holmes and A.I. Bezzerides from a story by James Benson Nablo
Produced by Samuel Bischoff and David Diamond
Cinematography by Harry Neumann
Film Editing by Leon Barsha

Cast:
Edward G. Robinson	Inspector Raoul Leduc
George Raft	Joe Victor
Audrey Totter	Joyce Geary
George Dolenz	Dr. Carl Macklin
Peter van Eyck	Eric Hartman
Toni Gerry	Yvonne Temblay
William Bryant	Jack Allen
John Cliff	Morrie
Steven Geray	Raphael Garcia
Joseph Vitale	Nick Johonus
Sally Blane	Marie Temblay
Peter Hansen	Fred
Kaaren Verne	Viveca Hartman
Henri Letondal	Dubois
Stan Malotte	Paul
Ralph Smiley	Paola
John Alvin	Constable Dan Percy
Charles Ferguson	Agent Crocker
William Henry	Michael
Carlyle Mitchell	Benson
Joel Smith	Rene
Sandra Stone	Rosie
Bill Hickman	Macklin's Bodyguard

Tina Carver	Counter Girl
Fred Coby	Radio Man
Roy Engel	Truck Driver
John Frederick	Police Constable in Car
John Goddard	Police Car Driver
Frank Hagney	Nightclub Bartender
Stuart Hall	Clothing Checker
Fred Libby	Booking Sergeant
Rory Mallinson	Rent-a-Car Clerk
Peter Mamakos	Ship Captain
Paul Marion	Detective Posing as Gardener
Ernesto Molinari	Card Player
Bill Neff	Sergeant
Jack Perry	Immigrant
Barry Regan	First Tail
Mal Alberts	Second Tail
Carmelita Gibbs	Cuban Girl
Frank Richards	Ship Officer
Suzanne Ridgway	Night Club Dancer
Carlos Rivero	Portuguese Waiter
Cosmo Sardo	Allen Henchman
Cap Somers	Gambler
Paul Toffel	10 Year Old Boy
Alan Wells	Armand
Sandy Sanders	Man

Released April 15, 1955
Bischoff-Diamond Corporation for United Artists
Running time: 84 minutes
Black and White

 A Bullet for Joey was originally called *Canada's Great Manhunt* inspired by a magazine article by Stephen Brott. That article was expanded into a story by James Benson Nablo. George Raft's old production company business partner Sam Bischoff optioned the story and planned to star Raft with Edward G. Robinson with Gloria Grahame as the female lead. Grahame was eventually replaced by Audrey Totter.

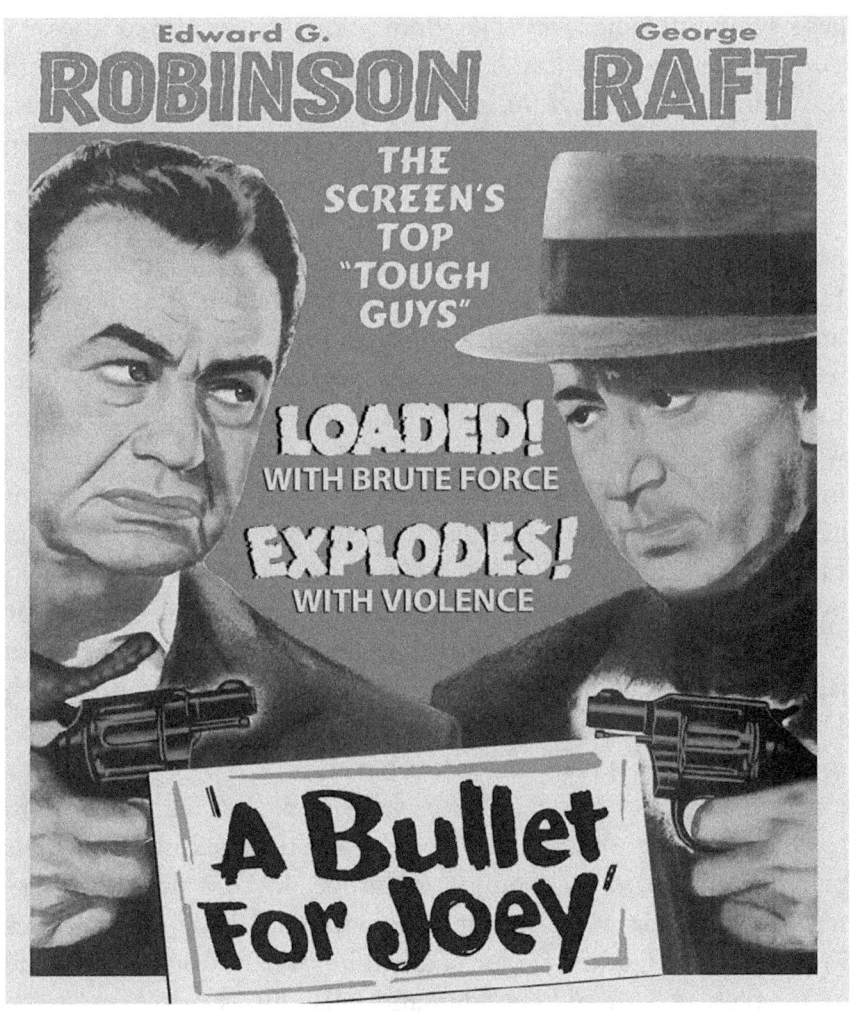

Movie ad for A Bullet For Joey

Having Edward G. Robinson and George Raft in a movie together held some promise. By 1955, televisions were in many American homes, and their older movies of either actor were appearing on the small screen. People who had not seen these films since their initial release were remembering how great the pre-war films had been, while younger viewers were discovering them for the first time. Neither Robinson nor Raft really looked all that different from 20 years ago. Both still had the same features and presence that they had established back in the 1930s. And despite both men no longer having the same level of stardom as they once enjoyed (for very different reasons, already discussed), they still had the talent and the charisma to make *A Bullet for Joey* a potentially exciting venture.

George Raft plays Joe Victor, an American racketeer who has been deported to Portugal and is hired by Communist agents in Canada to kidnap an atomic physicist. Dr. Carl Macklin (George Dolenz) has information the Communists can use, so their head man, Eric Hartman (Peter van Eyck) hires Victor for the job. Victor rounds up his old gang to be flow in, along with Joyce Geary (Audrey Totter), an ex-girlfriend of Victor's, who is coerced into helping him. Edward G. Robinson is Royal Mounted Police Inspector Leduc who is investigating the murder of a Mountie. The Mountie was murdered by one of Hartman's men, who was posing as an organ grinder with a monkey. This leads Leduc to the mission involving Hartman, Victor and the others. Macklin's secretary is murdered by one of Victor's men after he gets her to provide information by courting her. When she realizes she has been duped, she tries to run away and is shot in the back. Joyce becomes acquainted with Dr. Macklin, whom she ends up falling for, as he feels the same toward her. She is ready to collect her money and go, but drafts a letter to Inspector Leduc. Victor walks in on her and the two go to Macklin, where they find Hartman has drugged him and he is being taken aboard ship bound for Europe. Joyce is also taken hostage, as Victor has seen the letter she wrote to Leduc. As he closes in on his investigation, Leduc is taken hostage by Victor and some of his men. A ship, with Leduc and Macklin as prisoners, heads toward Europe. The Inspector tries to reason with Victor to not see this as just another crime caper, but as a mission that has a more profound affect. He reminds Victor that he is an American, and convinces him to turn on the Communists. Victor and Hartman kill each other in a gunfight, and Joyce is cleared.

A Bullet for Joey was a complete box office flop. Much of this was due to it generating little interest among exhibitors. In some cities it didn't play at all, while in others it barely got a mention in the ads that presented it as the second feature on double bills. In at least one city, it was incongruously paired with a revival showing of *The Wizard of Oz*, and it is likely the families going to see the MGM classic (which was not yet a TV staple) did not stay for this crime melodrama. The film's failure didn't affect Edward G. Robinson too greatly. Before going into *A Bullet for Joey*, Robinson had appeared in Phil Karlson's *Tight Spot* which was released about a month earlier. Ironically, it was a film noir inspired by a Senator trying to get Virginia Hill to testify against Bugsy Siegel. Thus, it was based on the lives of people George Raft actually knew. *Tight Spot* was a hit movie, and although Robinson is billed second (after the film's star, Ginger Rogers), he has a prominent role in the movie. Thus, appearing in a hit movie at around the same time as a flop, Robinson's appearance in *A Bullet for Joey* was easily overlooked. Raft, however was appearing in his only movie for that year, so it was the film by which he was judged. All of this is quite unfortunate, as *A Bullet for Joey* is a rather good movie, arguably as good as Raft's latest efforts, *Rogue Cop* and *Black Widow*.

While Raft and Robinson are playing roles that were very comfortable for either of them, their performances are exceptional. Both are old veterans in their respective areas. They have seen and experienced so much, they are as weary as they are knowledgeable. Interestingly, the characters that Raft and Robinson play do not actually meet until the final third of the movie. Their stories are parallel, with Joe Victor pulling off his mission, and Inspector Leduc investigating it. It is a tactic that was made especially noteworthy 40 years later by Michael Mann's *Heat* in which the stars, Robert DeNiro and Al Pacino, are together only for one explosive scene. While Raft and Robinson work together for more than one scene, they do have a very compelling one in which Leduc tries to convince Victor to turn against the Communists. Victor dies in Leduc's arms. While Victor's sudden turn when he decides to help Leduc seems a bit convenient, his death scene is remarkably well performed. Raft's eyes are filled with tears as Robinson holds him—it's a really emotional moment.

While Raft and Robinson had conflicted on the set of their previous movie, *Manpower* (1941), that was all forgotten by the time they appeared in this film. Accounts recall that they greeted each other warmly on the set, and could even be seen talking about the old days during breaks from filming. That doesn't mean there wasn't at least some rivalry left over. When Raft heard that Robinson paid the screenwriter to punch up his dialog, Raft did the same for his own dialog.

This is an especially good role for George Raft. Joe Victor is a man who was once a big shot and is now kicked out of his country and is seeking handouts in Portugal. He embraces the opportunity to pull one more job for a big payday. This is not too dissimilar from Raft having once been a big star who was hoping for a comeback now that his movie career was suddenly gaining momentum.

Unfortunately, that momentum was thwarted by this film's poor showing. Despite it having a lot of positives, *A Bullet for Joey* concluded George Raft's film career, and he realized that movies were no longer for him.

Later in 1955, Raft was offered to buy a 2% share of the Flamingo in Las Vegas. There was some trouble about his getting a gaming license due to his past associations with real life gangsters. The Flamingo had once been owned by his friend Bugsy Siegel. Eventually, Raft was allowed a gaming license and was the Flamingo's entertainment director. Raft also owned part of the Capri Casino in Havana, Cuba, and worked as a greeter there until Fidel Castro took over. Raft was in Havana the night the revolutionaries arrived.

Raft did return to movies in supporting roles and bit parts, mostly playing off his gangster image. He also did some TV appearances, including appearing in commercials. Even though his film career was effectively over, he kept appearing in movies and on TV till the end of his life.

SOME LIKE IT HOT AND THE LATER FILMS

George Raft was one of many cameos in Mike Todd's Oscar winning 1956 epic film *Around The World in 80 Days*, but his biggest break came a few years later when Billy Wilder offered him a role in his planned comedy *Some Like it Hot*. It was Raft's first real movie role in four years, and he was pleased at the opportunity to work with a prestigious director like Billy Wilder in a film that was to feature Tony Curtis, Jerry Lewis, and Marilyn Monroe. Lewis turned down the role:

George Raft as he appeared in Some Like it Hot

It was about two musicians who dress up as women after witnessing a murder so they don't get caught by gangsters, headed by George Raft. I didn't think dressing in drag for that much of a picture was funny so I turned it down. It turned out to be a terrific comedy and a big hit. After that every time Billy Wilder saw me, he'd look at me and say, "Schmuck!" I don't regret it, Jack Lemmon was absolutely magnificent in the role.[95]

Whether Lewis or Lemmon played in the co-starring lead opposite Tony Curtis meant nothing to George Raft. He was pleased to be the gangster whose men perform a St. Valentine's Day type massacre that is witnessed by the musicians, who hide from his pursuit by dressing as women and joining an all-girl jazz band, which includes Marilyn Monroe. Raft was pleased to be working again with Pat O'Brien, and briefly with George E. Stone whom he had worked with in Fritz Lang's *You and Me*. But despite being fun and amusing as Spats, a comical stereotype of his many gangster roles, Raft didn't end up reviving his screen career. He was hired by his old producer acquaintance Benedict Bogeaus for a supporting role in the indie film *Jet Over The Atlantic* that same year but what followed in the next couple of years were mere cameos.

The cameo appearances George Raft made in the 1960s started with *Oceans 11*, the first Rat Pack movie featuring Frank Sinatra, Dean Martin, Sammy Davis Jr, Joey Bishop, and Peter Lawford. Raft's cameo as a casino owner was an amusing in-joke as he had helped Bugsy Siegel finance the Flamingo Hotel and had very recently been its entertainment director.

Raft's next cameo was as himself in the Jerry Lewis comedy *Ladies Man*, which Lewis did as a favor:

When Dean Martin and I first got to Hollywood, we attended our first Hollywood party at George Raft's home. That was a pretty big deal to us, because not only were we fans of his, but we thought it was an honor that he was the first big Hollywood celebrity to welcome us to town. So now, years later, I have a big contract at Paramount and

---

95 Interview with the author

Jerry Lewis and George Raft

George is having trouble finding work. I wrote in a fun bit for him and I to do in *The Ladies Man*.[96]

The scene has Jerry's character refusing to believe that Raft is actually THE George Raft, causing the movie tough guy to plead with him to "believe me." He finally proves it by dancing a tango with Lewis.

Raft participated in a possible TV show with him and Maxie Rosenbloom playing co-owners of a nightclub, but the project was shelved. He did a walk-on in the teen comedy *For Those Who Think Young*, and another cameo with Jerry Lewis in *The Patsy* but by 1965 he was weeping about his financial problems. According to a UPI story in the *Chicago Tribune*:

---

96 Interview with the author

> George Raft, tough guy movie actor, broke down and sobbed today after a federal judge declined to sentence him to prison and instead fined him $2,500 for income tax evasion. United States District Judge Pierson Hall announced that he would not place Raft on probation or send him to prison. Raft had pleaded guilty Sept. 7 on one count of income tax evasion. Five other counts against him were dismissed today on the recommendation of the United States attorney's office. The count to which he pleaded guilty said he falsely claimed a $25,000 loss in a Cuban gambling casino, but Raft said it was a "bookkeeping error." The actor was shaking during the sentencing and he said later that he had clutched a 105-year-old rosary during the proceeding.[97]

Raft continued to work in films and TV, usually in small cameo roles, when in 1967 he once again made headlines regarding more troubles in his life.

> Actor George Raft said Friday he "might not go back to England now even if they let me." Commenting on the news that he had been barred from England by the British government, Raft said he was "shocked" and that he did not understand why the action was taken. "This is a great blow to me," he said., "After, all, what if I wanted to make a film in London and I couldn't go there. That would be horrible." Raft, who holds a part interest in a London gambling establishment, said his attorney in London told him "you knew some people years ago.". Raft said this seemed like a vague reference, "I know a lot of people." The actor, clad in a bathrobe, said the publicity surrounding the announcement has kept him from sleeping for the past 48 hours. "They treated me very well. I had a limousine and a chauffeur something I don't have here," he said. The actor said he had spoken to the management of the gambling establishment in London and they were unable to explain why he had been barred from the country. Raft left

---

97 George Raft is Fined, Sobs. *Chicago Tribune* September 29, 1965

England three weeks ago and had planned to return there Sunday. "I still have my clothes there," he said.[98]

George Raft's cameos continued in films like the James Bond parody *Casino Royale,* and the all-star flop *Skiddoo.* He appeared in a popular 1970 commercial for Alka-Seltzer, and in the elusive, oddball Peter Ustinov-directed feature *Hammersmith is Out.* Raft's final appearances in movies was another cameo as himself in Mae West's vanity project *Sextette* and a film about a Humphrey Bogart fan who gets surgery to look like his idol in *The Man With Bogart's Face* which was released in 1980, the year George Raft died.

When Raft died of emphysema on November 24, 1980, he was 79 years old, but many newspapers reported his age as 85, based on an erroneous date of birth that found its way into many biographies. George Raft, who had once been a major movie star during the heyday of classic Hollywood had not made out a will, and his estate consisted of a $10,000 insurance policy and some random belongings. These personal effects, including his wardrobe, were offered for sale via a Classified Ad asking $800 for everything.

George Raft made a significant impact during the golden age of 1930s and 1940s Hollywood movies, and is often included alongside such tough guy actors of the period as past co-stars Humphrey Bogart, James Cagney, and Edward G. Robinson. There are some essays that argue Raft could have been as well-remembered as Bogart had he not passed on roles in movies that later became lasting classics. There were times when Raft had a very astute understanding the best way he could present himself on screen, and chose appropriate projects accordingly. Other films in which he played a detective conducting an investigation seem to reveal that he might have been quite effective in the role of Sam Spade, for instance.

While it is fun to speculate, George Raft's film career is what it is. He made good choices and bad, appeared in enduring classics and forgettable programmers, and while his limits as an actor are often emphasized too negatively, he remains a significantly notable actor from a very important period in American cinema's rich history.

---

98 George Raft Told England Off Limits. *The Morning Call.* February 25, 1967

BIBLIOGRAPHY

BOOKS
Aaker, Everett. *George Raft: The Films.* McFarland, 2013
Behlmer, Rudy. *Inside Warner Brothers.* Viking. 1985
Cooper, Jackie. *Please Don't Shoot My Dog, Mister.* William Morrow. 1981
Dickens, Homer. *Films of Gary Cooper.* Citadel, 1971
Eames, John Douglas. *The Paramount Story.* Random House. 1987
Hyams, Joseph. *Bogie.* New American Library. 1966
Johnson, Nunnally. *The Letters of Nunnally Johnson.* Knopf, 1981
Kiriakou, Olympe. *Becoming Carole Lombard.* Bloomsbury Academic. 2021
Lang, Fritz. *Fritz Lang: Interviews.* Univ. Press of Mississippi, 2003
Martin, Len *The Columbia Checklist.* McFarland, 1991
McCabe, John. *Cagney* Carroll & Graf. 1999
Neibaur, James. *The Essential Mickey Rooney.* Rowman and Littlefield, 2016
Neibaur, James L. *The James Cagney Films of the 1930s.* Rowman and Littlefield, 2014
Neibaur James L. *The RKO Features.* McFarland, 1995
Neibaur, James L. *Tough Guy: The American Movie Macho.* McFarland, 1989
Okuda, Ted. *Grand National, Producers Releasing Corporation, and Lippert.* McFarland, 1989
Parish, James Robert. *The George Raft File.* Drake Publishers, 1973
Robinson, Edward G. *All My Yesterdays.* Hawthorn, 1973
Schulthorpe, Derek. *The Life and Times of Sydney Greenstreet.* BearManor Media, 2018
Sennett, Ted. *Warner Brothers Presents.* Arlington House. 1971
Sperber, A.M and Eric Lax. *Bogart.* William Morrow, 1997
Wallace, Stone. *George Raft: The Man Who Would Be Bogart.* BearManor Media, 2015
Watts, Jill. *Mae West, An Icon in Black and White.* Oxford University Press, 2001
Yablonsky, Lewis. *George Raft.* NY: McGraw-Hill, 1974

ARTICLES and REVIEWS
Actor George Raft Enters Hospital. *Los Angeles Times.* January 16, 1954
Amateur Show Latest Rage. *Los Angeles Times.* May 6, 1935
Arthur Pollock's Theater column. *Brooklyn Daily Eagle.* August 15, 1947
Bogart New Choice for Invisible Stripes. *The Los Angeles Times.* August 26, 1939
Bowery review. *The New Yorker.* 2011

Brook Goes Bad, Raft Straight. *The San Francisco Examiner.* September 17, 1933
Cagney and O'Brien Again. *Los Angeles Evening News.* July 27, 1949
Casting for Invisible Stripes. *The Brooklyn Daily Eagle.* September 6, 1939
Closeups and Longshots. Erskine Johnson column. Syndicated. July 30, 1952
Concentrates of the News. *The Los Angeles Times* October 24, 1939
Constance Bennett May Team With Raft. *The Los Angeles Times.* October 19, 1935
Each Dawn I Die review. *The New York Journal-American.* July 20, 1939
Each Dawn I Die review. *Variety* July 18, 1939
Every Night at Eight review. *New York Daily News.* August 3, 1935
Executive Says New Film Perfectly Cast. *The Los Angeles Times.* November 6, 1935
George Hansacker "Hollywood" column. Syndicated. January, 1949
George Raft Confined by Attack of Pleurisy. *Los Angeles Times.* February 12, 1946
George Raft-Humphrey Bogart Screen Test Denied. *The Los Angeles Times.* March 8, 1941
George Raft is Cast as Criminal. *The Times.* Hammond, Indiana. June 9, 1939
George Raft is Fined, Sobs. *Chicago Tribune* September 29, 1965 George Raft To Do Valentino Type Film Role. *Los Angeles Record.* February 8, 1933
George Raft Told England Off Limits. *The Morning Call.* February 25, 1967
Glass Key review. *The New York Times.* June 15, 1935
Hedda Hopper column. *The Los Angeles Times.* October 10, 1954
Hedda Hopper in Hollywood. Syndicated. April 9, 1947
Hollywood Chatter. *New York Democrat and Chronicle.* September 13, 1947
In Hollywood Today. *Sheila Graham.* Syndicated. April 2, 1946
Intrigue review. *The Los Angeles Times.* March 3, 1948
It Had To Happen review. *The Los Angeles Times.* February 23, 1935
Johnny Allegro review. *The New York Times.* May 31, 1949
Johnny Angel review. *Variety.* 1945
Leading Ladies in Demand. *Hollywood Citizen News.* April 18, 1939
Letters. *Photoplay* July, 1932
Limehouse Blues review. *The New York Daily News.* December 12, 1934
Louella Parsons column. Syndicated. Universal Service. April 19, 1933
Lucky Nick Cain review. *Variety.* February 28, 1951
Motion Picture Reviews. Women's University Club. March, 1935
Mr Ace. What The Picture Did For Me. *Motion Picture Herald.* Various, 1947
News and Gossip from the Stage and Screen. *Los Angeles Times.* May 7, 1933
Night After Night review. *The Pittsburgh Press.* October 15, 1932
Night After Night review. *The New York Daily News.* October 29, 1932
Othmann, Fredrick. Hollywood column. *The Hanford Sentinel.* April 28, 1941
Outpost in Morocco review. *Motion Picture Daily.* March 25, 1949
Pick-Up review. *The Hollywood Reporter.* March 13, 1933.
Quick Millions review. *Los Angeles Evening Express.* March 28, 1931

Raft and Bendix To Appear. *New York Daily News.* January 12, 1947
Raft Credits Director for Acting Fame. *Los Angeles Evening Citizen.* July 5, 1932
Raft Gets Vehicle in Race Street. *Rochester Democrat and Chronicle.* February 28, 1947
Raft in Familiar Role Goes Outside Law to Catch Racketeers. *Akron Beacon Journal.* June 12, 1952
Raft Weeps at 25-year Testimonial. *Oakland Tribune.* March 23, 1954
Raft's Services Retained. *The Los Angeles Times.* June 24, 1933
Schallert, Edwin. Raft May Do Bowery. *Los Angeles Times.* June 17, 1933
Sheila Graham column. Syndicated. February 28, 1951
Skolsky's Hollywood. Syndicated. March 19, 1942
Lloyd Sloan: And You Hear Such Interesting Stories. *Los Angeles Evening Citizen News.* April 9, 1949
Soanes, Ward. In The World of Stage and Screen. *Oakland Tribune.* June 2, 1933
Souls at Sea review. *Santa Ana Register.* August 28, 1937
Souls at Sea review. *Variety.* August 31, 1937
Stand-in Seals Off To New York for Personal Appearance. *Los Angeles Daily News.* September 2, 1938
Star Goes Into Souls at Sea. *The Los Angeles Times.* November 20, 1936
They Drive By Night review. *Motion Picture Daily.* July 15, 1940
Under-Cover Man Will Be Studied By Journalism Students. *The Shreveport Journal.* December 7, 1932
Virginia Vale column. Western Syndicate Press. June 6, 1946
Whistle Stop Review. *New York Times.* March 18, 1946
You and Me review. *The New York Daily News.* June 2, 1938
Yours for the Asking review. *Film Daily.* August 26, 1936
Zanuck likely to sign Raft. *The Los Angeles Times.* November 16, 1936

Interviews with the Author:
Jerry Lewis
Emil Sitka

Misc
Johnson, Nunnally (1969). Recollections of Nunnally Johnson oral history transcript. University of California Oral History Program
Twentieth Century-Fox Produced Scripts Collection at the UCLA Theater Arts Library

INDEX

Abbott and Costello 197, 252, 309
Adventures of Superman, The 299
Airport 325
All of Me 49-52
All Through The Night 190
Altman, Robert 262
Andrews Sisters 207, 216
Angels With Dirty Faces 3, 139
Arnold, Edward 82, 84
Around The World in 80 Days 333
Ayers, Lew 8
Babe Ruth Story, The 287
Background to Danger 199-207
Backus, Jim 292, 295
Bankhead, Tallulah 324
Bari, Lynn 223, 249, 251
Barnett, Vince 8
Barrier, Edgar 224
Barry, Don "Red" 287
Barrymore, John 135
Bartlett, Cy 138
Beavers, Louise 32
Beery, Wallace 38, 40, 41, 43, 45, 46, 47
Beetlejuice 241
Belle of the Nineties 15
Bendix, William 172, 266, 268, 270, 271, 287
Bennett, Constance 104
Bennett, Joan 3, 94, 99, 100, 164, 166, 167, 168, 169, 170, 220, 224, 225
Benson, Martin 298
Besser, Joe 309
Best Years of Our Lives, The 52

Bicycle Thief, The 298
Big Heat, The 318
Big House, The 144
Big Steal 294
Biroc, Joseph 302
Bischoff, Sam 252, 253, 254, 256, 272, 273, 274, 326, 328
Bishop, Joey 334
Bitter Tea of General Yen, The 97
Black Widow 320, 321-326
Blaine, Vivian 224
Blair, Janet 195
Blakely, James 98
Blazing Saddles 302
Blonde Crazy 25, 104
Blondell, Joan 151, 264
Blood on the Sun 241, 258
Bogart, Humphrey 117, 140, 154, 155. 158, 159, 161, 162, 163, 166, 170, 171, 173, 174, 175, 177, 178, 184, 185, 190, 197, 201, 233, 252, 282, 283, 292, 312, 337
Bogeaus, Benedict 239, 240, 241, 260, 262. 262, 334
Bohem, Sidney 318
Bohnen, Roman 243
Bolero 53-59
Bomba The Jungle Boy 325
Bonanza 251
Bond, Lillian 30
Bow, Clara 42
Bowery, The 38-48
Boyd, William 78
Boylan, Malcolm Stuart 138

Bradley, Grace 75, 77, 78, 79
Bradna, Olympe 114, 119, 120, 122
Brando, Marlon 313
Brecher, Egon 185
Brecht, Bertolt 128
Brent, George 264
Brewster's Millions 256
Bright, John 83
Broadway 190, 191-198
Brook, Clive 35, 36
Brown, Joe E. 312
Brown, Rowland 3
Brown and Carney 252
Bryan, Jane 146, 155, 158, 159, 160
Bullet for Joey, A 326, 327-332
Burke, Billie 98, 99
Burnett, W.R. 203
George Burns 313
Burr, Raymond 286, 287
Cagney, James 2, 3, 4, 6, 25, 29, 78, 83, 85, 104, 140, 141, 142, 144, 145, 147, 148, 157, 158, 166, 196, 197, 241, 257, 258, 289, 337
Calhern, Louis 10
Call of the Wild 104
Cantor, Eddie 6
Capone, Al 144
Capra, Frank 98, 302
Carey, Harry 129
Carmichael, Hoagy 230, 233
Carrillo, Leo 104, 105
Carroll, Nancy 23, 24
Carter, Helena 253, 256, 257, 259
Casablanca 201
Casino Royale 337
Castle on the Hudson 141
Champ, The 48
Chase, Charley 98
China Seas 100

Christmas Eve 260, 261-265
Christmas in July 254
City Chap, The 2
Clements, Stanley 289
Clyde, Andy 98
Cody, Lew 24, 25
Cohn, Harry 98
Connolly, Myles 166
Connolly, Walter 98. 99
Conway, Tom 237, 238
Cooper, Gary 17, 20, 29, 81, 113, 114, 117, 118, 119, 120, 121, 122, 134, 152
Cooper, Jackie 41, 42, 43, 44, 45, 47, 48
Cooper, Olive 138
Corsican Brothers, The 25
Costello, Dolores 109, 110, 111, 112
Crawford, Broderick 185, 195
Crawford, Joan 324
Cry Danger 302
Cummings, Constance 9, 10, 15
Curtis, Tony 333, 334
Curtiz, Michael 144
Cutwright, Jorja 238, 239
Dancers in the Dark 7, 10
Dangerous Profession, A 291-296
Davis, jr. Sammy 334
Day in the Country, A 309
Dead End 117, 163, 166
Dee, Francis 17, 114, 116, 119, 121, 122, 139, 151
Del Ruth, Roy 104, 283
Dell, Myrna 248
DeMille, Katherine 63
DeNiro, Robert 331
Denny, Reginald 262
DeSica, Vittorio 298
Devil Dogs of the Air 138
Diamond Lil 13, 15

Dietrich, Marlene 166, 180, 185, 186, 187, 188, 189, 190, 215, 216
Dinehart, Alan 106
Diplomaniacs 197
Dobkin, Lawrence 303
Dodd, Claire 82, 85
Domela, Jan 136
Doorway To Hell 3
Double Indemnity 218
Douglas, Mike 1
Drake, Frances 53, 55, 60, 62, 63, 64
Drew, Ellen 140
Durante, Jimmy 2, 15
Each Dawn I Die 141, 142-154, 157, 158
East Side Kids 236
Edwards, Alan 242
Edwards, Vince 318
Ellis, Edward 64
Enright, Ray 312
Evans, Clifford 308
Every Night at Eight 86, 87-93
Faye, Alice 88, 89, 90, 92
Faylen, Frank 271
Female on the Beach 251
Field, Virginia 264
Fields, W.C. 20, 207, 216
Flood, James 51
Foch, Nina 279
Follow The Boys 208-218
Fonda, Henry 131, 132, 133, 134, 135
For Those Who Think Young 334
Force of Evil 274
Ford, John 272
Ford, Wallace 100
Foreign Correspondent 170
Forrest, Steve 318
Francis, Anne 318
Francis, Noel 24, 25

Franz, Arthur 285
Frawley, William 53, 55, 58, 284, 289
French, Hugh 298
Friedman, Seymour 302, 307
G-Men 78
Gable, Clark 8, 40, 41, 104
Gallagher, Skeets 112
Gardner, Reginald 323, 324
Garner, Ava 236, 237, 238, 239, 274, 277
Garfield, John 141, 158, 184, 274
Garner, Peggy Ann 223, 224, 225, 226, 227, 321, 322, 324
Gay Paree 2
Genius at Work 252
George, Gladys 168
Gerrits, Paul 77
Ghosts on the Loose 236
Gibson, Wynne 10, 14, 17, 19, 20, 61
Gilligan's Island 295
Glaser, Benjamin 57
Glasman, Kubec 83
Glass Key, The 80-86
Gleason, James 112
Goldie 5
Goldner, Charles 298
Goldwyn, Samuel 117, 166, 275
Gorcey, Leo 163, 236
Grable, Betty 203
Grahame, Gloria 328
Grant, Cary 132
Grapewine, Charley 216
Gray, Coleen 298
Gray, Mack 2, 13, 39, 49, 54, 71. 80, 94. 142. 156, 165, 171, 184, 185, 189, 195, 212, 228, 234, 240, 246, 266, 285, 291
Gray, Sally 308
Greenburg, Max 2

Greenstreet, Sydney 203
Greer, Jane 237, 281
Griffith, Raymond 40
Griggs, Loyal 136
Guinan, Texas 2, 13
Gun Crazy 287
Hale, Alan 174, 178, 188
Hall, Thurston 145
Hammett, Dashiel 81, 83
Harding, Ann 262, 265
Harrigan, William 30
Harrison, Joan 248
Hart, Dorothy 303, 304
Hasso, Signe 230
Hathaway, Henry 53, 55, 114, 117, 131, 132, 135, 219, 223, 224
Havoc, June 253, 256, 257, 277
Hawks, Howard 3, 13
Heat's On, The 25
Heflin, Van 323, 325
Hell's Highway 144
Herbert, Hugh 140
High Sierra 184
Hitchcock, Alfred 170, 248, 251, 287
Hoffman, Bern 250
Hohl, Arthur 106
Holden, William 154, 155, 158, 159, 160, 161
Hope, Bob 297, 269, 289
Hopkins, Miriam 5, 49, 50, 57, 61, 62
Hopper, Jerry 136
House Across The Bay, The 163, 164-170
Hoyt, John 303
Hughes, Howard 292
Hush Money 5
Hymer, Warren 129
I Am a Fugitive From a Chain Gang 25, 37
I Am The Law 312, 322
I Married Joan 295
I Stole a Million 149-154
If I Had a Million 16, 17-21, 36, 139
I'll Get You For This (see *Lucky Nick Cain*)
I'll Get You 305, 306-309
Iling, Peter 298
I'm No Angel 15
In The Navy 254
Intermezzo 25
Intrigue 253-260
Invisible Stripes 154, 155-163
It All Came True 166
It Had to Happen 102-108
It Happened on Fifth Avenue 287
It Happened One Night 93, 97
Jeffreys, Anne 268
Jennings, Dev 136
Jennings, Gordon 136
Jet Over The Atlantic 334
Jewel Robbery 36
Jitterbugs 224
Johnny Allegro 276, 277, 278-283, 294, 302
Johnny Angel 228-239
Johnny Come Lately 258
Johnson, Russell 303
Jordan, Louis 217
Jory, Victor 145, 152
Judge, Arline 106
Junior Miss 325
Karloff, Boris 8
Karns, Roscoe 14, 17, 20, 22, 24, 25, 62
Kaye, Danny 289
Keaton, Buster 98
Keene, Tom 271
Keith, Brian 136
Keith, Rosalind 91

Kelly, Patsy 88, 89, 90, 92, 93
Kelton, Pert 42, 92
Kennedy, Edgar 49, 51, 109, 110, 111, 112
Kid From Brooklyn, The 289
Killer That Stalked New York, The 302
Knight, Fuzzy 135
Kolb, Clsrence 264
Krasna, Norman 123, 124, 126, 128
Ladies Man 334
Lady Killer 104
Lady for a Day 97
Lady's From Kentucky, The 137-140
Laffan, Patricia 308
Lamour, Dorothy 131, 133, 134, 135, 136
Landau, David 23
Lane, Charles 104, 254
Lang, Fritz 123, 124, 128, 129, 241, 334
Langdon, Harry 98
Langford, Frances 87, 88, 89, 90, 92
LaRue, Jack 33
Laughton, Charles 19
Laurel and Hardy 123, 197, 224
Lawford, Peter 334
LeBaron, William 126
Leigh, Janet 318, 319
Lemmon, Jack 333, 334
Les Miserables 52
Lewis, Jerry 333, 334, 335
Life Begins in College 197
Limehouse Blues 65-69
Lippert, Robert 301-302
Litel, John 176, 264
Little Caesar 3, 10
Little Giant (1932) 37
Little Giant (1946) 197

Loan Shark 300-309
Lockhart, Gene 287
Lombard, Carole 26, 28, 29, 31, 52, 53, 54, 55, 57, 69, 70, 72, 73, 74, 108, 123, 126, 132, 282
Lorre, Peter 199, 203, 204, 206
Lovable Cheat, The 325
Love, Montagu 66
Luber, Bernard 299, 301, 202, 305, 307, 309, 311
Lucky Nick Cain, 295, 296-299, 317
Lupino, Ida 109, 111, 112, 170, 171, 173, 174, 176, 177, 178, 184
MacDonald, Grace 216
MacDonald, Jeanette 207
Mack, Helen 51
MacLane, Barton 129, 289
MacMurray, Fred 108, 132, 223, 224, 292
MacReady, George 280
Madame Racketeer 8
Madden Owney 1, 2
Madhattan 2
Maltese Falcon 163, 185, 203, 205
Man From Cairo, The 309, 310-313
Man of a Thousand Faces 251
Man With Bogart's Face, The 337
Mann, Michael 331
Manpower 180-`90
March, Fredric 50, 52
Margo 72
Marin, Edwin 228, 232, 239, 240, 241, 244, 245, 246, 251, 253, 255, 258, 261, 262, 265, 266, 269, 272
Marriage of Convenience 195
Mars Attacks 241
Marshall, Brenda
Martin, Dean 334
Martin and Lewis 288, 313

Marx Brothers 197
Massen Ona 204
Maxwell, Marilyn 268, 270, 277
Mayo, Archie 169
Mayo, Virginia 286, 289
McDonald, Francis 63
McDonald, J. Farrell 231
McHugh, Frank 188
McLaglen, Victor 185, 234, 237, 238
McNamara, Richard 312 Iling, Peter 298
Meet Me in St Louis 241
Menjou, Adolph 60, 62, 63
Meredith, Charles 302
Merrily We Go To Hell 31
Mesenkop, Louis 136
Midnight Club 33-37
Milland, Ray 53, 56, 80, 82, 84, 85
Miller, Marvin 253, 255, 257
Million Dollar Legs 99
Mills, Harry D. 136
Miracle Mile 97
Monroe, Marilyn 333, 334
Moore Brothers (Tom, Owen, and Matt) 2
Morgan, Harry 266, 269, 284, 286, 287, 288
Morris, Adrian 130
Morrison, Joe 91
Most Dangerous Game, The 282
Mouvet, Maurice 56
Mr. Ace 239, 240-245
Muni, Paul 6, 8, 25, 158
Munsters, The 251
Murder My Sweet 254
Murphy, Byron 21
My Man Godfrey 57
Nigh, Jane 237
Night After Night 8, 9-16, 21, 25, 36

Night World 8
Nob Hill 219-227
Nocturne 245, 246-252
Nolan, Lloyd 75, 78, 94, 100, 117, 118, 136, 164, 166, 168, 169, 170
Normand, Mabel 25
Nothing Sacred 57
Oakie, Jack 20
Oberon, Merle 223
Oberst, Walter 36
O'Brien, Pat 157, 158, 195, 292, 293, 294, 334
O'Connor, Donald 207
O'Flynn, Damian 275
Oceans 11 334
Our Gang 32, 42
Out of the Fog 184
Outpost in Morocco 272, 273-277
Overman, Lynne 72, 135
Owen, Reginald 112
Pacino, Al 331
Padlocks of 1927 2
Paige, Mabel 251
Paivia, Nestor 195
Palm Beach Nights 2
Palmy Days 6
Papas, Irene 312
Parker, Jean 65, 66, 67, 69
Parsons, Louella 35, 203, 224
Patent Leather Kid 140-141
Patrick, Lee 163
Patsy, The 334
Peck, Gregory 325
Phipps, William 302
Pick-Up 27-33
Pidgeon, Walter 168, 169, 170
Pine, Phillip 286
Piper, Fredrick 308
Pitfall 254
Pitts, ZaSu 140
Platinum Blonde 251

Plunderers, The 25
Politics 138
Porcasi, Paul 194
Postman Always Rings Twice, The 100
Powell, William 36
Princess and the Pirate, The 289
Public Enemy 3, 10
Queen of the Nightclubs 2
Quick Millions 2-4, 10, 21
Race Street 265, 266-272
Rackin, Martin 301
Raines, Ella 292-293
Rand, Sally 56, 57
Ratoff, Gregory 24, 223
Rear Window 287-288
Rebel Without a Cause 295
Red Light 283, 284-290
Regas, Pedro 176
Return of the Badmen 2
Ridges, Stanley 243
Ritz Brothers 197
Roberti, Lyda 92
Robinson, Edward G. 4, 25, 37, 140, 151, 179, 185, 187, 188, 203, 287, 326, 327, 328, 329, 330, 331, 337
Robinson, Willard 205
Robles, Rudy 249
Rogers, Ginger 323, 324, 331
Rogue Cop 314, 315-320
Room Service 196
Rosenbloom, Maxie 147, 313
Ruggles, Charles 19
Rumba 70-74
Russell, Gail 304
Russell, Rosalind 195
Ryan, Robert 287
Ryder, Loren 136
Saps at Sea 123

Scarface 3, 4, 6, 7, 8, 10, 15, 21, 25, 33, 74, 197, 203, 274, 319
Schary, Dore 313
Schulberg, BP 99, 123
Schulthorpe, Derek 206
Sciola, Kathryn 84
Scott, Randolph 132, 215, 261, 262. 264, 268
Seiter, William 195, 196-197
Sen Yung, Victor 289
Sennett, Mack 285
Seymour, Dan 256
She Couldn't Take It 94-101
She Done Him Wrong 15
Shea, Gloria 55
Sheridan, Ann 171, 174, 175, 176, 177
Sidney, Sylvia 29, 30, 31, 32, 123, 124, 126, 127, 128, 129, 239, 240, 241, 242, 244
Side Street 2
Siegel, Bugsy 331, 334
Sitka, Emil 283
Skiddoo 337
Skipworth, Alison 8, 9, 10, 15, 17, 20, 34, 36
Smart Money 25
Some Like it Hot 295, 333
Song is Born, A 289
Sons of the Desert 196
Souls at Sea 113, 114-123
Spawn of the North 131-136
Spiral Staircase 264
Staiola, Enzo 298
Star is Born, A 52
Star Trek 251
Stewart, Paul 302
Stolen Harmony 75-79
Stone, George E. 124, 129, 334
Story of Temple Drake, The 33, 61
Street Scene 32

Struss, Karl 239, 240, 241
Sunset Boulevard 256
Swanson, Gloria 256
Tall Texan, The 309
Talmadge, Richard 135
Tamiroff, Akim 133, 275
Tate, Reginald 308
Taxi 6, 104
Taylor, Kent 66
Taylor, Robert 314, 317, 318, 319, 323
Tetzlaff, Ted 74, 108, 282
They Drive By Night 170, 171-179, 184
Thin Man, The 86
Thomas, Frankie 163
Three Ring Circus 251
Three Stooges 97, 283, 309
Tierney, Gene 323, 324, 325
Tight Spot 331
Time of Your Life 258
Tiomkin, Dimitri 135
To Have and Have Not 233
Todd, Thelma 92
Toler, Sidney 64
Totter, Audrey 328, 330
Towering Inferno, The 302
Tracy, Lee 194
Trapped by Boston Blackie 302
Tree Grows in Brooklyn, A 227, 325
Trevor, Claire 151, 153, 230,
Trumpet Blows, The 26, 58, 60-64
Tully Tom 255
Tuttle, Frank 82, 152, 153
Twentieth Century 57
Under-Cover Man 22-26, 52
Up in Arms 289
Valentino, Rudolph 7, 28, 54, 59, 61, 64
Van Eyck, Peter 330
Vice Squad 326

Vinson, Helen 36
Violent Men, The 326
Wallace, Jean 292
Wallace, Richard 126
Walsh, Raoul 41, 43, 47, 48, 61, 86, 87, 89, 136, 139, 171, 174, 180, 184, 188, 199
Wanger, Walter 166
Warner, Jack 201, 313
Weekend With Father 325
Weidler, Virginia 119, 122
Weill, Kurt 128
Welles, Orson 216
West, Mae 12, 13, 14, 15, 25, 57, 337
Westcott, Helen 302
Wheeler and Woolsey 197
Whistle Stop 233, 234-239, 244, 277
White Heat 258, 289
White, Jules 98, 283
Wilder, Billy 218, 333
Williams, Bill 292
Williams, Guinn 80, 83, 84, 86, 124
Wilson, Clarence 30, 32
Windsor, Marie 275
Wings 99
Winner Take All 2, 104
Wizard of Oz, The 331
Wong, Anna May 68, 69
Wray, Fay 42, 43, 44, 45, 48
Yablonsky, Lewis 3, 57, 58, 116, 117, 123
You and Me 123, 124-130
Young, Loretta 6, 265
You're Never Too Young 288
Yours For The Asking 109-113
Zanuck, Darryl F. 40, 43, 47, 50, 92, 102, 117, 313

Zorina, Vera 208, 210, 212, 216, 217, 218
Zucco, George 118

www.ingramcontent.com/pod-product-compliance
Lightning Source LLC
Chambersburg PA
CBHW050331230426
43663CB00010B/1822